PORTRAIT OF CAMBRIDGESHIRE

Portrait of
CAMBRIDGESHIRE

by

S. A. MANNING

Photographs by Richard Jemmett

ROBERT HALE · LONDON

ISBN 0 7091 7133 1

Robert Hale Limited
Clerkenwell House
Clerkenwell Green
London EC1

PHOTOSET, PRINTED AND BOUND
IN GREAT BRITAIN BY
WEATHERBY WOOLNOUGH, NORTHANTS

CONTENTS

I   The Cambridgeshire Scene   9

II   Waterways   30

III Farming and Research   47

IV   Industry   67

V   Nature in Cambridgeshire   87

VI   Cultural and Leisure Activities   106

VII Cambridge   125

VIII The Cathedral Cities   144

IX   Cambridgeshire Worthies   161

X   Some Cambridgeshire Villages   180

     Index   203

ILLUSTRATIONS

Between pages 48 and 49

The chapel, Corpus Christi College, Cambridge
The River Cam below Jesus Green lock, Cambridge
Parker's Piece, Cambridge
The River Cam above Silver Street, Cambridge
The University Botanic Garden, Cambridge
Peterborough Cathedral: north aisle
The Old Guildhall, Peterborough
Peterborough: view from beneath the Old Guildhall

Between pages 96 and 97

St Ives: the ancient bridge over the River Ouse
A corner of St Neots
Ely Cathedral: west front
Ely Cathedral: west and south-west towers
River scene near Stretham
The Senate House, Cambridge
Market Hill, Cambridge
King's College, Cambridge
The Round Church, Cambridge
Clare College and bridge, Cambridge
Training on the river at Cambridge

Between pages 144 and 145

Riverside scene at Ely
The Maltings, Ely
Peterborough: the cathedral from the gardens

Peterborough: gateway to the cathedral
Wisbech: the North Brink
Riverside scene at Godmanchester
March: the Church of St Wendreda
The Old Nene passes through March
Ye Olde Ferry Boat Inn, Holywell (foreground: rushes being
    dried)
Potato clamps in fenland farm country
The village college at Linton
Typical fenland farm country
A corner of Hinxton
An ancient house at Houghton
Landbeach: All Saints' Church
Grantchester: thatch among the trees

PICTURE CREDITS

All photographs by Richard Jemmett

Map   pages 200–201

I

THE CAMBRIDGESHIRE SCENE

"THAT'S WHERE I LIVE!" exclaimed the young soldier looking from the Norwich-bound train and pointing to a small house, the only building in a vast, level expanse of virtually treeless fenland just beyond Ely.

His companion's reaction was one of total amazement, his reply, brief and to the point, completely unprintable. He was in no doubt that neither man nor beast could possibly exist, let alone live, in such a place.

A few days later, travelling the same stretch of railway, I shared a compartment with two other young men who had obviously just completed a short course in Cambridge.

Glancing back towards the famous university town, one said "Look, it's really no more than a village!" The other asked, "Whatever would you do if you were there on *a week's course?*"

"Oh, you'd have to get out of it," replied his friend, "You'd need a car."

I was not completely surprised by these reactions, for while living in Cambridge I became accustomed to London friends bemoaning the fact that I was "buried in the sticks"! The plain fact is that many people genuinely believe that Cambridgeshire *is* a dreary waste, an empty wilderness, where towns and villages are all but absent. Even the recent addition to the county area of Peterborough, a lively and growing cathedral town, does not seem to impress them.

One has to admit that, compared with many other parts of Britain, the whole of Cambridgeshire, now including Peterborough and the former Huntingdonshire and Cambridgeshire and the Isle of Ely, is flat and low-lying, some areas being below sea-level. Although the land rises gradually in the south and west, reaching 200 feet and more in places along the edges of the county, there is no scenery that is wildly spectacular.

This is a land of great open skies where the sight of vast flocks of starlings wheeling and coalescing at dusk makes a thrilling spectacle. This is not a landscape for the motorist with his quick glance. It is one which can only be enjoyed by those prepared to get to know it gradually and intimately, viewing it at different times of day throughout the changing seasons.

The subtleties of the Cambridgeshire landscape are numerous. Level in one part and very gently rolling in another, highly cultivated over large stretches and virtually left to nature along ancient chalky earthworks and where small remnants of fenland remain, it has been modified considerably by man throughout its long, rich history. Nowadays, of course, man has at his disposal so much knowledge and so many powerful machines and mechanical devices that it is possible to change a landscape, even to destroy it, more quickly and effectively than ever before.

During the Stone Age, when man could not control his environment, primitive people lived, according to the evidence of thousands of flint hand-axes, in the valleys of the Cam, Nene, Ouse and other rivers. Man was still living in the Cambridgeshire area during the Mesolithic (eighth – fourth millennium B.C.) when Britain became an island. Vital information concerning his presence was obtained at Peacock's farm, Shippea Hill, where microliths (very small blades made for mounting in wooden handles) and other small flint implements were found. At this important site Cambridge University scientists, using radio-carbon dating and pollen analysis, also added to our knowledge of the Neolithic. During this period, that succeeding the Mesolithic, men had arrived in Britain by boat from western Europe, bringing to a land of hunters, fishers and food-gatherers knowledge of simple farming that was to become the basis for our civilization.

A small Neolithic community is thought to have first occupied the site at Shippea Hill, where limited clearances of trees and shrubs were made, some time during the period 3400 – 3000 B.C. There were, of course, other Neolithic settlements in Cambridgeshire where, for example, pottery has been found in a Neolithic pit at Chippenham and where several finds have been made of the coarse, heavy, decorated pottery characteristic of the Neolithic culture called 'Peterborough' after its type site. By the way, as an indication of the advances that had been made, it is important to appreciate that the Peterborough folk were flint miners, flint workers, hunters, potters, traders, and stock-raisers, and may even have grown corn.

Beaker folk, named after the characteristic shape of their drinking vessels, arrived from the Continent after about 2000 B.C. introducing single burials in round barrows and the use of copper, soon to be followed by bronze, for tools and weapons. They are represented here by burials at such places as Ely, Chippenham and Ramsey St Mary's. Evidence of man's activities in Cambridgeshire during the Bronze Age derives largely from funerary sites, individual finds of daggers, socketed axes and other metalwork, and bronzesmiths' hoards, one of which contained over 6,500 pieces of metal at Isleham.

A knowledge of iron reached our area about 500 B.C. with the arrival of people from the Low Countries who settled in dry places along the edge of the fenland and along the valleys of the Rivers Cam and Little Ouse. Signs of one important settlement of the later Iron Age, a hill-fort, are still visible on the Gog Magog Hills at Wandlebury, an estate just outside the Cambridge city boundary whose owners, the Cambridge Preservation Society, make much of it available to the public. Here the hill-top is crowned by two circular banks with a ditch between them, enclosing about fifteen acres. These remains represent the earliest fortifications on this site (probably third century B.C.), later defensive works having been demolished during the eighteenth century. Not far away, at the War Ditches site on the hill above Cherry Hinton, what would have been another Iron Age fort was destroyed during construction and its defenders killed, probably by the Belgae. These Celtic-speaking tribes of north-east Gaul first invaded Britain soon after the mid second century B.C. They worked clay soils with a heavy plough, produced efficient wheel-made pottery and struck coins.

Evidence of the Belgic presence, largely restricted to places outside the Fens, has come to light in several parts of present-day Cambridgeshire, examples being the traces of a settlement on Castle Hill in Cambridge and Belgic pottery from lower levels of Roman sites in the old county of Huntingdonshire. In A.D. 43, the year of the Roman invasion of Britain, control of the Cambridge region was in the hands of Belgae. These Catuvellauni, as they were called, had put up considerable resistance to Julius Caesar in 54 B.C. and their anti-Roman attitude was an important factor in producing the Roman Conquest, which eventually brought some 300 years of peace and prosperity to our region.

The area was opened up, at least in part, by new roads, four of which crossed at Cambridge where a Roman settlement, probably a fort, commanding the river developed on Castle Hill by the road to Godmanchester. There was a probable fort or road station at the last-named place. Also sited on a river bank, Godmanchester was at the junction of three Roman roads – Ermine Street (on the line London to Lincoln and beyond), the Via Devana from Cambridge, and the road from Braughing (Hertfordshire). That the Romans brought their own form of civilization to these parts is evident from the discovery of second-century baths near Pinfold Lane, Godmanchester.

North-west of Godmanchester, where Ermine Street crosses the River Nene, the Romans developed an important centre of activity. Here, in the area around Water Newton, was their settlement of Durobrivae, a fortified site and one of the principal potteries in Britain during the third and fourth centuries. To the east, at Longthorpe, two miles west of Peterborough, there was a Roman fort on the north bank of the Nene. Traces of their activity have been found in other parts of Cambridgeshire, but perhaps the most effective reminder of Roman enterprise and initiative is the stretch of Car Dyke, remains of a canal constructed to carry grain and other supplies to the north, at Waterbeach, near Cambridge. The severance of the official connection between Britain and the Roman Empire in A.D. 410 was followed by the collapse of Roman traditions of government, economy and culture. Later the conquest of Britain by heathen Anglo-Saxons led to the Dark Ages.

The return of Christianity, official creed of the Roman Empire for about 100 years before Roman soldiers had finally left Britain, was marked by the establishment of religious communities in the Cambridgeshire region. According to the *Liber Eliensis*, St Felix, Bishop of East Anglia, who died about 647, founded a monastery at Soham, site of an Anglo-Saxon cemetery of the pagan period.

Early in the second half of the seventh century Peada, eldest son of Penda, the king of Mercia who had championed heathenism against Christianity, founded a Benedictine monastery, now a cathedral, at Peterborough. Oswy, King of Northumbria, who was baptized in Iona, gave Peada his daughter in marriage conditionally on his acceptance of Christianity. Also in the seventh century religious establishments appeared at Thorney and Ely, islands in the fens, then a wilderness of "much water and few reeds". Very little remains of the monastery at Thorney, but at Ely the great cathedral, the third longest church in England, dominating both town and countryside, stands over the tomb of St Etheldreda who founded Ely Abbey for both monks and nuns in or about the year 673.

During the second half of the ninth century the religious foundations at Soham, Peterborough, Thorney and Ely were sacked and destroyed by the Danes. St Felix's cathedral at Soham was never rebuilt and many years passed before the other buildings were put in order. Eventually Cambridgeshire was in that part (about half) of England occupied by the Danes, which was subsequently termed the Danelaw.

During the reconquest by Edward the Elder and his sister, the lady Ethelfleda of Mercia, the Danelaw was divided into shires, among them those of Huntingdon and Cambridge, and Huntingdon was fortified, as was Wigingamere, identified by some archaeologists with Wicken, a village north-east of Cambridge. A period of peace and prosperity returned to what was now, in fact, a united England whose people, Anglo-Saxon and Dane alike, formed 'a community of interest'. Later to do so much for the reclamation and colonization of the fenland, the monasteries at Peterborough, Ely and Thorney were rebuilt during this second half of the tenth century and new religious foundations established at Ramsey and St Neots.

Danish attacks on England were resumed early in the reign of the weak and foolish King Ethelred. He was replaced as king by Sweyn Forkbeard, King of Denmark, but not before the Anglo-Saxons of Cambridgeshire bravely but unsuccessfully threw themselves against the Danes who harried the region, burning Cambridge and the fens, slaying men and livestock.

Following the deaths of Sweyn and Ethelred, the brief struggle for the throne of England between their sons, Cnut and Edmund Ironside, and the death of the latter, Cnut became king. England was to remain under Danish rule until 1042. Despite a heathen upbringing, Cnut became a powerful force in the suppression of heathenism and a great upholder and benefactor of the Church. When visiting Ely, Cnut and his queen gave a purple cloth worked with gold and set with jewels for the shrine of St Etheldreda. The association with Ely of this King of Denmark, Norway, England and the Hebrides is commemorated in the words of an ancient song:

> Merry sungen the monkës in Ely
> When Cnut King rowed thereby.
> Row, cnichts, near the land
> And hear we these monkës sing.

Although much has disappeared, there are some visible monuments of this Late Saxon Age. A place of prayer and worship since about the reign of King Cnut, the Church of St Benedict stands not far from Cambridge market-place. The tower, nave and, it is thought, part of the chancel of St Benet's, as this church, the town's oldest, is generally called, date from Saxon times. At Barnack the Church of St John Baptist, its tower early eleventh-century, has a beautiful piece of sculpture, a seated Christ in Majesty, dating from about 1000–1050, while All Saints at Wittering has a Saxon chancel arch. The Church of Holy Trinity at Great Paxton is of great interest for it was cruciform with a true crossing and aisled, very rare features in Anglo-Saxon England. Armed with the appropriate volumes of Professor Sir Nikolaus Pevsner's *The Buildings of England* series, visitors will find other monuments of pre-Conquest times: crosses at Elton, Fletton and Stanground, for example.

With the death of King Harthacnut, son of King Cnut, in 1042 the English line returned to the throne in the person of Edward the Confessor who, as a child, was brought up at the monastery of Ely. Edward, son of a Norman princess, entertained William, Duke of Normandy (afterwards William I), at his court, appointed Normans to important positions in the land, and may be said to have prepared the way for the Norman Conquest.

On the eve of this historic event, during the very short reign of Edward the Confessor's successor Harold, the area covered by modern Cambridgeshire was largely within the earldoms of Gyrth, Earl of East Anglia, and Waltheof, Earl of Huntingdon and Northampton. Gyrth was said to have asked to be allowed to lead the army against William, Duke of Normandy, who, in the event, was reported to have struck him down at Hastings, but not before he had slain the Conqueror's horse. Taken to Normandy after the Conquest, Waltheof became, in English eyes, a martyr when, ten years later, he was executed after his arrest on suspicion of having invited the Danish fleet to the Humber.

The Norman conquerors soon began to make their presence felt. Then, in 1070, a party of Danes, who had taken to the Fenland after King William had agreed to their wintering around the mouth of the Humber, joined up with the English landowner Hereward the Wake and his followers. Together they sacked the great monastery at Peterborough, after which the Danes left in their ships. Hereward returned to the Isle of Ely where Morcar, earl of the Northumbrians, and other English rebels joined him. He escaped when, in 1071, the Conqueror's forces broke into Ely, last centre of English resistance to the Normans, but others were not so fortunate.

Soon after the Conquest William, determined to exercise control, had ordered motte-and-bailey castles to be built at Cambridge and Huntingdon. At Cambridge the motte, a large earth mound, stands in front of the Shire Hall, while at Huntingdon remains of the motte survive behind Castle Hill House. Giving further emphasis to their presence, the Normans introduced their own leaders and officials into many positions of responsibility. At Ely, for example, one of William's kinsmen, Simeon, Prior of Winchester, was appointed Abbot in 1081 and, although already in his eighty-seventh year, set about planning a larger church and reconstructing the monastic buildings. Work was still in progress when Simeon died twelve years later. Almost another hundred years passed before it was completed, but Ely Cathedral (the monastery was given this rank in 1109), a site of considerable importance to students of Norman architecture, remains to this day an active centre of worship and prayer.

During the reigns of William I's sons William Rufus and Henry I religious houses continued to be established and parish churches built. A chapel remains from the Augustinian priory founded close to Cambridge Castle in 1092 and later transferred to Barnwell, now part of north-east Cambridge. Also in that town, Jesus College, a late fifteenth-century foundation, includes parts of the Benedictine nunnery of St Radegund, a house established prior to 1135, whose suppression was authorized by Henry VII. Of the surviving Norman parish churches those at Castor (consecrated 1124) and Ickleton must be accorded special mention here.

In 1142 there was more trouble in the Isle of Ely. Geoffrey de Mandeville, first Earl of Essex, Constable of the Tower of London, and grandson of one of the Conqueror's supporters, helped King Stephen to put down the insurgents. But Geoffrey had been playing a double part, hunting with the hounds and running with the fox, and the following year Stephen had him arrested. Forced to give up his castles, Geoffrey was released. He left the King's presence "like a vicious and riderless horse, kicking and biting", and disappeared into the Fens, emerging with his supporters to rob and pillage. After occupying the Isle of Ely without opposition in 1143, he took and strengthened the monastery at Ramsey and established strongpoints at Wood Walton and Benwick. Thus protected, Geoffrey and his growing band of supporters terrorized the district, even sacking and burning Cambridge. Arriving to deal with the situation, Stephen, forced to withdraw from the Fens, decided to build a number of castles to contain the rebels. It was while reconnoitring the one at Burwell that Geoffrey, now hated by those who once welcomed him, was fatally wounded. The Isle of Ely was reasonably quiet again, but not for long.

In 1173, at the time of the rebellion against Henry II, Cambridge castle was refortified and Wisbech Castle manned, but the rebels, Hugh Bigod, Earl of Norfolk, and Robert de Beaumont, Earl of Leicester, did not reach the district, having been intercepted *en route*, near Bury St Edmunds where Robert of Leicester was captured. Surviving to negotiate a truce, Hugh continued his rebellious behaviour, surrendering to Henry when, having successfully besieged Huntingdon, the King advanced on the Bigod castle at Framlingham in Suffolk.

The hostility between King John and the barons brought the opposing armies to Cambridgeshire, which was ravaged by the barons and punished by the King who burned Peterborough and Oundle. During the course of this punitive expedition of 1216 John, now a sick man, marched on to Wisbech and, surviving with only a few of his knights the crossing of the Wash, became very ill and died a few days later. John's nine-year-old son, Henry III, succeeded him, and less than a year later the treaty of Kingston-on-Thames brought the end of the civil war and a general amnesty.

During Henry's long reign Franciscans or Greyfriars, Dominicans or Blackfriars, and Carmelites or Whitefriars arrived in Cambridge, bringing a new spirit to religion at a time of strong anti-papal feeling. Scholars from Paris arrived there in 1229, following others from Oxford who had come some twenty years previously. In 1252 the King and his son Prince Edward visited Ely Cathedral for the dedication of the presbytery of Bishop Northwold who had escorted Eleanor of Provence to England in 1235, the year before she and the King were married.

Prince Edward was in Cambridgeshire on business of a very different nature in 1267 when his capture of the Isle of Ely, then occupied by disinherited rebel lords, brought the collapse of organized resistance and the end of the civil war that had flared up three years earlier.

Having succeeded his father in 1272, the prince took the throne as Edward I, concerning himself with the law and becoming "a royal definer of things legal". Early in Edward's reign Hugh de Balsham, whose election by the monks as Bishop of Ely displeased Henry III but was confirmed by the Pope, obtained a charter to introduce studious scholars into his Hospital of St John, Cambridge, instead of the secular brethren already living there. Four year later, in 1284, he obtained a charter to separate his scholars from the brethren of the hospital and founded and endowed for them the earliest of Cambridge colleges. Sited by the Church of St Peter-without-Trumpington Gate, now the Church of St Mary the Less or Little St Mary, the college was called the House of St Peter or the Hall of the Scholars of the Bishop of Ely. Now it is simply Peterhouse, part of a university which continues to spread and grow.

Edward II has been called innocent-minded, lazy, incapable, unbusinesslike and unhappy, and is said to have been of artistic temperament. Be that as it may, he found time to interest himself in Cambridge, undertaking to maintain certain scholars to be sent there by him.

In 1337 Edward III converted his father's grant into King's Hall, one of the establishments later replaced by Trinity College. The following year Elizabeth de Clare, daughter of the ninth Earl of Clare, created Clare Hall, now Clare College. Nine years later Pembroke College was founded by Mary, widow of Aymer de Valence, Earl of Pembroke. Then, in 1348, Gonville Hall, later the nucleus of Gonville and Caius College, was founded by Edmund Gonville, an East Anglian rector.

Immediately after the Black Death of 1348-9, when plague decimated the population, the clergy included, Trinity Hall was founded as a college for students of canon and civil law by William Bateman. This Bishop of Norwich, twice the Pope's representative in attempts to reconcile the French king and Edward III, was often employed by King Edward in political negotiations. Corpus Christi College was founded in 1352 by the combined town gilds of Corpus Christi and St Mary for the training of clergy. The founders' original intention was, it seems, that these clergymen should be compelled to celebrate Masses for the souls of departed gild members. Apparently the fees charged for such services had risen considerably due to the shortage of clergy following the Black Death. Corpus Christi was the last college to be established in Cambridge for almost a century. There was a reminder of the catastrophe associated with its foundation when the need to make up losses among the clergy resulting from the Black Death was mentioned in the statutes Elizabeth de Clare gave her college in 1359.

Early in the reign of the young Richard II the colleges of the growing university of Cambridge were, like people and buildings in certain other parts of the country, subjected to violence during the Peasants' Revolt of 1381. Locally the rising was suppressed by Thomas Arundel, Bishop of Ely. In 1401, two years after crowning the usurper Henry IV, Arundel, as Archbishop of Canterbury, visited Cambridge to question and warn the chancellor, doctors and masters of the university concerning lollards, heretics holding views like those of the religious reformer John Wycliffe, a number of whom were cruelly put to death in England.

The founding in 1441 of King's College, Cambridge, by the nineteen-year-old Henry VI, a pious and gentle king who involved himself in much of the detailed planning, was seen as a powerful act of support by conservative elements in the church. Its great chapel, whose foundation stone was laid by Henry himself in 1446, was, among other things, "a princely reprimand to all lollards and questioners". In 1445 Henry married Margaret of Anjou. Three years later she lent her patronage to Andrew Doket, Rector of St Botolph's, Cambridge, who was authorized by royal charter to found "the College of St Bernard of Cambridge", later called Queens' College in honour of Margaret and Edward IV's queen, who agreed to become "foundress by right of succession".

Delays in building the new colleges at Cambridge were caused by the Wars of the Roses, but in 1473, two years after their main phase ended, St Catherine's College was founded by Robert Wodelarke, then Provost of King's. Within the next twelve years Edward IV died, his son Edward V was deposed after a few months, and Richard III was killed at the Battle of Bosworth, which ended the Wars of the Roses.

During the reign of Henry VII, whose accession in 1485 marked the end of the Middle Ages and the start of the Tudor Age, Cambridgeshire became increasingly important in the affairs of both England and Europe, largely through the growth in size and influence of Cambridge University. Jesus College was founded by the suppression of St Radegund's nunnery and the appropriation of its buildings and revenues, and Christ's College, originally founded in 1442, was re-founded by Lady Margaret Beaufort. This wealthy and pious mother of Henry VII founded St John's College soon after her young grandson Henry VIII came to the throne.

Towards the end of this king's reign Buckingham College, a hostel for Benedictine monks, was refounded as Magdalene College, and about a month before he died Henry himself established Trinity College. Based on several earlier found-ations, it is a living reminder of the 'pope-king' and his part in the Reformation whose development in England was greatly influenced by the spread in the university of Cam-bridge of the new spirit of enquiry and discussion there of new doctrines from the Continent.

The suppression of the orders of monks and friars, op-ponents of the 'new learning', and the dissolution of the monasteries brought changes to Cambridgeshire. There was much destruction of monastic property, including cloister and monastic buildings at Ely where, however, the monastery school, now The King's School, was refounded by Henry VIII as a part of the new foundation of the cathedral church of the Holy and Undivided Trinity.

A period of confusion followed the death in 1547 of Henry VIII, "King of England, France and Ireland, defender of the faith and of the Church of England and also of Ireland on earth the supreme head". Henry's nine-year-old son became Edward VI but died before reaching his sixteenth birthday. Then the proclamation of Lady Jane Grey was met with rejoicings in Cambridge market-place and other centres. A mere fortnight later Jane was deposed and Mary Tudor became Queen a few days after escaping from Sawston Hall, home of the Catholic Huddlestons, before it was burnt by Protestant citizens of nearby Cambridge.

Under Mary, who was determined to restore papal authority in England, some three hundred men and women were burnt in less than four years. John Hullier, curate, whose memorial tablet is at Babraham church, was burnt in Cambridge after being bound with chains and set in a pitch barrel, and the 'Cambridge Martyrs', Archbishop Cranmer and Bishops Latimer and Ridley, all reformers long associated with Cambridge and its university, were burnt at Oxford. In these more tolerant times the persecuting Mary is almost forgotten, but her physician John Caius is honoured as one who re-founded Gonville Hall, now Gonville and Caius College – Caius ('Keys') for short.

After Mary's death the accession of Elizabeth I brought a resumption of the breach with Rome. As is evident from the parish accounts of the town of March, altars, destroyed under Edward VI and set up again under Mary, were once more destroyed. The Bishops of Ely and Peterborough were de-prived, and in due course penalties of one kind and another were intermittently imposed on Catholics and also on Protestants who did not conform to the usages of the Church of England (those later called dissenters or nonconformists). Thomas Cartwright, Lady Margaret professor of divinity at Cambridge, who lectured and preached against the constitution of the Church of England, was deprived of the professorship and of his fellowship at Trinity College and eventually im-prisoned as a puritan for two years. John Udall, a puritan and Master of Arts of Trinity College, was sentenced to death in 1591 and pardoned the following year, dying soon afterwards. Among other martyrs made by Elizabeth's State Church were the Cambridge graduates Henry Barrow (whose principles required the admission of the supreme authority of Jesus Christ and of Holy Scripture), John Greenwood and John Penry, all hanged as seditionists.

Cambridge University, destined to prosper and to see the foundation of Emmanuel and Sidney Sussex Colleges during her reign, welcomed the Queen in 1564. She was attended by her Secretary of State William Cecil, afterwards Lord Burghley, Chancellor of Cambridge University for nearly forty years. His large mansion, Burghley House, stands in the north-west of the county, a monument to one who for a time was imprisoned in the Tower but survived to reach high office.

While the great ones and the learned people of Cambridge concerned themselves with matters political, religious and intellectual, the men of the Fens, a region still largely undrained, continued with their fishing, fowling and grazing. According to Camden, the Elizabethan antiquary and historian, they were of "brutish unciviliz'd tempers".

After the death of Elizabeth, James VI of Scotland became James I of England. On his way south to be enthroned he stayed at Hinchingbrooke House, one mile west of Huntingdon. The house, now a school, was the home of Sir Oliver Cromwell, uncle of the future Lord Protector, then aged three. The rather bookish King visited Cambridge on several occasions, supporting the university against the townspeople, refusing to grant the town the status of city. While staying in Trinity College during his last visit he ratified the marriage of his son Charles with "the zealous Romanist" Princess Henrietta Maria of France.

This son, the Prince of Wales, became King Charles I in 1625 and soon imposed his authority on the colleges and university at Cambridge. In 1638 the king was involved in disputes arising from the completion of the Old Bedford River, a new twenty-one-mile relief waterway forming the first major stage in the drainage of the fens. A group of 'adventurers' led by the fourth Earl of Bedford, with the Dutchman Cornelius (later Sir Cornelius) Vermuyden as engineer, had undertaken the work. A court held at St Ives in 1637 agreed to their being rewarded with large tracts of fenland, but reversed its decision a year later on the grounds that, while the drainage had been improved, the area was still subject to occasional flooding. The commoners, championed by Oliver Cromwell, had regarded the earlier decision as an act of enclosure. King Charles sympathized with them, declaring that after drainage they would retain their customary rights. Little further work was done until after Charles's death when Vermuyden, assisted by engineers and Scottish and Dutch prisoners, went on to complete other vital drainage channels. Today Vermuyden's 'rivers' serve as his memorial in the Fens.

Some people in the wider Cambridge area were not ready to commit themselves to total acceptance of King Charles's authority. The villagers of Melbourn, for example, resisted the demands of the King's collectors for the tax known as ship-money in 1640. This was the year Oliver Cromwell, previously Member of Parliament for his native town of Huntingdon, was returned as Member of Parliament for Cambridge.

When, two years later, the conflict between Crown and Parliament erupted into civil war, it was Cromwell who prevented much of the Cambridge college plate from reaching the King. It was Cromwell, too, who organized the forces of the Eastern Association and recruited zealous puritans when Cambridgeshire, Huntingdonshire and five neighbouring counties combined in the Parliamentary cause. History books include many details of Cromwell's part in the civil wars. Suffice it here to say that even his enemies remarked on his courage, industry, great spirit and resolution. As temporary president of the Council of State after the end of the civil wars and the execution of Charles I, and later as Lord Protector, Cromwell also made his mark, though Cambridge Universtiy felt threatened and certain people were persecuted because of their religious beliefs at this time.

After the Restoration Charles II smiled on "Our University of Cambridge". Parliament, determined to deal with dissenters, engaged in religious persecution. One dissenter, John Ray, the blacksmith's son who, as his biographer put it, "laid the foundations of modern science in the many branches of zoology and botany", was obliged to resign his Fellowship of Trinity College, Cambridge, when the Act of Uniformity (1662) came into force. His tomb stands in the quiet church-yard at Black Notley in Essex and the learned Ray Society still bears his name.

Cambridgeshire has its own reminder of this particular

period of intolerance at Oakington, site of the graves of
Francis Holcroft, Joseph Oddy and Henry Osland, puritan
ministers who lost their livings for their preaching. A fellow of
Clare Hall, Cambridge, Holcroft was ejected from Bassing-
bourne in 1662. Seized while preaching to those who held
steadfast to puritanism, he was tried and banished the realm.
Lord Anglesey's intercession with Charles II resulted in Holcroft being allowed to remain in this country. Nevertheless he
lost his liberty, being imprisoned as an insolvent debtor at
Cambridge and in the Fleet. Despite all his sufferings, he
resumed his preaching for a few years after James II fled the
kingdom.

Under James II Cambridgeshire had seen Protestants in
positions of authority replaced by Roman Catholics. This was,
of course, all part of the king's utter disregard of the law and
of his policy of 'Romanization', a course completely opposed
by many English Catholics. Finally the acquittal by a jury of
the Seven Bishops – the Bishops of Ely and Peterborough and
five others, put on trial by the King for publishing a seditious
libel, encouraged the Protestant leaders to summon William of
Orange, and led eventually to James's flight from the country
and the establishment of William and Mary on the throne.
One result of the Glorious Revolution, as the series of events
leading to James's flight came to be known, was the passing of
a Toleration Act allowing Protestant nonconformists their
own places of worship, teachers and preachers, subject to
certain oaths and declarations. The old Congregational Chapel
at Melbourn was founded about this time.

A much wider degree of religious toleration was achieved
towards the end of the Georgian period when, in 1829,
almost all disabilities of Roman Catholics were removed. The
Georgian Age had begun in 1714, following the death of
Queen Anne and the arrival of George I, and was to cover
the century and a quarter to the accession of Queen Victoria.
The Georgians were great builders and Cambridgeshire has
examples of their work. One of the best of them, Peckover
House, a fine house facing the River Nene on the North
Brink at Wisbech, dates from 1722 (George I). Now the
property of the National Trust, it was the home of Jonathan

Peckover, a Quaker banker from Norfolk, and his descendants for 150 years.

Though apparently scheduled for eventual demolition, Addenbrooke's Hospital stands behind cherry trees and massed cars, a memorial to John Addenbrooke, its founder, who died during the reign of George I. Originally intended for the poor, it is known the world over, as is the new Addenbrooke's Hospital, a complex of modern buildings overlooking open country close to the Cambridge boundary. The building of Downing College, Cambridge, started during the latter part of the Georgian period. At its very end work commenced on the Fitzwilliam Museum. One of the oldest public museums in Britain, it was the result of the magnificent bequest of the seventh Viscount Fitzwilliam whose own fine art collections and library form the nucleus of a museum of international importance.

1816, the year Viscount Fitzwilliam died, saw the ruthless suppression of the Littleport Riots when, faced with unemployment, high prices and near starvation, farm labourers and soldiers returning from the Napoleonic Wars gave vent to their anger and frustration in the small Ouse-side town. Later, armed with simple farm implements and preceded by a wagon bearing fen punt guns, the rioters marched to Ely. Here some were arrested and others dispersed by the military. Eventually many were imprisoned, five were transported to Botany Bay, and five, who are commemorated on a tablet at St Mary's Church, Ely, were publicly hanged.

In an area that was (and still is) distinctively agricultural life for the poorer people continued to be difficult, dreary and laborious long after Queen Victoria commenced her reign. Many of the girls left home early, going into service in country houses or households in the towns, and even towards the end of the Victorian period gangs of women and girls were still being hired out to work long hours in the fields of Cambridgeshire.

In the Fens, where many windmills were employed to drive scoopwheels and lift water, increasing use was made of steam engines in Victorian times. The importance of this development in fen drainage was emphasized in the following words:

These Fens have oft times been by water drown'd,
Science a remedy in water found.
The power of steam she said shall be employ'd
And the destroyer by itself destroy'd.

Work continued on the fenland drainage system itself, a number of improvements to Vermuyden's work being carried out.

The arrival of the railways just before the middle of the nineteenth century connected Cambridge and Ely with London, and led to the opening of branch lines to such places as March, Peterborough and Wisbech. Apart from opening up the area and extending its communications, the railways created employment. March, strategically placed and eventually to have one of the largest mechanized marshalling yards in England, benefited in this way, as did Peterborough where 226 cottages for railway workers were erected on New England estate in 1854–66.

During the Victorian age Cambridge University reformed its statutes and widened its field of learning. Three new colleges were established: Selwyn for men, and Newnham and Girton, not at first officially a part of the university, for women. Lectures for women had been started at Cambridge in 1870, largely due to the efforts of Henry Sidgwick, the famous philosopher, whose wife succeeded Miss Anne Clough as principal of Newnham in 1892. Newnham College was first established in 1871. The Association for Promoting the Higher Education of Women in Cambridge was formed in 1873, and that year Girton College moved to Cambridge from Hitchin where it had been founded four years earlier.

The year 1874 must surely be regarded as most important not only for Cambridgeshire but also for science and the world, for it was then that the Duke of Devonshire, Chancellor of Cambridge University, founded the Cavendish Laboratory. At this Cambridge institution Sir J. J. Thomson founded a new school of physics dealing with the structure of the atom. Its work led to the discovery of the fission of the uranium nucleus, which made the atomic bomb possible. Thomson, elected to this distinguished post while still in his twenties, was succeeded in the Cavendish professorship of Experimental Physics at Cambridge by Ernest (later Lord) Rutherford, himself one of the great pioneers in the field of atomic physics.

The extension of experimental research in Cambridge Universtiy and elsewhere during the latter part of last century brought a demand for scientific instruments. This resulted in the founding of companies by Charles Darwin's son Sir Horace Darwin (Cambridge Instrument Co.) and William George Pye, formerly at the Cavendish Laboratory, whose name is now borne by a large group producing scientific instruments, two-way radios, television sets and transmitters, and other electronic equipment and components. These developments were of great consequence for an area which has never been heavily industrialized and were to become important both nationally and internationally.

Pyes made a significant contribution to the war effort in 1914-18 by manufacturing precision gun-sights, Aldis signalling lamps, and other equipment for the armed services. The First World War, with its dreadfully heavy toll of young lives, affected countless families in Cambridgeshire, just as it did so many others throughout the length and breadth of the country. Another result of this Great War, with its food shortages and lack of knowledge of crop varieties and of methods of preparing and preserving foodstuffs, was the setting up at Cambridge of the National Institute of Agricultural Botany and the Low Temperature Research Station, both still actively engaged in research.

With the return of peace Cambridgeshire devoted attention to its educational needs. At Cambridge new buildings were needed by both university and colleges to accommodate the increased numbers of students. In the county itself Henry Morris's idea of the village college, a regional centre combining school and facilities for adult education and social and cultural needs, bore fruit when Sawston Village College was opened in 1930. Between then and the start of the Second World War other village colleges were built at Bottisham, Linton and Impington, this last-named being in Professor Sir Nikolaus Pevsner's opinion "One of the best buildings of its date in England, if not the best".

There was much quiet activity in other fields, too. For example, Aero Research, a company formed at Duxford in 1934 by Dr de Bruyne, who designed, built and flew his own low-wing monoplane, was working on synthetic resin adhesives for use in bonding aircraft structures. During the Second World War its wood glues were used to assemble Mosquito aircraft and gliders, and its new metal-to-metal adhesive in tank clutches and many types of aircraft.

With the loss of shipping space and sources of supply the Second World War was a time of serious shortages for Britain. Happily the agricultural areas of Cambridgeshire made significant contributions to home food production whose vital importance tends only too often to be overlooked in times of peace.

Cambridgeshire has a number of reminders of the Second World War and of those who gave their lives then. Outstanding among them is the American Military Cemetery at Madingley. Here on a hillside are the Memorial Wall inscribed with the names of 5,125 servicemen who lie in unknown graves and the chapel containing a large mural map of the war in Europe.

When hostilities ceased the people of Cambridgeshire, like others throughout the country, looked forward to resuming their normal lives and activities. But for those living in the fenland relief was shortlived, for early 1947 brought the great flood whose waters covered 37,000 acres by the end of March and caused considerable damage to the flood banks. It was June by the time the land was pumped dry and December before the flood banks were ready. An extensive flood protection scheme was put in hand, but not before several years had been spent in argument and discussion!

During the years following the Second World War Cambridgeshire has become an increasingly vital centre of research. Laboratories have been established here by the British Welding Research Association whose work has yielded data employed in the construction of nuclear reactors and the Concorde airliner – to mention but two great projects. Metals Research Limited was formed to grow single metal crystals and undertake research in metallurgy and solid-state physics, while Tube Investments Ltd opened laboratories at Hinxton Hall to study major metallurgical research problems. The Agricultural Research Council started an institute for the study of the fundamental physiology of farm animals at Babraham Hall, and the Medical Research Council has founded several units, some in conjunction with Cambridge University.

In recent years old colleges have been extended in Cambridge and new ones such as New Hall, Churchill and Darwin have appeared. Expansion is the keyword not only at Cambridge but in the growing town of Peterborough and in other parts of the county. Let us hope that reasonable care is taken to preserve essential evidence of the past, the very foundation of the present and of the future also.

II

WATERWAYS

Writing about the waterways of Cambridgeshire, one feels bound to give pride of place to the River Cam, if only because its name is embodied in those of the famous university city and the county itself.

The branch of the River Cam known as the Rhee (or Ashwell Cam) rises at Ashwell, just over the county border in Hertfordshire, where springs emerge from the chalk of a steep hillside.

In Cambridgeshire it flows by Meldreth where the Church of the Holy Trinity has traces of Norman work and there are reminders of past ages – stocks and whipping post, the stump of a wayside cross, and great firehooks once used for pulling burning thatch off cottages. There is, too, a modern boarding school for spastic children. The Rhee passes the long village green at Barrington where the Church of All Saints has a window in thankfulness for a happy childhood spent there. There is also a reminder of the harsher side of life, the memorial to the fallen, including the name of George Coote, one of six hundred men who went down when, on 1st January 1915, the *Formidable* was sunk by a German submarine.

Next the river flows by Harston where the past is represented by a church of flint and stone rubble and a beautiful Tudor manor house, and the present by the laboratory and offices of Fison's Pest Control. The Rhee then goes on to Haslingfield where Henry VIII's physician, Thomas Wendy, built a house. Monuments to members of the Wendy family and a memorial window to Bishop Mackenzie, who died as a missionary in Africa in 1862, are features of All Saints' Church. A good viewpoint and an interesting element in the riverside landscape here is the spur of chalk known as the White Hill (for an obvious reason) and also as Chapel Hill from the medieval shrine that attracted pilgrims to this spot.

East of Cantalupe Farm the Rhee joins the combined waters of the Saffron Walden Cam and the Linton Cam (also called the Bourn River, not to be confused with the Bourn Brook) which come down from the chalk uplands and unite not far from the railway at Shelford. Flowing on towards Cambridge, the river, the combined waters of the Ashwell, Saffron Walden and Linton Cams, is joined at Byron's Pool by the Bourn Brook from the Eltisley fields beyond the village of Bourn. Byron's Pool, where the poet is said to have practised his swimming feats, is reached by a footpath from the road leading from Trumpington to Grantchester.

These two places, separated by the river, are still well worth visiting. Trumpington church has the second oldest brass in England, that to Sir Roger de Trumpington who went with the future King Edward I on crusade and died in 1289. In the churchyard is the tomb of one nearer our own time, Henry Fawcett the blind reformer, whose wife, Millicent Garrett, was one of the first advocates of votes for women. Blinded in a shooting accident at the age of twenty-five, Fawcett nevertheless took up his fellowship at Trinity Hall, Cambridge, became a professor of economics and an author, entered parliament as an independent, and was made Postmaster-General by Mr Gladstone. Fisherman, horseman, walker and skater, he used to tell his friends: "Do not patronize those who are blind, treat us without reference to our misfortune; and, above all, help us to be independent." What a splendid example to those who, in full possession of sight and faculties, spend their lives planted in front of a television set complaining about the poor programmes or the number of 'repeats'!

Grantchester is famed for its association with Rupert Brooke, the young poet who lived there after leaving Cambridge University and who, in 1915, died at the age of twenty-eight on the Greek island of Scyros. People have often wondered why this young man became something of a cult-figure, almost a folk-hero. The answer must surely be that, as a poet, he spoke for many thousands of young men who lost their lives in one of history's most costly and futile wars. These lines of his make further comment unnecessary:

> If I should die, think only this of me:
>   That there's some corner of a foreign field
> That is for ever England. There shall be
>   In that rich field a richer dust concealed;
> A dust whom England bore, shaped, made aware,
>   Gave, once, her flowers to love, her ways to roam . . .

Also called Granta, as in Grantabridge which became Cantabridge and finally Cambridge, the Cam flows on to the famous university city. One may walk by it across the meadows from Grantchester to Newnham on the edge of the city, through a land of ancient pollard willows where one may be rewarded by the sight of swans in flight.

The river runs through Cambridge, passing 'the backs', the area behind certain colleges, which is particularly attractive in spring and when sunshine plays on trees and ancient buildings. After "the most superb half-mile scene in the whole of Europe, if not in the world", as Rodney Tibbs the Cambridge writer put it, the Cam goes under Magdalene bridge, flowing past the college of that name and the grassy acres of Jesus Green, with its riverside walks. The stretch of river between Chesterton, a mixture of 'village' church, old buildings and modern Cambridge housing, and Baitsbite Lock has served as training water for generations of Cambridge rowing men and as setting for bumping races and other events for the college eights.

Fen Ditton lies by the Cam, not far from Chesterton. Standing at one end of the Fleam Dyke, an ancient defensive earthwork, its name is said to mean Fen Ditch-town. The Church of St Mary, large and dignified, has fourteenth-century features, including an octagonal font bearing the shield of Bishop Arundel.

Further along the river, on the same side, is Horningsea whose Church of St Peter has a fine Elizabethan pulpit with tester. Opposite this place is Milton where All Saints' Church has a Norman chancel arch and a sixteenth-century brass to Sir William Coke and his wife. South of the church is a timber-framed house, once the home of the Rev. William Cole, the eighteenth-century antiquary and friend of Horace Walpole.

Beyond Milton and Horningsea are Landbeach and, nearer the river, Waterbeach. A seventeenth-century rector of Landbeach, William Rawley, served Francis Bacon, statesman, essayist and philosopher, as chaplain while the great man was Lord Chancellor, and after his death edited his unpublished papers and wrote a memoir of him. He deserves to be remembered for his sense of personal loyalty. One cannot say this of Bacon who helped to bring about the conviction and execution of Robert Earl of Essex, whom he had served as confidential adviser and from whom he received an estate at Twickenham.

At Waterbeach, the village on the beach or shore of the river, past and present rub shoulders, as in so many parts of Cambridgeshire. Here are airfield and barracks, sections of the Roman canal known as the Car Dyke, and an ancient church where enlargement and rebuilding took place last century. Incorporated in farmhouse and barn are the remains of Denny Priory, the most important architectural evidence of a house of Franciscan nuns of the Order of St Clare in this country. Founded as a cell of Ely in 1160 and later transferred to the Templars, Denny passed to the nuns of St Clare about the middle of the fourteenth century.

Across the river from Waterbeach the fenland is marked by a series of lodes, artificial drainage and transport channels connecting villages and farms with the Cam. Bottisham Lode, running between Bottisham Fen and Queen's Fen, leads from the river to the village of Lode and the magnificently wooded grounds of Anglesey Abbey, with its priceless collection of books and works of art formed by the first Lord Fairhaven and left by him to the National Trust.

Lord Fairhaven started life as Huttleston Broughton, son of Urban Broughton, who made a fortune in the United States and later returned to England. He was educated in America and then at Harrow, and served with the 1st Life Guards in the First World War. In 1926 he bought Anglesey and began to transform the house, which was founded for eleven

Augustinian canons in 1135, and to create in the fen landscape a garden that, in Sir Arthur Bryant's words, "can compare with the great masterpieces of the Georgian era". In 1929 Huttleston Broughton, man of duty with interests in the worlds of art and sport, was granted the barony intended for his late father.

Bottisham, the village from which the lode takes its name, stretches between the B1102 road and the A45. Here the church has monuments to members of the Jenyns family whose home, Bottisham Hall, was rebuilt in 1797. One is to the memory of Colonel Jenyns who survived the Valley of Death at Balaclava.

The lode on the other side of Bottisham Fen extends from the Cam to Bottisham's neighbour, Swaffham Bulbeck, whose northern part, Commercial End, with its warehouses and wharves, was a prosperous trading centre before the railways took traffic away from the rivers. Swaffham Bulbeck has one church, St Mary's, with an Early English west tower, but neighbouring Swaffham Prior has two, St Mary's (with a Norman octagonal tower) and St Cyriac's, standing in one churchyard up above the village street.

Beyond Swaffham Bulbeck Lode, on the far side of Swaffham Prior Fen, a lode connects the river with Reach, a village at the north-west end of the Devil's Dyke (or Ditch), a huge ancient earthwork extending for miles across country, passing by Newmarket Heath racecourse on its way to Stetchworth. The mayor of Cambridge still travels to Reach, once a busy little inland port and centre of trade, to open the fair, formerly one of the county's most famous annual events, scattering coins to the children. In recent years a local man has claimed that Reach is a self-governing kingdom under the terms of a charter in which King John gave the village its freedom and guaranteed it for ever.

The lode up to Reach is connected with another leading to the ancient village of Burwell whose church is, in Pevsner's opinion, "the most perfect example in the county of the Perpendicular ideal of the glasshouse". West of St Mary's is the deep moat of the twelfth-century castle. It was here that, as recounted in the first chapter of this book, Geoffrey de

Mandeville was killed by an arrow. A chat with a local historian produced the extraordinary story that the rebel's corpse was excommunicated by the Pope and kept unburied for years until the Pope was satisfied that his sons had made reparation for his sins!

North of Reach is Wicken whose lode to the river runs through the well-known National Trust nature reserve. The little church is of interest as the last resting-place of the Lord Protector's son Henry Cromwell, "an honourable figure" (as Carlyle called him), who became Governor-General of Ireland, and was later allowed to live at Spinney Abbey, which stands just north of Wicken Fen on the site of a house founded in the thirteenth century for Augustinian canons.

Flowing northwards for a few more miles, the Cam joins the Old West river, part of the original Great Ouse, at Fish and Duck corner where, at the inn of that name, travellers may refresh themselves.

The Great Ouse, a most important river, rises in Northamptonshire, flows through Buckingham and Bedford, and enters modern Cambridgeshire through St Neots, a town whose development arose from the presence of a tenth-eleventh century Benedictine priory. No visible trace of this remains, but St Mary's Church, large and late medieval, has survived not only as a place of worship but as a reminder of things past.

Beyond St Neots the Great Ouse passes between the two Paxtons whose churches are of considerable interest. Holy Trinity at Great Paxton is an Anglo-Saxon building that can, as Professor Pevsner has pointed out, truly be called grandiose. Dating from pre-Conquest times, this aisled and cruciform church with a true crossing is a very rare type. The Church of St James at Little Paxton has Norman features and in the churchyard stands a stone to John Buonarotti Papworth, the nineteenth-century architect who served the King of Württemberg and whose more important works included St Bride's Avenue in Fleet Street, London.

The Great Ouse passes Offord D'Arcy where St Peter's Church has a Norman arcade and several old brasses. At Offord Cluny, where Cluny Abbey in Burgundy was lord of the manor until early in the fifteenth century, an intake and pumping station on the river ensure that the nearby Grafham Water is kept filled. This important reservoir, made by damming the valley of Diddington Brook, covers the best part of 2,000 acres, its shoreline extending to nearly ten miles. With a storage capacity of 13,000,000,000 gallons, it serves an area of 2,000 square miles. Through the co-operation of the Anglian Water Authority, there are facilities at Grafham Water for fishing, sailing, bird-watching and other forms of recreation. Car parks and picnic areas are provided, and there is a nature reserve comprising the western end of the reservoir plus part of the northern shore.

Flowing on, the river reaches Huntingdon and Godmanchester, ancient towns joined by a raised causeway rebuilt in 1637. At Huntingdon, a Saxon burgh, are the house where Oliver Cromwell was born and the grammar school he attended, now the Cromwell Museum. Both All Saints' Church and St Mary's embody. Norman work. Other noteworthy buildings include the late seventeenth-century red-brick Walden House, Cowper House, where the poet of that name lived, and the eighteenth-century red-brick Town Hall. At Godmanchester, a Roman station and later a great county town, St Mary's Church has stalls, with a good set of misericords, that are believed to have come from Ramsey Abbey. There are timber-framed houses here, the best being Tudor House (1600–03) with its gabled wings and overhangs, and riverside scenes in which houses of various heights and styles naturally form a harmonious whole.

On to Hartford where the Great Ouse is but one element in a scene whose charm stems from the presence at the waterside of All Saints', a restored church, and the trees of the Georgian Hartford House. Then comes Wyton whose seventeenth-century Three Jolly Butchers, timber-framed and plastered, provides moorings and certain other services. Houghton, next on the river, boasts a stone-spired church, St Mary's, with a tower that becomes octagonal, unusual but by no means unique in Cambridgeshire. One wonders how to classify Potto Brown who lived at Houghton and occupied the timber water-mill, now owned by the National Trust and let to the

Youth Hostels Association. He took his ledgers to chapel, so the story goes, and told God the names of all his debtors!

Now for the delightful Hemingfords with attractive old buildings and river scenery that is really English. St Margaret's at Hemingford Abbots, a church of brown cobbles, has a monument to Joshua Barnes, the seventeenth-eighteenth century Cambridge professor, whose inscription is partly in Greek, one of the languages to which his scholarly life was devoted. St James's at Hemingford Grey, its tower facing the river, is but a short distance from the ancient manor house whose garden goes down to the water. Another riverside link with the past is the great plane tree planted in 1702, only ten years before the death of Joshua Barnes. Truly a single tree can outlive generations of men!

The Ouse next reaches St Ives where it flows under a narrow and ancient bridge, a structure almost unique in England in that it carries one of the very few remaining bridge chapels. St Ives itself, quaint and still busy in a quiet sort of way, was prosperous in the Middle Ages when its Easter Fair was one of the most important in the country. Its large church of All Saints, with its beautifully proportioned steeple, dates largely from the fifteenth century, and there are a few other buildings of interest. Oliver Cromwell, very much a man of these parts, is commemorated in the name of an early Victorian yellow brick terrace and by a bronze statue.

From St Ives the river flows towards Holywell, site of the Ferry Boat. One of the oldest in the country, this famous inn, said to be haunted and to have associations with Hereward the Wake, stands at the waterside. Not far from it is Anchor Cottage, once the Anchor Inn. The charming village got its name from the well which, sited in the churchyard, gained holy associations.

Taking a north-easterly direction by Middle Fen, the Ouse passes to the west of Over, the village on the fen edge. Its church, ornate with friezes, mouldings and carvings, belonged to Ramsey Abbey. Stone seats run round the walls, calling to mind the old saying: 'the weakest to the wall'. A bit further along, on the opposite side, lies Bluntisham where St Mary's has an extremely rare feature for an English church, a polygonal apse of the period *c.* 1290–1350.

East of Bluntisham, Earith lies by the river. It is a vital point for both the Great Ouse and the entire fenland, for it was here in the seventeenth century that Vermuyden made his two new straight cuts. The first, the Old Bedford River, seventy feet wide and twenty-one miles long, was dug from the Great Ouse at Earith to Salters Lode, west of Denver, on the tidal river. A sluice regulated the amount of water diverted from the original course of the Ouse, and the tail sluice resisted inflow from the tidal water and the sea.

Twenty years later the second cut, the New Bedford River or Hundredfoot Drain, was made parallel to the first. At that time, too, the first Denver Sluice was built across the Ouse, excluding tidal water from the river's original course and turning it up the Hundredfoot. The great tract of land between the two cuts was made to serve as a reservoir for flood waters by the construction of high barrier banks. Now known as the Ouse Washes, this is not only a vital factor in flood control but a site of international ornithological importance with areas safeguarded by the Wildfowl Trust, the Cambridgeshire and Isle of Ely Naturalists' Trust and the Royal Society for the Protection of Birds.

Vermuyden's artificial channel to Denver cut off part of the natural course of the Ouse, the loop via Ely, whose waters are navigable but non-tidal. This original course of the Ouse is known as the Old West River from Earith to its confluence with the Cam, as the Ely Ouse from the Cam to Littleport, and as Ten Mile River from Littleport to its outfall into the tidal river at Denver.

Leaving Earith, the Old West, a section extending for $11\frac{1}{4}$ miles, flows between Aldreth and Willingham, passing such places as Milking Hills, Adventurers Head and Frog's Hall, whose very names stir the imagination. Aldreth, like so many places in fenland, has associations with Hereward the Wake and within its bounds is the site of St Etheldreda's Well. At Willingham the nave of the church has a magnificent roof with carved and moulded beams and spandrels pierced with tracery. Here, too, on rising ground, is the ancient earthwork named after Belsar, the Norman commander who came here in search of Hereward.

Further on Wilburton, where Henry VII was entertained by the rector, Thomas Alcock, lies to the north of the river, while from the opposite bank a lode leads up to Cottenham. This was the birthplace of Thomas Tenison, Archbishop of Canterbury and one of the 'seven bishops', who earlier had bravely remained at his post in Cambridge throughout the Plague. This village was also the birthplace of John Colledge, a man who, loving liberty, crossed the Atlantic and became ancestor of a President of the United States, John Calvin Coolidge.

Stretham, not far from the confluence of the Old West and the Cam, has a fourteenth-century church tower and a fifteenth-century village cross. As a reminder of the long struggle to drain the fens it has a scoop-wheel pumping station containing the original steam beam engine. Replacing four windmills, this engine could, at a normal work rate and use of a ton of coal for every six hours at work, raise some 30,000 gallons of water per minute. Never replaced by diesel or electric pumps, the Stretham steam engine has ceased working and is now preserved by a trust and open to the public.

At Fish and Duck corner the waters of the Old West and the Cam meet and flow northwards as the Ely Ouse through a land dissected by catchwaters and drains, whose names are self-explanatory, and by green roads known as droves.

Very soon the Ely Ouse flows by the small hamlet of Thetford (not to be confused with the ancient Norfolk riverside town of this name), from which Bronze Age causeways ran to Fordy and perhaps also to Barway on the other side of the river. By the water beyond Barway is Stuntney beside whose causeway, built by the monks of Ely and now part of the A142 road, a Bronze Age hoard was found in 1939, Roman remains having earlier been discovered on the opposite side of the road. Stuntney Old Hall, an early seventeenth-century gabled house, was the home of Cromwell's mother and Oliver inherited it from his uncle.

Next the Ouse flows by Ely, subject of part of a later chapter. Thanks to the foresight of the local authority and their construction of a riverside walk, it is possible to enjoy pleasant strolls beside the Ouse in this historic fenland city.

Just beyond Ely, on the same side of the river, is Chettisham where the small Early English chapel contains pieces of Norman sculpture, one a grotesque head. Across the river is Prickwillow where seven extra steps were made up to the front door of the rectory to allow for shrinkage of peat from around the building, which, like the Victorian church, is set on piles. Situated quite close to the Cambridgeshire border, Prickwillow is on the River Lark whose waters flow north-west from the village for a few miles before discharging into the Ely Ouse.

Across the Ouse, north-west of its confluence with the Lark, lies Littleport, scene of the nineteenth-century riots, already mentioned. The tower of its large church, St George's, is a prominent landmark for miles. From Littleport bridge the Ouse flows alongside the A10 road through rich fenland, very soon to pass across the county border on its way to the Denver complex of sluices and channels. Here water from the Ely Ouse is transferred through aqueducts and improved river channels to Abberton and Hanningfield reservoirs in Essex or led off to the tidal length of the Great Ouse discharging into the Wash near King's Lynn.

Also running into the Wash, to the west of the Ouse estuary, is the Nene, a river connected to the Great Ouse by navigable waterways of the Middle Level system.

Rising in Northamptonshire, the Nene, sometimes called the Nen, enters Cambridgeshire through its north-western corner. It flows into Wansford, where there is a fine old bridge with arches dated 1577, a church with Saxon window and Norman font, and a seventeenth-century inn, The Hay-cock, whose size reminds us that the village was on the Great North Road.

On to Stibbington and its Hall with the fine Jacobean façade, and then to Water Newton with the Church of St Remigius and an eighteenth-century watermill. Here, where their Ermine Street crosses the Nene, the Romans built a forty-four-acre walled town, Durobrivae. Between it and Water Newton they constructed kilns and other buildings, part of a great pottery industry carried on in the area. Aerial photography has revealed much, but sadly there is very little to see on the ground. The same is true of Ailsworth on the other, northern, side of the Nene, where the site of a Roman villa with mosaic floor and tessellated pavement was discovered last century.

Part of another Roman villa was excavated in 1822 at a site above the river at Castor, where remains also exist of a group of Roman buildings built round a large courtyard. Plainly visible at Castor is the very important Norman parish church dedicated, uniquely in England, to St Kyneburga, daughter of Peada, under-king of the South Mercians and founder of the monastery at Peterborough. A cruciform church, it has many features of considerable interest, its fine crossing tower, consecration inscription of 1124, and pieces of Saxon sculpture being but a few of them.

Continuing its journey to the sea, the Nene passes the two Ortons: Orton Waterville, whose Church of St Mary has a beautiful Elizabethan pulpit, and Orton Longueville, site of Orton Hall, house of the Gordons, Marquesses of Huntly, Earls of Aboyne. On the opposite side of the river, at Longthorpe, are the twenty-eight-acre site of a Roman fort and Longthorpe Tower, where extensive fourteenth-century wall paintings of biblical and other subjects remained undiscovered until after the Second World War.

Two miles east of the Tower is the centre of Peterborough. From a point near this town, subject of part of a later chapter, artificial cuts, roughly parallel to one another, were made in the fifteenth and eighteenth centuries to shorten the Nene's course and thus help to speed its waters to the Wash. Modified many times since it was first cut, the first of these, Morton's Leam, is still used, but the main river now flows through the second cut, a more direct channel to the north of the earlier one.

Soon after leaving Peterborough, the Nene passes between two places whose roots go deep into history: Thorney to the north, Whittlesey to the south. There was a monastery at Thorney in the seventh century. Destroyed by raiding Danes in 870, it was refounded as a Benedictine house in 972. After the Norman Conquest the abbot gave instructions for the rebuilding of the church, and it was ready in 1108. Consecrated twenty years later, the abbey church became the centre of a monastic community whose piety and industry drew praise from William of Malmesbury, the twelfth-century historian. Thanks to the monks, this island in the fens was, he said, a very paradise bearing trees. The abbey gateway was "one of the hundred celebrated places" in fourteenth-century England, and the abbot sat in the House of Lords. Then came the Dissolution and the almost complete destruction of the church and monastic buildings.

Almost a century passed and then in 1638 the ruined church was restored. Few people now realize that nine saints either lived at Thorney or were buried there. Just as few have heard of Tatwin, the hermit of Thorney, who took St Guthlac by boat to Crowland where he spent fifteen years as a hermit and where the great abbey was built over his shrine. Guthlac with the scourge is shown with two other English saints in a stained-glass window at St Mary's, Whittlesey. This little town on the Nene's southern side has several important old houses, and from the seventeenth century its butter cross and Black Bull Inn. Whittlesey was the birthplace of a number of distinguished men. One of them, William Whittlesey, became Archbishop of Canterbury in 1368 after holding the bishoprics of Rochester and Worcester. Another, Sir Harry George Wakelyn Smith, served at Waterloo, was victor of Aliwal, where he led the charge against the Sikhs in 1846, and became Governor of the Cape in 1847. Commemorated in South Africa in the names of the towns of Harrismith, Whittlesea and Aliwal, he died in 1860 at the age of seventy-three and was buried in his native town where, in St Mary's Church, there is a monument with bust.

East of Whittlesey, on the same side of the Nene, lies March, site of a Roman settlement. Now a busy little town, it has three nineteenth-century churches and, at the south end, the medieval Church of St Wendreda, its magnificent double hammer-beam roof richly carved with nearly two hundred angels. With its pleasant riverside roads, March lies on the Old Nene, an old course of the River Nene which passes through the neighbouring parish of Upwell and then along the Cambridgeshire-Norfolk border.

The main River Nene continues through a land whose scattered farms bear such names as Chestnut Farm, Goosetree Farm and Speedwell Farm. To the north is the village of Wisbech St Mary where the medieval church was restored and partially rebuilt late last century. To the south lies Elm, site of several Roman settlements and of a church with a fine tower, and Friday Bridge where, at Needham Hall, Oliver Cromwell is said to have slept on an oak table "so that he should be no better lodged than his soldiers".

North of Elm and adjoining the village of Wisbech St Mary is Wisbech, through which the Nene passes, making its own contribution to the pleasant atmosphere of this attractive town. In the town centre, within two hundred yards of the bridge, Peckover House, the Georgian showpiece of Wisbech, stands facing the river on the North Brink, itself one of the finest Georgian streets in the entire country. Built in 1722, and once known as Bank House, it became the home of the Peckover family at the end of the eighteenth century, when it was bought by Jonathan Peckover, the Norfolk quaker and banker. In 1948 the Hon. Alexandrina Peckover, the last member of the family, presented the house to the National Trust together with sixty-two acres of land, now playing fields and pasture, across the road to the north. Both the south front and that facing the garden at the rear lend an atmosphere of quiet, unhurried dignity to Peckover House whose interior has many examples of rich plaster decoration, panelling and carving.

Across the river, along South Brink, are more houses worthy of note. One (that now numbered 7-8) was the birthplace of Octavia Hill, the philanthropist and housing reformer, who, together with Sir Robert Hunter and Canon H. D. Rawnsley, founded the National Trust in 1895. Important as Octavia Hill's work was, it is evident that, to Wisbech, its most famous person is Thomas Clarkson, to whom the town erected a great neo-Gothic memorial.

Son of the headmaster of the grammar school, Clarkson was born here in 1760. He took an early interest in the subject of human liberty and published a prize essay against slavery in 1786. The following year he joined a committee to work for the suppression of the slave trade. A friend of Granville Sharp and William Wilberforce, he travelled widely, enlisting support, and helped to found the Anti-Slavery Society. With the triumph of the cause, Clarkson became a Freeman of the City of London and in a sonnet William Wordsworth addressed him as "duty's intrepid liegeman" and as "firm friend of human kind".

Wisbech lost its ancient castle long ago, but there is a reminder of it in the great old Church of St Peter and St Paul in the form of a large brass (one of the biggest in England) of Thomas de Braunston, Constable of the castle, who died in 1401.

The growth of Wisbech as a town and marketing centre must have been influenced greatly by the presence of the original castle. Its development as a port was naturally affected by the state of the Nene, silting being the cause of serious trouble for many years. The cutting of Morton's Leam late in the fifteenth century seems to have improved the flow of the river, leading to an increase in trade and the presence of small ships. Early in the seventeenth century, however, silting and flooding again caused severe problems. Later that century Vermuyden made a sluice on the river to prevent sea floods and a long straight cut to stop silting and improve navigation. Trade and prosperity followed.

By the second half of the eighteenth century there were years troubled by silting and flooding, and others when water all but disappeared from the river. By the end of the century ships, and with them prosperity, returned following the construction of Kimberley's Cut, an embanked channel for the river below Wisbech. The canalization in 1794 of the Well Stream, a waterway running south-east of the town along the present Cambridgeshire-Norfolk border, also contributed to the trade and prosperity of Wisbech. In 1825-6, at a time when Wisbech was the most important cereal-exporting port in the country, 1,209 ships entered the port.

In 1830 the well-known engineers Rennie and Telford were responsible for the new Nene Outfall Cut to Crabs'

Hole. This project diverted the river, now much straighter between Wisbech and the sea, from its old channel amongst the shifting sands of the Wash. One problem solved by the opening of this new outfall was that of the bore. Some idea of the effect of this tidal wave can be gained from this entry in Ralph Thoresby's diary for 1680:

> This morning before we left Wisbech, I had the sight of an Hygre or Eager, a most terrible flush of water, that came up the river with such violence that it sunk a coal vessel in the town, and such a terrible noise that all the dogs in it did snarl and bite at the rolling waves, as though they would swallow up the river, the sight of which (having never seen the like before) much affected me. Each wave surmounting the other with extraordinary violence!

A decline in the ship-borne trade of Wisbech followed the arrival of the railway in 1847, but the town still serves as a port, though its facilities do not appear to be overstretched. One day in August 1977, local newspapers headlined the fact that, for the first time since 1968, there were ten ships in port, eight with barley from West Germany, one with petroleum from Immingham, and another with packaged timber from Stettin.

People who know Cambridgeshire intimately will, like others who have consulted detailed maps of the county, readily appreciate that this chapter gives a simplified account of its waterways. This is inevitable, for there are so many cuts, channels and other completely artificial waterways that even an attempt to do justice to them all would require the space afforded by a full-length book.

The vast and complex systems of channels start with ditches draining farmers' land. Water from these vital primary channels passes into main drains, and then into main rivers, being pumped from one to the other in the fens and low lying coastal areas where land levels are below river or tide levels (the vastness of the task of constructing and maintaining flood embankments in such places can be imagined).

Extending for ten and a half miles from near Ramsey, through Benwick, Doddington and Chatteris parishes to

Welches Dam on the Bedford River, the Forty Foot Drain is an important cut. Dating from Vermuyden's time, it is leased by local angling clubs whose members are attracted by such species as bream, roach and rudd. For boating enthusiasts it forms part of a good route from the River Great Ouse to the River Nene.

The Sixteen Foot Drain, another part of the fenland drainage system dating from the seventeenth century, stretches for nine miles from near Chatteris north-west to Upwell, running parallel to the B1098 road. It is connected with waterways branching into Norfolk and up along the Cambridgeshire border with that county. Also popular with anglers, its waters are leased by an angling association.

Two more major cuts that must be mentioned are the New South Eau (1631) from Thorney parish in the extreme north of the county, and its extension, the North Level Main Drain (1831-4). Carrying water from parts of south Lincolnshire and north Cambridgeshire into the Nene near the north-eastern tip of the county, their combined length is about fifteen miles.

Of course, the work of those responsible for maintaining and exploiting the Cambridgeshire waterways, both natural and artificial, is never finished. By constant vigilance and application, they endeavour to promote drainage and to prevent flooding, to provide water for domestic, industrial and agricultural purposes, and to cater for people interested in boating, angling, bird-watching and certain other outdoor pursuits. In these last-named activities, they are assisted, encouraged and at times prodded by such voluntary organizations as the county naturalists' trusts (two cover our area) and the East Anglian Waterways Association.

Nowadays it is often said that there are few fields of activity left where individuals and small organizations can make effective contributions. It is a pleasure, therefore, to end this chapter with the encouraging fact that it was the initiative of the East Anglian Waterways Association that led to help from the Royal Engineers in clearing out the Old West River, once again a useful part of the waterways of Cambridgeshire.

III

FARMING AND RESEARCH

CAMBRIDGESHIRE, one of the eastern counties forming 'the granary of England', is a fertile area, much of which is classified in the first two of the Ministry of Agriculture's five grades of land. Farming here is efficient and productive but is more dependent on effective land drainage than in any other part of Britain. But with the potential loss of water by evaporation from the leaves of plants being greater than the average summer rainfall (10–14 inches), it is often necessary to irrigate the lighter lands.

The county's better land is the silt fenland in the extreme north, a region devoted to horticulture and general arable farming, and the peat fenland and islands to the south of this, where growers concentrate on cereals, root-crops and vegetables. Both these fenland areas are covered by small to medium holdings. To the west of the peat fenland are the Peterborough loams and sands whose small to medium units are under general arable crops and the Peterborough lime-stones and clays where units of varied size are given over to cereals and mixed farming.

Further south, on the Huntingdon boulder clays in the west of the county, is an area of general arable farming, its units of varied size. Adjoining this are units of similar size on the gravels, greensands and clays of the mid-Cambridgeshire fruit-growing area (general arable farming is also carried on here). Medium to large units occupy land classified mainly as grade 2–3 in the rest of the county, cereals and general arable crops being grown on the boulder clay loams of west Cambridgeshire and the low clays and silts of mid-Cambridgeshire and cereals and sugar-beet on the south Cambridgeshire chalky soils.

Of course these general statements give a somewhat

47

simplified picture, tending to obscure, for example, the difficulties of farming in parts of the fenland where loss of the peat, which steadily oxidizes away and is also affected by wind erosion, exposes the underlying soils, sometimes creating cropping problems. The difficulties of farming these changing soils is being studied at the Arthur Rickwood Experimental Husbandry Farm at Mepal, one of the chain of centres operated by the Agricultural Development and Advisory Service of the Ministry of Agriculture, Fisheries and Food. Here, in a flat area lying below mean sea-level, black fen peats of varying depths overlie sand, gravel and silty clay subsoils. An important part of the work involves investigations into the effects of raising and mixing different amounts of subsoil with the existing peat soil. The results to date indicate that sugar-beet is the most consistently responsive crop. Cereals have also benefited from mixing, spring wheat particularly on mixed sandy subsoils, winter wheats on both sandy and silty subsoils.

The serious fenland problem of wind erosion and blowing is also being tackled at the Arthur Rickwood Experimental Husbandry Farm. A hedge of a variety of purple willow planted in 1970 is already beginning to show its value, wind speed recordings taken on the leeward having shown encouraging reductions of the order of 10–60 per cent during 1976–77. Inter-row nurse crops of barley, mustard or rye and rows of straw 'planted' by machine are being used in other experiments aimed at reducing the damage to crops caused by fen blows.

Farms in other parts of Cambridgeshire are beset by difficulties peculiar to their own particular areas. There are bound to be many such local problems in a county with such a large area of agricultural land, 720,673 of its 840,419 acres (its total area, excluding water) being classified in this category. Some 637,000 acres are devoted to arable farming, almost two-thirds of it to cereal production. Wheat takes up more than 246,000 acres and barley another 158,000 acres.

Most Cambridgeshire-grown wheat is used for human food and livestock feed. Official figures give an estimated yield of 41.6 cwt of wheat per acre in Cambridgeshire (1974), the comparable figure for England being 39.5. Much of the

The chapel, Corpus Christi College, Cambridge

The River Cam below Jesus Green lock, Cambridge

Parker's Piece, Cambridge

The River Cam above Silver Street, Cambridge

The University Botanic Garden, Cambridge

Peterborough Cathedral: north aisle

The Old Guildhall, Peterborough

Peterborough: view from beneath the Old Guildhall

county's barley is grown for malting, the malt products themselves being sold to the brewing, bakery and food manufacturing industries, but some of the grain is fed to livestock. At an estimated 31.7 cwt per acre, the yield of barley in Cambridgeshire is just above the average figure for England.

About 9,000 acres are sown with oats while very much smaller areas are cropped with mixed corn and rye for threshing and maize for grain or for feeding to livestock either in its green state or as silage.

The sugar-beet is of considerable importance in Cambridgeshire, some 70,000 acres being under this crop there. Until recent years the sugar-beet crop involved considerable labour when hand singling was undertaken in the spring and when the roots, source of the sugar for which the beet are grown, were lifted and trimmed by hand in the autumn. Now monogerm varieties and seed pelleting, precision seed drills, selective herbicides and mechanical harvesting have all helped to eliminate most of the hand work.

Sugar, previously obtained solely from cane grown in tropical areas, was extracted from beet in Prussia in 1747, but many years passed before the discovery was exploited with commercial success in Britain. Pioneering attempts to do so failed in Essex and Suffolk during the nineteenth century, and then the university department of agriculture at Cambridge and the then Board of Agriculture established by experiments that sugar-beet could be grown successfully here. A processing factory was built in Norfolk in 1912 and, initial difficulties having been overcome, another seventeen, including those at Ely (1925) and Peterborough (1926), were erected by 1928.

In 1936 all the sugar factories were acquired by the British Sugar Corporation which, assisted by farmers in Cambridgeshire and certain other parts of the country, saved valuable shipping space during the Second World War by producing not only sugar but animal feeding-stuffs in the form of sugar-beet tops and pulp.

Now sugar-beet is grown under contract between individual growers and the British Sugar Corporation, the only beet sugar producer in the United Kingdom, the largest single beet sugar company in the western world, whose central offices are at

Peterborough. During the growing season crops are supervised by British Sugar's agricultural staff, the fieldsmen who advise farmers, look out for aphids and other pests and issue spray warning cards. Harvesting begins in September and continues into January, the farmers delivering to the factories the swollen roots in which the plants have stored sugar made in their leaves. During this period, the campaign, as it is known, the sugar factories in Cambridgeshire and elsewhere work twenty-four hours a day, seven days a week, extracting and refining sugar for domestic and industrial use.

The by-products of home sugar production are themselves valuable. Green tops removed on the farms are fed to livestock or ploughed back into the soil. Dried molassed beet pulp from the factories makes high-energy animal feed and there are large quantities of molasses for use in various industrial processes. Soil washed from the beet at the factories is sold, as is lime, a co-product of sugar processing that farmers use to reduce soil acidity and improve subsequent crops.

A large area of potatoes (some 42,000 acres in 1974) is grown in Cambridgeshire, the crop being especially important in the fenland and on the silts. Some of the main varieties seen in the county are King Edward, whose introduction dates from 1902, Pentland Crown, a product of the Scottish Plant Breeding Station, and Maris Piper. Bred at the Plant Breeding Institute in Maris Lane, Trumpington, Cambridge, the last-named variety is favoured in the fen area, its resistance to the yellow potato cyst eelworm, a common pest, being a valuable characteristic. Mainly medium-sized and with very good cooking quality, the tubers (the actual potatoes) of Maris Piper are very suitable for washing and pre-packing. Substantial amounts of Cambridgeshire-grown potatoes are sold in this way, often through centralized grading and marketing organizations, but many more are grown on contract for processing as crisps, frozen and par-fried, dehydrated and canned potatoes.

Vegetables (excluding potatoes) grown in the open account for almost another 35,000 acres of agricultural land in Cambridgeshire. Just under a half of this acreage is cropped with green peas. Those from about 500 acres are sent to market in the pod, peas from another 6,000 acres are canned, quick frozen or dehydrated, and those from yet another 8,000 acres are harvested dry. Processors of peas demand a very high standard and their fieldsmen keep a close watch on growing crops. Like all other plants, peas are affected by a number of pests. The pea moth is most serious on peas that are dry harvested and the pea midge, a tiny fly, can be a real nuisance in parts of the area.

Carrots occupy more than 5,000 acres in the county. Light clean soils produce carrots of good shape that are easily harvested and washed, and so the Chatteris area, with its light peat soil, has long been an important centre for this crop. Some of the carrots produced in Cambridgeshire are canned or processed in other ways, but the majority, many of them pre-packed, are marketed fresh.

In terms of the space devoted to them (some 4,000 acres), onions, a traditional crop in the black fens, are another of Cambridgeshire's main crops. Those from about 100 acres are grown as a green salad vegetable, but the majority are harvested dry as bulb onions for pre-packing or pickling. Onions can be dried artificially but, given suitable weather in autumn, they are lifted and left in the fields to ripen. French beans, mainly for processing, take up the best part of 3,000 acres. Broad beans, again mainly for freezing or canning, occupy nearly 700 acres, and runner beans, most of them for market, about a tenth of this area.

In Cambridgeshire celery is cultivated on 1,600 acres, an area amounting to almost a half of that devoted to this crop in England and Wales. Celery seedlings are produced by specialist growers from seed sown under glass and transplanted by machines in the spring. They do particularly well on the peat of the black fens. The county also makes a substantial contribution to the production of 'greens' of various types, by far the largest area being under Brussels sprouts (2,000 acres), cabbages (650 acres) and lettuce (450 acres). Root crops not already mentioned include beetroot (nearly 500 acres, the greater part for processing), parsnips (200 acres) and turnips and swedes (90 acres).

Beans, greens and roots for stock feeding use another large

part of the county's agricultural land. 4,000 acres are sown with mustard, a crop grown for seed, fodder or ploughing in, and rather more land is under oil-seed rape grown for its vegetable oil.

Although arable farming takes priority over much of the county, there are some 64,000 acres of permanent grass, largely confined to riverside marshes and washes and the heavier clays, 6,000 acres of rough grazing and 20,000 acres of temporary grass. About 23,000 acres of this land are mown, the grass harvested in this way being conserved for livestock feed.

Dairying and beef production are carried on in Cambridgeshire, but the number of cattle and calves (some 66,000 in 1974) amounts to a very small fraction of the national total. As in so many parts of the country, the black and white British Friesian, holder of many records, is the most familiar dairy breed in Cambridgeshire. By appearing in agricultural shows, such as the East of England Show at Peterborough, some of the county's Friesians not only attract interest in the breed but carry with them the names of Cambridgeshire parishes. Thus from J. H. Martin & Sons, Littleport, have come Littleport Celia, Littleport Pincher and Littleport Crocus, and from Horrell's Farmers Ltd., Longthorpe, Peterborough, Longthorpe Nestling, Longthorpe Babs, Longthorpe Pickle and others.

A much smaller number of Guernseys, the Channel Islands breed producing very rich milk, is kept in Cambridgeshire. Animals from the Guernsey herd owned by Horrell's Farmers Ltd have, like their Friesians, been given Longthorpe as a prefix to their names. Another great dairy breed, the hardy Ayrshire, has representatives in the county, among them Raveley Rose, Raveley Lillian and other animals from the herd of A. T. McCreadie & Sons, the Great Raveley breeders. Dairy Shorthorns are also kept in Cambridgeshire where a well-known herd (prefix Phorpres) is that of the London Brick Company at Yaxley, Peterborough.

Among beef cattle kept in Cambridgeshire are Herefords, red with broad white faces, and Charolais, the large white French breed. Bulls of these and certain other beef breeds are crossed with dairy cows, the cross-bred calves being more suitable for rearing for beef production than pure-bred ones.

At 50,000 the number of sheep and lambs is comparatively small. On the other hand, with nearly 260,000 on Cambridgeshire holdings in 1974, pigs form quite an important element in the county's farming activities. The popular breeds are Large White, Landrace and Welsh, but others are kept and often used to produce hybrids.

Cambridgeshire's poultry population of just under 2½ millions is small compared with that in, say, Norfolk (more than nine millions), but its output is by no means negligible. Most of the birds are classified as fowls and nearly half of these chickens, as the layman would call them, are reared as broilers for the table, the majority of the others producing eggs for eating. Most of the remaining 59,000 poultry are turkeys, the numbers of ducks and geese being small.

With more than 7,000 acres of them, Cambridgeshire has the fourth largest acreage of commercially grown orchards in England, only Kent, Hereford and Worcester, and Essex surpassing it. Dessert apples account for some 1,800 acres. Cox's Orange Pippin is the main variety and there are smaller acreages of Worcester Pearmain, Discovery, Golden Delicious, Egremont Russet, and other varieties. Cooking apples take up about the same acreage as dessert types, the greater part of the ground being planted with Bramleys Seedling, a speciality of the Wisbech area where the industry is based on processing. Pears are grown on 959 acres, the second largest acreage for England and Wales, exceeded only by Kent with its 8,000 acres of pear orchards. The chief variety in Cambridgeshire is Conference (800 acres), with smaller areas devoted to Williams Bon Chretien, Doyenne du Comice, and others. A few acres of perry pears are also grown, but cider apples are of no commercial importance in the county.

Cambridgeshire, with 2,600 acres, has the third largest area of plum orchards in England and Wales, most of the fruit being sold for processing. The Victoria plum is the main variety, but the Pershore (Yellow Egg) plum, damsons, greengages, and other plums are also grown. The county has thirty acres of cherries, about one-third sweet varieties, the remainder acid.

Small fruit take up almost another 2,000 acres in Cambridgeshire, putting the county fourth, after Hereford and Worcester, Kent and Norfolk, for this type of crop. Strawberries account for more than 1,200 acres and less areas are under raspberries, blackcurrants. gooseberries and other small fruit. The area of gooseberries, 476 acres, is the second largest in the country, only Kent exceeding it.

Bulbs, flowers and hardy nursery stock are grown on 2,000 acres of open agricultural land in Cambridgeshire, while glasshouses, more than half of them heated, cover another 160 acres.

As mentioned several times in this chapter, much Cambridgeshire-grown produce is sold for processing. This is not an entirely recent development here, for the county is something of a pioneer in these matters. The pea-vining machine sited at Smedleys of Wisbech in the 1920s was the first of its kind installed in England and probably in Europe. Later, in 1937, when they began quick freezing at Wisbech, Smedley's frozen foods were the first to be introduced to the English housewife.

The Smedley story, an important one for both growers and consumers, developed soon after the First World War when Samuel Wallace Smedley, a successful fruit merchant, opened a factory at Wisbech where gooseberries, raspberries, strawberries, plums, apples, and other fruits were canned and bottled. In the 1920s modern American pea-canning machines, including viners, were installed. Smedleys went on to develop other processes and new products, among them celery hearts, carrots and mixed diced vegetables. Additional factories were opened in other parts of the country and a wide range of quick frozen fruits and vegetables were packed and sold throughout Britain by retail shops, each with a refrigerated cabinet.

During the Second World War, when quick freezing was suspended, Smedleys produced greatly increased quantities of canned foods, including soups and jams, some of which were sent in Red Cross parcels to prisoners of war. In 1945 quick freezing started again at Wisbech, and meat, fish and potato chips were added to the list of products. Now Smedley-HP Foods Limited is part of the great Imperial Group, and the factory at Wisbech is one of six producing Smedley canned foods, HP baked beans and some Ross frozen foods. The founder's grandson is Managing Director and those growing fruit and vegetables for the company include sons and grandsons of Smedley's earliest suppliers.

Pioneer work in canning was also undertaken in Cambridgeshire by Chivers whose factory in the ancient village of Histon, near Cambridge, now one of those in the Cadbury Schweppes Food Group, is the manufacturing centre for preserves sold under the Chivers, Hartley, Moorhouse and Rose's labels. Members of the Chivers family have farmed in the Histon area since at least the early years of the nineteenth century. Originally they appear to have concentrated on cereal crops, turning to fruit growing between 1860 and 1870 when grain prices dropped during an agricultural depression.

Eventually the quantities of fresh fruit available exceeded those sold locally and through the great market at Covent Garden in London. New outlets were found in Yorkshire but, in 1873, when they discovered that much of their fruit was being used for this purpose, Chivers themselves decided to start making jam at Histon. Their products were well received and Chivers and Sons, a limited company by 1875, went on to develop canned fruit and vegetable processes, opening factories at Huntingdon, where canned peas were a speciality, and Montrose in the Scottish raspberry-growing area. It is nearly twenty years since Chivers sold their business to Schweppes, but members of the family still farm and one of the pleasures of living in Cambridge is to be able to drive out to Histon to buy their excellent apples.

Not all Cambridgeshire-grown fruit and vegetables go to processors. Comparatively small volumes of produce are sold by farm shops and direct to the public on a 'pick your own' basis. Large quantities are disposed of by commission salesmen in the wholesale markets or marketed by independent packhouses or through some form of co-operative. One fenland farmers' co-operative, the March-based Fenmarc Potatoes, has packhouses at Littleport and Chatteris. Founded in 1969, it has forty-five members and handled produce to the value of more than £4,000,000 during the 1976-77 season. Another such co-operative, Fengrain, has 170 members, its premises at Wimblington, near March, being the largest custom-built farmer-owned store in the country.

Problems affecting marketing are constantly borne in mind not only by growers and their organizations but also by the staffs of institutions engaged on experimental · work and research in Cambridgeshire. Workers at the Arthur Rickwood Experimental Husbandry Farm, already mentioned, have on many occasions shown their concern for such practical considerations. For example, in reporting the results of crop variety tests, attention is called to varieties of carrots whose smooth skin, bright colour and uniform shape make them a good proposition for canning or pre-packing.

Apart from soil studies and crop variety testing, the experimental programme at the Arthur Rickwood Experimental Husbandry Farm lists work on celery, cereals, leeks, onions, potatoes and sugar-beet. Investigations on potatoes include methods of controlling potato cyst eelworm whose three known races can cause very severe losses in yield, gangrene, a fungal infection of tubers which can result in serious losses during storage and after planting, aphids, transmitters of virus infections, and cutworm. Work on this and other crops is concerned with planting, treatment, harvesting and storage, as well as pests and diseases.

The second of the Cambridgeshire Experimental Husbandry Farms, another of the centres operated by the Agricultural Development and Advisory Service, is at Boxworth, mid-way between Cambridge and Huntingdon, between 25 and 67 metres above sea-level. Selected as the experimental husbandry farm for the clay soils on the drier side of England, Boxworth is mainly concerned with experimental work on arable husbandry, mainly cereal growing, dairy farming with autumn-calving Friesians of the herd established in 1952, and the production of beef from Friesian steers. Parts of the farm are managed to produce grass for grazing and forage for conservation, while others are continuously cropped with cereals (certain fields have carried wheat for up to twenty-six years consecutively) or devoted to break crops such as beans or oil-seed rape followed by two winter wheat crops.

In recent years the experimental programme has included many investigations into various aspects of winter wheat, the main cereal crop at Boxworth, methods of cultivation and husbandry, control of weeds and diseases of cereal crops, break crops, fodder conservation, management of dairy cattle and rearing of calves.

A number of miscellaneous crops have been grown in order to assess their potential. Lucerne, a purple-flowered leguminous plant, is one of them. Also known as alfalfa, a name derived from the Moorish for 'best of fodders', it has been some-what neglected in this country despite its popularity with seventeenth-century farming improvers. Workers at Boxworth have shown that lucerne, long-rooted and drought-resisting, has several advantages over other fodder crops. 'Fixing' this element, a gas making up four-fifths of the atmosphere, through bacteria in its root nodules, it requires no additional nitrogen and thus there is a saving in fertilizer. Lucerne, with its high protein content, has enabled dairy cattle to be fed more economically at Boxworth, where crops succeeding it have benefited from the residual effect of the nitrogen compounds in its root nodules. As at the Arthur Rickwood Experimental Husbandry Farm, variety testing of crops is carried out at Boxworth in conjunction with the National Institute of Agricultural Botany (N.I.A.B.).

With its headquarters and main trial grounds in Cambridge and fourteen regional centres in the main crop production areas of England and Wales, N.I.A.B is a vital force in modern British agriculture and horticulture whose work has an added international importance. Charged with improving the general level of crop variety and seed quality, it was set up in Cambridge in 1919 after deficiencies in these respects had been found to be limiting home food production during the First World War.

N.I.A.B. tests on a field scale over a number of years all new varieties of most agricultural and horticultural crops (fruit and flowers are notable exceptions). Assessments are made by specialist officers of field characters, quality and yield over a range of sites, soils and seasons. Eventually, after close and expert scrutiny of results, annually-revised lists of the best varieties available in this country are issued for the guidance of farmers and vegetable growers. Varieties are recommended for general use, special use and particular parts of the country, and attention is called to varieties becoming outclassed.

N.I.A.B. fully describes and classifies each new variety, a very necessary activity as every one must have some unique characteristic in order to be legally saleable in this country. N.I.A.B is also the technical co-ordinator and operator of the United Kingdom Seed Certification Scheme. This requires all seed sold here to be true to variety and to meet high standards of purity and germination capacity. To ensure that the regulations are being observed, seed samples are tested in the Official Seed Testing Station at N.I.A.B. Although most of the funds are provided by the Ministry of Agriculture, N.I.A.B. is an independent body managed by a governing council. Its fellowship scheme is open to all interested in agriculture, enabling them to receive newsletters of up-to-date information and leaflets as they are published.

N.I.A.B. maintains close contact with the Plant Breeding Institute (P.B.I.) at Maris Lane, Trumpington, on the outskirts of Cambridge. Founded in 1912, this organization produces improved varieties of arable and forage crops and engages in related research in breeding methodology, pathology, genetics, cytogenetics, cell biology and plant physiology. Financed mainly by grants from the Agricultural Research Council, it has a staff of 170 plant breeders, plant pathologists, physiologists, entomologists, geneticists, biochemists and other scientists and one hundred other people whose numbers are increased from time to time by visiting research workers. More than 400 acres are available for experimental work, another 70 acres on local farms being used as trial grounds. In addition there are laboratories, extensive glasshouses and controlled environment chambers.

High yield, freedom from pests and diseases, and the improvement of quality are basic objectives of all P.B.I breeding programmes, but the requirements of maltsters, farmers, sugar refiners, manufacturers of potato crisps and other industrial processors are given due attention. P.B.I. varieties are named and marketed under the registered trademark of Maris (for example, Maris Huntsman and Maris Freeman are P.B.I-bred winter wheats). In 1976 Maris varieties appeared thirty-three times on the N.I.A.B. Recommended List, a further twenty-four were on the National List, and thirty-five varieties of cereals, potatoes, kale, oil seed rape, beans, maize, grasses and lucerne appear on the official lists of twelve overseas countries. Added recognition of the great value of its work came in 1973 and 1975, two years when the P.B.I. received the Queen's Award to Industry for outstanding achievement in technological innovation.

One cannot consider the achievements of the P.B.I. without stressing the vital importance of the pioneering activities of Rowland Harry Biffen who was later knighted and made a Fellow of the Royal Society, for his work and foresight led to the beginning of agricultural plant breeding at Cambridge and to an understanding of the need to adopt scientific methods. After graduating in natural sciences at Cambridge, he was appointed in 1899, at the age of twenty-five, to the new university department of agriculture where he studied Mendelian inheritance in wheat and barley by hybridization with the object of breeding improved varieties for commercial use on farms.

Early in his career Biffen crossed a popular English wheat, Squareheads Master, with Ghirka, a Russian variety resistant to the fungus disease yellow rust. From the progeny of this cross he selected his variety Little Joss and made this winter wheat, with its yellow rust resistance, available to farmers in 1910. (It remained on the N.I.A.B Recommended List until 1956.) Biffen was made professor of agricultural botany at Cambridge in 1911, and the following year director of the newly established Cambridge University Plant Breeding Institute. In 1916 he made available his important new winter wheat Yeoman. Combining baking quality, high yield and good standing power, this hybrid between the North American wheat Red Fife and the English variety Browick set a new high standard and remained a recommended variety for forty-one years.

Biffen, who had continued to develop the activities of the institute, engaging staff to work on wheat, barley, oats, peas and other crops, retired in 1936. Soon after the Second World War the P.B.I became independent of Cambridge University and moved to its present premises and land at Trumpington.

New barleys of malting standard were bred, among them
Proctor. Awarded the N.I.A.B. Challenge Cup for the best
home-bred cereal variety of the year in 1953, and taking up
half the barley acreage by 1956, Proctor received many national
malting barley championships. Now becoming outclassed, it
has contributed to increased barley production in this country
and to the parentage of such recommended varieties as Maris
Otter, a high malting quality barley bred at the P.B.I., and
Lofa Abed, a spring barley produced in Denmark.

Maris Peer, the first potato bred at the P.B.I., was added to
the N.I.A.B. Recommended List in 1963. Produced by crossing
Ulster Knight, a variety of the cultivated *Solanum tuberosum*,
with an unnamed seedling derived from *Solanum demissum*, a
wild Mexican species of potato, this outstanding early variety is
widely grown. High yielding, its medium to small tubers are
suitable for pre-packaging and canning, and its resistance to
several diseases also serves to recommend it. A second variety,
Maris Page, followed in 1965, and then, in 1966, came Maris
Piper, a variety bred for the very valuable characteristic of
resistance to potato cyst eelworm. Others have since been bred
and, as with other crop plants grown at the P.B.I., more will
follow.

The work of multiplying, promoting and marketing crop
varieties produced by the P.B.I. and other official plant breeding
stations of the United Kingdom is undertaken by the National
Seed Development Organization (N.S.D.O.). Incorporated in
1967 and based at Newton Hall, Cambridge, this government-
owned company is also involved in the patenting of plant
breeding techniques evolved at the research stations and in the
licensing of their use. N.S.D.O. normally grows basic seed and
plants of the varieties for which it is responsible and sells them
to the seeds and nursery industries for further multiplication
and sale to farmers and growers. Its overseas activities have
secured the admission of many varieties bred in Cambridge and
other parts of Britain to national lists in France, Belgium,
Denmark and other countries.

International links have also been established by a number of
Cambridgeshire research organizations concerned with farm
livestock. The Agricultural Research Council's Institute of

Animal Physiology (I.A.P.) at Babraham, Cambridge, receives many visiting foreign scientists and research students, and members of its own staff attend conferences and symposia in various parts of the world.

The establishment of I.A.P. in 1948 resulted from the Agricultural Research Council's concern that progress towards the improvement of animal health and production was hindered by lack of knowledge of the fundamental physiology of farm animals. Babraham Hall with 450 acres of land was purchased and the first departments set up. The original nineteenth-century building, housing offices and library, is the centre of an organization whose laboratories, livestock buildings, workshops, forty-six staff houses and farm form part of an estate provided with its own water supply and sewage plant. Officially described as long term strategic research to extend knowledge of the basic physiology and biochemistry of farm livestock as a foundation for improved animal production, I.A.P.'s work also involves basic studies on other species, including small laboratory animals. Although I.A.P. issues biennial reports of its work, the detailed accounts of research results appear in scientific periodicals. Thus during a recent two-year period (1974-75) 391 of these scientific papers were published.

Cattle, sheep, pigs and goats for research are bred on the farm, surplus animals being disposed of commercially or to other research institutes, universities and hospitals. Besides supplying animals to the laboratories, the herd of Jersey cows has formed the basis for several research projects, including the development of a pregnancy diagnosis test by progesterone estimation in milk, now available for large scale use in dairy herds, and the detection of mastitis by the milk conductivity test. Animals from the herd, which has achieved distinction in all Channel Islands classes of the county competition, have been exported to the Sultanate of Oman, Libya, Iran and other countries.

Sheep are represented at I.A.P. by a large prize-winning flock of Clun Forest ewes and smaller numbers of Soay, Merino, Jacob and other types. There is also a 100-sow unit of Large White pigs and herd of eighty Saanen goats.

The I.A.P. scientific staff numbers about 150 and there are some thirty visiting scientists and about twenty people doing postgraduate research. From the records of publications and accounts of outside activities in the biennial reports it is clear that these highly qualified men and women bring to their work a strong sense of dedication.

Professor Ivan de Burgh Daly, formerly professor of physiology in Edinburgh, served as first director from 1948 until his retirement in 1958. His successor, Sir John Gaddum, retired after six years and then Dr Richard Keynes held office until 1973 when he returned as professor to the physiological laboratory in Cambridge. The present director, Dr B. A. Cross, has served as president of the International Society of Neuro-endocrinology and on the committees of a number of scientific societies. At I.A.P. he has established a director's group for neuroendocrinological research. "Neurobiology has," he writes in his introduction to the eighth biennial report, "been a neglected area in agricultural science which has tended to treat livestock as if they were ambulatory crops. We hope that the presence of neurochemists, neuropharmacologists, neuro-physiologists and neuroendocrinologists in the laboratories will enhance our ability to exploit the newer concepts of brain science in the service of animal production and welfare."

Towards the end of 1976 the Animal Research Station (formerly the Agricultural Research Council unit of repro-ductive physiology and biochemistry) at Huntingdon Road, Cambridge, became part of I.A.P. Here about thirty scientists undertake research into the morphology, physiology and biochemistry of germ cells and the reproductive tract and the application of scientific knowledge to animal breeding.

The causes and control of avian diseases, particularly those causing serious economic losses to the poultry industry, and interrelated biochemical, physiological and husbandry problems are investigated at the Agricultural Research Council Houghton Poultry Research Station. With headquarters near St Ives and satellite breeding units at Boxworth and Girton, it produces for experimental purposes its own supply of eggs, embryos and hatched birds from flocks whose health is checked regularly. Close contact with the poultry industry and scientific

organizations enables Houghton to be kept fully aware of
current poultry health problems and to offer its assistance
accordingly.

Established by the Animal Health Trust in 1948 (it is now
financed entirely by the Agricultural Research Council), the
Station has acquired a reputation for scientific achievement. As
early as 1949 it identified the agent, a fungus, responsible for
moniliasis in turkeys, and since then there has not been a year
without some important development. Taking just a few
examples, we find two vaccines against fowl typhoid developed
in 1956, the practicality of breeding for resistance to Marek's
disease and lymphoid leukosis confirmed in 1966, the development of a vaccine against Marek's disease reported in 1968, and
a link between gizzard erosion and certain fish meals established six years later.

Since 1974 Houghton Poultry Research Station, with its staff
of over 200, has been directed by Dr P. M. Biggs, who has
served as president of the British Veterinary Poultry Association and as secretary-treasurer of the World Veterinary
Poultry Association, and was elected a Fellow of the Royal
Society in 1976 for distinguished contributions on tumours of
chickens, on the virus causing Marek's disease and on the
development of a successful vaccine against this condition. Like
so many of his colleagues, Dr Biggs assists in the dissemination
of knowledge by publishing the results of his research in
scientific journals, contributing to meetings of national and
international scientific societies, and helping with lectures and
courses.

Similar contributions are made by several other centres of
research and development in Cambridgeshire. Among them
are a number of Agricultural Research Council units not
already mentioned, such as those for developmental botany
and soil physics. Cambridge University has departments concerned with agriculture, land economy, applied biology and
veterinary medicine. Then there are the regional laboratories,
veterinary investigation centre and field drainage experimental
unit of the Ministry of Agriculture, Fisheries and Food at
Cambridge.

Information from these various sources reaches farmers

through the Ministry's Agricultural Development and Advisory Service, the agricultural Press, radio, television and advisory officers of marketing boards and commercial concerns. Happily there is a growing appreciation of the need to keep the public informed on farming matters and for the interest of children to be aroused and developed from an early age.

The East of England Show, held annually at Peterborough, forms a vital link between all sections of the farming world, the general public and schools, providing exhibits of technical, educational and cultural interest, as well as all the other features one expects to find at such a great outdoor exhibition. In 1977 it attracted a total three-day attendance of 154,700, some 10,000 being schoolchildren.

The show is organized by the East of England Agricultural Society. With a membership of some 7,300, this body, formed in 1970 by a merger of the Cambridgeshire and Isle of Ely, Huntingdonshire, and Peterborough Agricultural Societies (it has since been joined by others), derives much of its strength from the fact that it is not only concerned with farming but also with people, proclaiming two facts that are often overlooked, namely: "Farming is the nation's greatest single industry; people are its greatest asset." Emphasizing the interdependence of people and farming, the society presents long service awards to farm workers and silver medals for ideas and innovations contributing substantially to farming technology.

Bought for just under £25,000, and provided with ring areas, buildings, eleven miles of roadways and essential services at a cost of £303,000, the East of England showground covers 300 acres bounded by the A1 and A605. A centre of great interest and activity throughout the summer show, it has attracted an increasing number of trade stands over the years (631 in 1977). In 1977 there were more livestock entries than in any previous year. In addition to 1,404 light horses and ponies, there were 114 heavy horses (the showground is the home of the Shire Horse Society), 818 cattle, 118 sheep, 168 goats and 378 pigs. While the more familiar ones, those of greatest commercial importance, are exhibited in force, other breeds also appear in the show, and the Rare Breeds Survival Trust puts on live and static displays featuring lesser-known kinds of domestic livestock, illustrating their history and place in the modern world.

It may strike some people as more than a little curious that anyone should expect those engaged in farming, an industry now so highly mechanized and complex, to be concerned about the preservation of endangered types of British farm animals. But it is a fact that there are farmers interested in such matters. Many of them also have sympathy for the nature conservation cause, though some may on occasion display hostility towards certain people calling themselves conservationists.

One must never be surprised by the reactions of individual farmers to these or indeed other issues. For, as is the case with all other groups of people, one cannot be dogmatic about them and one must certainly not think in terms of 'the typical farmer' or 'the farmer's point of view'. This is evident from the results of research carried out at the University of Essex by a team of four sociologists investigating the social situation of farmers in East Anglia. Their typology of East Anglian farmers is of considerable interest. Though, like all such schemes, it may over-simplify a complex human situation, one recognizes their farming types in Cambridgeshire.

First there is the 'gentleman farmer' who takes little direct part in the actual working of the farm whose management is not strongly affected by changing market conditions. He may employ a manager or agent and devote much of his own time to civic or charitable work. Occasionally he combines an active interest in hunting or shooting with a genuine concern for wildlife.

Then there is the family farmer. Like the gentleman farmer, he does not always worry too much about market orientation but, unlike him, he is personally and actively involved in the running of his farm, spending a lot of his time working on the land. He is often sympathetic to environmental and nature conservation issues, though he does not suffer gladly people lacking detailed personal knowledge of farming and its problems.

The remaining two types of farmers are very much concerned with market conditions and the need to make money. They differ in the extent to which they are personally involved in the actual operations of husbandry. The agri-businessman has very little, if any, time for manual work. He keeps busy with market reports, statistics and accounts, and his farm often has the look of an efficient and well kept factory. The active managerial farmer is not only a businessman but he is personally active on the farm, supervising here, checking there, advising on one problem, helping physically with the solution of another. Sentiment plays little part in the farming lives of these businessmen-farmers, but they are potentially valuable allies of those who, having studied the facts, are prepared to discuss ecological, conservation and other issues against a background of reality. They have no time for anyone who would treat the countryside as a museum or as a playground for townspeople. Certainly in Cambridgeshire it is not, and cannot, be seen in this light. All the same, there is much in the county to interest visitors who come prepared to appreciate its great contribution to British agriculture, a result stemming largely from the determination of generations of men to drain the land and keep the waters under control.

IV

INDUSTRY

ALTHOUGH it is predominantly an agricultural county, Cambridgeshire makes, notably at Peterborough and Cambridge, important contributions to the output of Britain's manufacturing industries and helps in no small way to swell the country's exports.

Many centuries ago the presence of suitable supplies of clay made the Peterborough area an outstanding centre for the production of pottery. These same natural resources led to the manufacture of bricks, the Fletton type having, in fact, derived its name from the village, now an industrial suburb of Peterborough, where it was first made in 1881. The London Brick Company Ltd (L.B.C.), whose enterprise and initiative have enabled it to build up the largest brick-making operation in the world, has brick works in the Peterborough and Whittlesey areas (and also, of course, in places not covered by this book) and owns and farms stretches of clay-bearing land, its land bank of clay reserves.

L.B.C. saved a considerable acreage of valuable clay-bearing land when, in 1968, it decided to replace the nineteenth-century King's Dyke Works at Whittlesey and to build a new production unit on the floor of the pit, 85 feet deep and 55 acres in extent, created during 114 years of excavation for clay. The success of this operation led to the proposal to site a second new works in the same area. The use by L.B.C.'s subsidiary company London Brick Land Development Ltd of worked-out brick pits for the disposal of industrial waste and household refuse may well enable land that would otherwise remain derelict to be reclaimed and returned to agricultural use.

Almost twenty years ago L.B.C. pits in Peterborough were among those investigated for future water storage. They were not called into service and the great reservoir of Grafham

Water was made by flooding hundreds of acres of agricultural land. During the dry summer of 1976, however, the Anglian Water Authority approached L.B.C. on the likely need to draw off water from their large flooded pit, Stewartby Lake, in neighbouring Bedfordshire!

The geological structure of Cambridgeshire is such that in places there are raw materials suitable for the manufacture of Portland cement. At Cherry Hinton, on the eastern side of Cambridge, Associated Portland Cement Manufacturers Ltd, the parent of a major international group of companies known as the Blue Circle Group, has one of its smaller works. Originally built about 1904, it employs just over a hundred people and produces some 112,000 tonnes of cement each year. Norman Works, as it is known, has always been proud of the fact that its fine quality cement has been used in many important construction projects, among them Stockport Town Hall, Blackbrook Dam (Loughborough), Great Yarmouth waterworks reservoir and the Empire Stadium at Wembley. There is another cement works, the property of Rugby Portland Cement Co. Ltd, at Barrington.

Cambridgeshire has much highly fertile soil and, as in certain other parts of the country, manufacturing processes depending on agriculture and farm produce have developed. Malting, milling and brewing are examples of old-established activities still represented in the county.

Paines of St Neots, a private limited company established in 1831 by James Paine who farmed at Toseland Manor near Paxton, have earned an excellent reputation not only in this country but overseas. Malt extract manufacturers, millers and brewers, they use cereals grown mainly in local areas to high quality specifications. Their malt extract factory is in continuous operation throughout the year, producing a complete range of malt extracts for use in brewing (hopped malt extract for home brewing is a major part of the company's output), food and confectionery manufacture and for medicinal preparations. The founder started by brewing beers in his own house and now the company brews for both home and export markets a range of beers comprising bitter, EG traditional ale, mild, old English, pale ale and gold medal. As leading specialist millers, Paines manufacture speciality flours from cereals, soya and malt for use in the processed-foods manufacturing industry.

At Wisbech the independent company of Elgood and Sons Ltd, whose brewery is situated on the North Brink of the River Nene, maintains a tradition established there in the eighteenth century when Dennis Herbert and John Cooch bought a seventeenth-century mill and granaries and converted the buildings into a brewery. In 1877 ownership of the business passed into the hands of John Elgood, a maltster from Huntingdon who was mayor of Godmanchester, and has remained in the family ever since. Today the brewery, modernized and extended, owns and supplies fifty-eight public houses, all within thirty miles of Wisbech, and much of its beer is still classed as 'real ale'.

Flour milling, already given as one of the industries of St Neots, and the manufacture of animal feeding-stuffs are carried on in Peterborough, Cambridge and elsewhere in the county. At Cambridge the Foster Mills were built near the railway station by the Foster family, millers and bankers, towards the end of the last century. Just after the Second World War the premises were acquired by Spillers (now Spillers-French Milling Ltd), who replaced the existing equipment by a complete modern plant, including the first pneumatic conveying system in the country, and built a second silo whose capacity of more than 5,000 tons of grain is twice that of the original silo. Close to Foster Mills is the research and technology centre where quality control and product and process development and improvement are dealt with for the whole of the Spillers group. There is also a nutritional centre at Kennett, near Newmarket, whose staff conduct research into food for human consumption and into feeding for all kinds of animals.

Industrial activities based on sugar-beet and certain fruits and vegetables were dealt with in the last chapter. Others associated with agriculture and horticulture include the manufacture of machinery. At Ely the Dorman Sprayer Company produces crop-spraying machinery and equipment for the home and export markets. Machines made by the company, pioneers in the application of selective weed-killers to sugar-beet on the band-spraying principle, a system for which its equipment is now used overseas, ensure the accurate application of chemicals to growing crops to control weeds, pests and diseases. With its rapid expansion, the company left the small premises in Cambridge where it started in 1948 and moved to larger ones in Ely in 1964.

Lurmark, the agricultural engineers who are considered to be the largest British manufacturer of these products, make spray nozzles used on agricultural equipment. Established in 1954, this small company exports about a third of its output to nine countries. Root Harvesters, the Peterborough agricultural engineers, make potato harvesters and other equipment, while Simplex of Cambridge Ltd manufacture grain storage, dairy and horticultural equipment and forage stores at Sawston. Diesels built by Perkins Engines, the large Peterborough company, are serving agriculture in many parts of the world. Produced in three, four, six and eight cylinder configurations with outputs from 30 to 180 b.h.p., they are used by such leading manufacturers as Allis Chalmers, Balthus Farm Equipment, International Harvester and Massey-Ferguson.

Demands for livestock housing and storage facilities for produce and materials have stimulated the manufacture of farm buildings in the county. There are companies active in this field of production at such places as Balsham, Peakirk and Peterborough. The Cozy-Shel (Insulation) Co. of Whittlesey carries out *in-situ* sprayed insulation, a method that prevents condensation forming on the underside of tin roofs and saves space in potato stores by making the use of bulky straw bales unnecessary.

At least two large companies in Cambridgeshire are concerned with agrochemicals. The Agrochemical Division of Fisons Ltd has a chemical works at Hauxton, and the Agrochemical Division of Ciba-Geigy (UK) Ltd, a subsidiary of Ciba-Geigy Ltd of Basle, Switzerland, deals with the sale and development of its products at Whittlesford.

The Plastics Division of Ciba-Geigy at Duxford specializes in synthetic resins and adhesives. A. E. and N. Ashton & Co Ltd, a company whose decision to move there from the

London area in the 1960s created additional employment in Ely, constructs chemical plant in plastics materials. As engineers in reinforced plastics, they made and installed, for example, the tanks and pipelines for a nickel refinery.

There are in Cambridgeshire several companies producing plastic toys and toy kits. One of them, Lesney Products, who moved to Peterborough a few years ago, are well known as makers of 'matchbox' toys. Their new factory was established at Woodston to carry out production of plastic model kits, a toy line then entirely new to the company. Now they make about a hundred different kinds of plastic models - aircraft, cars, boats and so on, most of which are exported.

Printing, one of Cambridgeshire's oldest industries, also helps to increase Britain's exports, taking the names of the county and its principal towns to many parts of the world. As early as the year 1534 the right of the University of Cambridge to print and sell all manner of books was granted by Henry VIII in Royal Letters Patent. Today Cambridge University Press, a charitable enterprise, self-financing and generating its own funds, has the same objectives as the university itself, namely: "The acquisition, advancement, conservation and dissemination of knowledge in all subjects; the advancement of education, religion, learning, and research; and the advancement of literature and good letters."

The Press is governed by a committee of senior members of the university (under a chairman appointed by the Vice-chancellor as personal deputy) whose approval is needed before any new book, journal or Bible can be published there. More than half of the staff of nearly a thousand are employed in Cambridge, where the headquarters, printing division and part of the publishing division are located, the remainder working in London.

With branches in Australia and the U.S.A., Cambridge University Press exports large numbers of the 400 new books it publishes each year. It supplies over 500 different Bibles and prayer books, being one of the three English presses which may lawfully print the authorized version of the Bible and almost certainly the oldest Bible printer and publisher in the world. In addition some 4,000 scholarly books are maintained in stock. Besides working for its own publishing division, the university and the colleges, the Press's printing works prints for learned societies and examination boards in this country and overseas.

Similar work for learned societies is undertaken in Cambridge by Heffers Printers Ltd who, offering a comprehensive design and printing service, has increasingly turned its attention to the growing market for printing resulting from the industrial and commercial development of certain parts of the country. Heffers' printing activities began in 1911 when William Heffer, who in 1876 had opened a little shop selling postcards and other small items, acquired a small printing works. Enlarged twelve years later, the premises were rebuilt in 1935 and further extended in 1956. Finally in 1973 Heffers moved to a new purpose-built factory with 40,000 square feet of modern plant two miles from the centre of Cambridge. Heffers Printers Ltd, with a staff of over 200, is one of the Heffer Group whose four bookshops are vital links with the world of books for countless scholars and readers not only in this country but overseas.

Three of Heffers' bookshops, the main one and those for children's books and paperbacks, are in Trinity Street. This narrow and busy thoroughfare is blessed with three other bookshops. The premises of one of them, that of Bowes and Bowes at No. 1, will always be associated with the great publishing house of Macmillan, for it was to this building that Daniel Macmillan, founder of the firm, moved in 1845. Two years earlier he had set up for himself as bookseller at no. 17 Trinity Street where he added publishing to the business in 1844. Sad to say, Daniel Macmillan died at the tragically early age of forty-four in 1857, the year he published *Tom Brown's Schooldays*.

Newspaper and periodical publishing and contract printing are undertaken on a large scale at Peterborough by companies of the East Midland Allied Press Group, producers of *Angling Times, Garden News, Motor Cycle News* and twelve other nat ional publications and of *Lincoln, Rutland and Stamford Mercury* (founded *c.* 1712) and twelve other provincial newspapers. The group was inaugurated after the Second World

War by R. P. Winfrey whose father, Sir Richard Winfrey, Liberal Member of Parliament for Norfolk and Lincolnshire constituencies from 1906 to 1924, acquired his first newspaper, the *Spalding Guardian*, in 1887. In 1965 it took new premises at Woodston, Peterborough, to house one of the first offset-litho printing and colour presses designed for newspapers. Colour pages for insertion in national newspapers and the group's own publications are pre-printed and re-reeled. The pre-print plant is believed to be the biggest and most modern in Europe, and the Woodston complex, with its new presses and advanced computerized photocomposition of text and production of printing plates, is an important centre of technical innovation and achievement.

R. P. Winfrey, who was chairman of East Midland Allied Press until 1973, had seen a 'Spearhead' web-offset press made at Westwood Works, Peterborough, by Baker Perkins who gave up, for the time being, the manufacture of these machines after the sudden death of John Crabtree who had supplied the designs. In 1961 Winfrey visited the Danish family of Aller, who gave such great impetus to offset, with its advantages over the letterpress method of printing, and decided to have a web-offset plant installed in his own printing works. Advocating Anglo-Danish collaboration, he suggested that Baker Perkins should acquire the British rights of Aller offset machinery. Several years were spent in negotiation but – to cut a long story short – Baker Perkins had become the most important makers of web-offset printing machinery in Europe by the end of 1967. Their web-offset presses are exported to many parts of the world, notably to the United States, and in Australia *Reader's Digest* is printed by one such Peterborough-built machine, a giant weighing over 450 tons.

Another company in Peterborough, Crosfield Electronics, manufactures specialist graphical and press control machinery. Brotherhoods have made bank-note printing presses, just one of many products designed and built by these Peterborough manufacturers, who are proud to know that precision machinery built in Cambridgeshire by their skilled engineers is working efficiently and reliably in at least eighty countries all over the world. Brotherhoods have erected in the Soviet

Union, Turkey and elsewhere fibre-spinning machinery made at Peterborough and, to quote another example, they have made stainless steel filters for use in a factory in Chile. Their steam turbines and air and gas compressors are well known throughout the world. One large contract involved supplying fifty-one turbines for sugar refineries in South America, another compressors for an ammonia fertilizer complex in Central America.

Perkins Engines, all of whose United Kingdom factories are in Peterborough, was mentioned earlier in connection with its services to agriculture. But, vitally important as these are, they represent only part of its output, Perkins diesel engines also going into commercial vehicles, fork-lift trucks and marine craft. Perkins had moved into new manufacturing facilities at Eastfield, Peterborough, in 1947 when production reached a hundred engines a day. Within three years it had formed subsidiary companies in Australia, North America and France. Nine years later Perkins was acquired by one of its major customers, Massey-Ferguson Ltd of Toronto, Canada. In 1962, when 80 per cent of its production was exported, Perkins produced its one millionth 'export' engine in Peterborough and only a few years later it received its first Queen's Award to Industry for its export achievements.

Perkins continues to develop throughout the world, but its Peterborough manufacturing facility remains the largest engine-producing unit in the entire group. The main Eastfield production plant and the V8 engine plant at Fletton had a combined output of 269,437 engines (87 per cent were exported) and 123,000 CKD (engine assembly) kits in 1976, and are supported by extensive components manufacturing, packing and warehousing facilities. With an eye to the future, Perkins has expanded at Peterborough, introduced new machine tools, completed a 100,000 square-foot area for marshalling engines prior to despatch and a new, air-conditioned computer facility, and constructed a new engineering complex for research and development.

Certain of the products of Baker Perkins (not to be confused with Perkins Engines, just mentioned) have already been described, but we must find space for some, at least, of their

other activities in Cambridgeshire, bearing in mind that the
Baker Perkins Group also includes companies based in other
parts of Britain and overseas. Food machinery, particularly
equipment for the bakery industry, is manufactured in Peterborough. The company supplies complete automatic plants
covering every step in the baking process, including mechanical handling and packaging, and individual machines forming
part of the system. It makes equipment for the production not
only of bread but of cakes, swiss rolls, biscuits and similar
foods. As is the case with many of its other products, much of
the confectionery processing machinery built by Baker Perkins
is exported. These machines are remarkable examples of the
designer's art. There is even a chocolate coater that can be
computer controlled and will work continuously for over a
week without an operator! Chemical processing and foundry
machinery are also supplied by Baker Perkins whose Westwood foundry at Peterborough manufactures in a variety of
metals castings of all sizes and complexity for engineering
customers.

Obviously a vast modern organization like Baker Perkins is
constantly initiating new ideas and, not surprisingly, often
finds itself developing or pioneering new processes or techniques. To give but two examples, it developed the 'Fascold'
process of making moulds and cores in foundries in association
with the British Cast Iron Research Association, and helped to
pioneer group technology, a modern works technique.

There are, of course, a number of other companies concerned with engineering in Peterborough. Employing from a
few to several hundred people, they play a vital role in our
mixed economy, manufacturing various types of machinery
and equipment and undertaking many kinds of work. The
Peterborough Die Casting Co., aluminium high-pressure die-
casting specialists, is one that provides a service to such larger
organizations as Hotpoint, Perkins Engines and Black and
Decker. Perkins Engines is, as we have seen, based in Peterborough, as is Hotpoint who manufacture their well-known
domestic appliances there.

Away from Peterborough, Cambridgeshire's great engineering centre, there are many companies active. Marshall of

Cambridge, a large employer, owns and operates Cambridge airport and airport works. With a chain of car and commercial vehicle sales and service centres throughout the east of England, it designs and manufactures commercial and military vehicles, buses, aircraft and airborne containers. Cambridge and the district are greatly indebted to Marshall who allow the public to use its commercial airport and Customs facilities.

The Pye Group, famous for its radio and television associations (actually it supplies many other products and services), is still firmly based in Cambridge where it was founded in 1896 by William George Pye, who left the position of chief mechanic at the Cavendish Laboratory to start his own business, the design and manufacture of equipment and instruments for use in schools and laboratories. Now Pye of Cambridge is an industrial group of some fifty companies in Britain and overseas, employing over 25,000 people with an annual turnover of £240 million. The group's individual character stems from the fact that each company is a specialist in its own particular field employing no more than 2,500 people (in fact, the majority employ only a few hundred).

Pye turned to radio sets after the First World War and, in 1922, announced the opening of a Wireless Department at their works. The radio and instrument sides of the business were separated a few years later when Charles Orr Stanley, who eventually built up the company into an international group, formed Pye Radio Ltd. This company played a pioneering part in the development of television, setting up a special section to design and produce tubes and valves in 1935 and marketing a commercial television set with a 9-inch screen a year later.

The Pye organization made a significant contribution to the national effort throughout the Second World War, eventually employing 14,000 people, many working in their homes. The television side concentrated on the development of all forms of radio location and radar, setting up Britain's first electronic detection device at Walton-on-the-Naze, Essex, in 1939. The radio side concentrated on communications equipment, including two-way wireless sets for use by infantry and tank crews.

With the cessation of hostilities and the reopening of a public television service, Pye designed its first post-war television receiving set. This was followed by the first transformerless television set and later by black screen television, two Pye 'firsts'. Then came automatic picture-control, an innovation followed in the 1950s by the 27-inch screen and the incorporation of the Pye printed circuit in television. Pye attended the Brussels Trade Fair of 1947 with a complete television transmitting station. Soon the B.B.C. Television Service was using its outside broadcasting units and several different countries bought television equipment built at Cambridge. Colour television, introduced to Britain by Pye at the 1949 Radio Show, soon became a valuable tool in teaching hospitals and industrial and commercial applications of closed-circuit television were developed.

Meanwhile, Pye had entered the commercial market in telecommunications and in 1947 put radio-telephones in a fleet of Cambridge taxis, the first mobile radio scheme licensed in Britain. Now over 80 per cent of all British radio-telephones are built by Pye at Cambridge. Pye introduced that revolutionary electronic device the transistor to Britain. This enabled the company's engineers to effect a considerable reduction in the size and weight of the Pye portable radio, a 'first' when it was introduced in 1926. Among its many other achievements Pye introduced stereo on record in Britain (another 'first'), produced a 5-foot guided-missile which can be carried by one man and used against armoured vehicles and fortified emplacements, and developed the soniscope, an electronic stethoscope capable of amplifying required sounds in the body and of excluding extraneous noises, and the Barnet ventilator, an electronic lung.

The headquarters of Pye of Cambridge Ltd, the parent company managing all the companies of the Pye Group in the United Kingdom and overseas, are situated in Cambridge. Here, too, are several subsidiary companies. Cambridge Data Processing Ltd, the largest computer service bureau in East Anglia, offers a complete range of programme packages, data-preparation services, computer-processing facilities, computer-programming systems analysis and design. Cathodeon Ltd is active in the field of glass/vacuum electronic engineering, producing such things as hollow cathode lamps, photocells, infra-red detectors and glass-to-metal seals.

Labgear Ltd, manufacturer of television distribution and test equipment for use in flats, hotels, office blocks and towns, was the first company to announce its intention of manufacturing a unit which will enable teletext, the dial-a-page magazine format television information service, to be received by the majority of households. Pye Business Communications Ltd, a company formed as recently as 1970, markets communications equipment mainly for commerce and industry. In recent years it has installed twenty-nine cameras plus monitors as part of a £60,000 security and traffic surveillance contract at the National Exhibition Centre, Birmingham, and closed-circuit television and sound-reinforcement systems at Westminster Abbey. Pye Engineering Services Ltd provides a fully comprehensive engineering service to both the Pye Group and outside companies in the design and manufacture of high-class press tools, jigs, fixtures and special-purpose machines, prototype production runs and the mass production of sheet-metal components. Their facilities also include a competitive model shop, a welding section, a plating and painting shop and the manufacture of printed circuit boards.

Formed immediately after the Second World War, Pye Telecommunications Ltd manufactures radio-telephone systems, including mobile and personal equipment, together with associated base stations, point-to-point link equipment in V.H.F., U.H.F. and H.F., with ancillary equipment and radio paging systems. This company, employer of some 2,400 people, gained a £5 million contract from the Ministry of the Interior, Kuwait, for the supply, installation and commissioning of a V.H.F. mobile radio system. It has also installed many two-way radio-telephones for Securicor Ltd, one of Britain's largest users of such equipment. Other customers include police, fire, ambulance, security, transport, taxi and farming organizations.

Pye Thermal Bonders Ltd manufactures radio frequency generators and presses for dielectric heating and low-voltage heating equipment. It also makes complete installations for wool-warming, drying adhesives on paper, curing of glue in paper filters and drying of paints and varnishes. Pye TVT Ltd specializes in sound and television broadcasting equipment, providing equipment for complete studios, transmitting stations and outside broadcast vehicles. It also makes a range of specialized products for nuclear closed-circuit television applications, professional tape recorders for sound and television broadcast studios, equipment for flight simulation and other television large screen projection applications.

Pye Unicam Ltd is concerned with the development, manufacture and international marketing and sales of a wide range of analytical and measuring equipment, including gas and liquid chromatographs, spectrophotometers and electro-chemical instruments. Cathodeon Crystals Ltd, the Pye Group company based at Linton, a village on the county border, south-east of Cambridge, supplies the small, precisely manufactured crystals used for frequency control in communications equipment. This brief outline has inevitably been confined to the main activities of Pye companies in Cambridgeshire. Suffice it to say that those active elsewhere add to the knowledge and experience of the group, itself a living and growing monument to its founder and a great credit to all who work within it.

The Cambridge Scientific Instrument Co., later to change its name slightly, was formed in Cambridge towards the end of the last century when Horace (later Sir Horace) Darwin, youngest son of the famous naturalist Charles Darwin, formed a partnership with Dew-Smith and set out to design and manufacture scientific equipment for the various departments of Cambridge University. Soon their apparatus was being supplied to scientists in other parts of the world and Darwin turned to industrial instruments, pioneering work that brought considerable opposition, particularly from working people. Darwin took up many other inventions and by the time he died in 1928 the company had won considerable prestige, having been responsible for some thirty 'firsts' in commercial instrument manufacture for both science and industry.

These 'firsts' included the seismograph (1891) devised by

James Alfred Ewing, the professor of mechanism and applied mechanics at Cambridge who became Principal and Vice-chancellor at Edinburgh, and the first commercial automatic temperature controller (1909). In the first quarter of this century 'Cambridge', as the company is often called, was concerned with crack extensometers for St Paul's Cathedral, London, and apparatus for investigating the explosive effects of coal dust in mines. It also manufactured Dr G. A. Shakespear's katharometer, an instrument used during the First World War for measuring hydrogen leakage from balloons and later for other gas mixtures.

After Darwin's death the company and its list of 'firsts' continued to develop. In 1933 it made R. M. Mallock's calculating machine and during the Second World War recording sound ranging outfits and degaussing test gear for ships for combating magnetic mines. In 1954 'Cambridge' made apparatus for measuring copper strip for the first Atlantic telephone cable and also the vector cardiograph. Five years later it produced the first commercial electron probe X-ray microanalyser. Since then other vital developments have included the first commercial scanning electron microscope, image analysers, one of whose many uses is measuring the area of the grey matter in the brain, and electron beam micro-fabrication systems.

In October 1975 the shareholders of Scientific and Medical Instruments Ltd, the holding company of Cambridge Scientific Instruments Ltd, accepted a government-supported offer to combine with Metals Research Ltd to form the Cambridge Instrument Co. Ltd, which now markets materials, materials science equipment and scientific and medical instruments.

Since the Second World War several other manufacturers of laboratory and industrial equipment have established themselves in Cambridgeshire. Techne (Cambridge) Ltd was founded by Dr N. A. de Bruyne, F.R.S. in 1948 and two years later moved into the former rectory, since extended, in the village of Duxford. Techne has a workforce of about a hundred in Cambridgeshire, while its American associate company employs some twenty people who market Duxford-made products and do some manufacturing.

With its products largely in the scientific field, Techne has specialized in the manufacture of instruments to control liquid (usually water) temperature for laboratory applications, but it has also introduced a range of fluidized baths for high-temperature precision calibration, general purpose laboratory heating, and removing plastic residues from dies, breaker plates and extruder screws in the plastics industry. Techne, whose products are used in hospital, university and industrial laboratories and elsewhere throughout the world, has also developed and produced modified units for temperature controllers and circulators for photographic colour processors, for control systems for kidney-dialysis machines and other specific applications.

Grant Instruments (Cambridge) Ltd, another successful and well-known manufacturer of laboratory equipment employing about a hundred people, has premises south-west of Cambridge, at Bulbeck Mill, Barrington, and at its modern factory in the neighbouring village of Shepreth. The company was formed soon after the Second World War by Peter Ward whose hobby of repairing and making mechanical singing birds had earlier led to his working for a scientific instrument maker. The company's name, Grant, is a constant reminder that its first products, laboratory water baths, were made in the village of Grantchester, where Peter Ward worked alone at the bottom of the Old Vicarage garden in a Gothic folly, a building given to his father by the mother of the poet Rupert Brooke.

Eventually the lone worker entered into a partnership with Cecil Chapman, Grant's present managing director. With turnover rising, they moved from Grantchester to the old water mill at Barrington and engaged their first employee, then an engineering undergraduate at Cambridge, now Grant's production director. By 1958 it was obvious that production had to develop to satisfy the increasing volume of orders and a second company, Grant Instruments (Developments) Ltd, was set up so that Peter Ward, who wished to avoid becoming enmeshed in commercialism, could pursue his objectives and develop a range of thermistor thermometers and temperature recorders.

In 1977, the year Peter Ward retired and the development company was reabsorbed into the main one, Grant received from the Royal Society of Arts an award for design management. Now, with its name familiar to laboratory workers in industry, education, medicine and research throughout the world, Grant's main products are temperature controlled baths and miniature temperature recorders, but it also manufactures equipment for measuring the amount of blood loss during surgery, special baths for bringing blood to the correct temperature prior to transfusing and equipment used to freeze down plasma collected from blood donor sessions. Some 40 per cent of production is exported, the biggest overseas customer being the U.S.A. followed by Australia and Iran. Trade in Europe is also developing rapidly and a West German branch, the first outside England, was opened in 1975.

Several other companies based in Cambridgeshire are helping to satisfy the demand for laboratory and industrial equipment, instruments and accessories. They usually employ well under a hundred people and, sadly, one must record that many of them do not answer enquiries about their achievements or their products. (This comment also applies to many companies operating in completely different fields and it is obviously time that British industry thoroughly examined its whole attitude to administration, information and publicity services. Much of it gives the impression of being unaware of the fact that it has such a lot to be proud of!)

As with Grant, just mentioned, it was an outstanding and dedicated individual who founded the London Instrument Co. which became known as Cantabrian, from the trade name under which its equipment was made, in 1973, the year the business was acquired by Lillywhites of Piccadilly (part of the Trust Houses Forte Group). This was Henry Rottenburg, inventor and lecturer in engineering at Cambridge University, who moved the company from East Molesey, Surrey, where he had established it in 1912, to premises above a tailor's shop in Cambridge (it moved to Newnham Mill and then, in 1974, to its new factory at Ditton Walk).

Rottenburg, whose inventiveness ranged from cigarette holders to stereoscopic cameras, from adjustable darts to equipment for sawing people in half (for the Magic Circle!), turned more and more from products for the theatrical world, activity that disturbed the establishment of the day, to the manufacture of athletics equipment. His introduction to the needs and demands of this sport came through one of his students, Harold Abrahams, who later became an Olympic gold medallist and chairman of the British Athletics Board.

The problem of starting races caused Rottenburg much concern and he produced a starting gate, but this found more favour with racehorses than athletes. By 1937, when he introduced British athletes to the starting block, Rottenburg's company was making standards and measuring equipment for high jump and pole vault and scoreboards and experimenting with datum measurement for hammer, discus and javelin. He and his chief draughtsman, Barry Bartholomew, having become the measurers and judges for major athletics meetings all over England, it was not surprising that, soon after the Second World War, Rottenburg should have been given the responsibility of getting together the necessary equipment for the 1948 Olympic Games to be held in London. In about eighteen months he designed and made most of this equipment in his own factory. Cantabrian equipment continues to be used in the Olympiads. Since 1950 it has been used in the Commonwealth Games and the European Championships and from later dates in the Pan American Games, Asian Games, South East Asian Games, Pan African Games, Southern Pacific Games and the Central American and Caribbean Games. As part of its growing range of products, Cantabrian Ltd has developed an educational and collegiate grade of equipment. That the company is seriously interested in the export market is obvious from the careful way in which its catalogues are issued not only in English but French and German also.

Long recognized throughout the world for the excellence of its tennis, squash and badminton racquets, hockey sticks and other sports equipment, Grays, now a member of an international group of companies, was established in 1855 in Cambridge and is still based there at Playfair Works. H. J. Gray, who became champion racket player of England in 1863, was the rackets coach at St John's College, Cambridge, when he decided to found his sports business and it seemed only natural to take as his trademark a representation of this historic institution's gateway.

Under the management of Horace George Gray, who took over when his father, the founder, retired in 1896, the firm grew from a small family business to a larger limited company. In 1908 it introduced a tennis racquet on the lamination principle, an idea that revolutionized the manufacture of these bats. As the years passed other members of the family assumed responsibility for management and Grays continued to expand, taking over other companies.

In 1973 a reorganization took place and Grays of Cambridge (International) Ltd became the holding company for the group, which includes Grays of Cambridge Ltd, Grays of Cambridge (Pakistan) Ltd, Gray Nicolls (Australia) Pty Ltd, Sams-Atlas Ltd, Tonbridge Sports Industries Ltd and others. Now, as it continues to design and produce new ranges of sports equipment, the business whose founder supplied bats to that great cricketer W. G. Grace has the satisfaction of knowing that its racquets, bats and sticks are used by finalists in many of the great championships.

Spicers Ltd, a member of the Reed Group, has its head office and office services division at Sawston. Here it employs some seven hundred people who work in the offices and the two factories, one of which manufactures envelopes, the other producing account books, exercise books, student notebooks, duplicate books, writing pads and other forms of commercial stationery.

Sawston was a centre of paper-making for several centuries, but Spicers no longer make paper there, having closed the paper mill of Edward Towgood and Sons, which was located on a part of their 400-acre estate, as recently as 1974. In 1836 Edward Towgood bought the mill, once known as the Borough Mill and later as Sawston Paper Mill, from the widow of Charles Martindale who is believed to have installed there one of the first paper-making machines introduced into Britain. Under the Towgood management steam power and another paper-making machine were installed. Sawston Paper Mill soon became one of the leading paper mills in the country, its reputation for the manufacture of the finest grades of paper, particularly ledgers and fine writings, being second to none.

The Towgood family is remembered for such good works as rebuilding the Sawston National School, paying for the vicarage, and holding an annual children's school treat fair with band and swings and guards posted along the river to stop the children falling in. When Spicers Ltd bought Sawston Paper Mill in 1915, they continued to run it under the name of E. Towgood and Sons Ltd and maintained the old tradition with, for example, a substantial contribution to Sawston Village College and the conversion of 6 acres of the estate into a sports ground.

Their modernization programmes enabled the mill to continue producing paper of outstanding quality for more than another half century, but this aspect of Spicer's past is now part of our wider industrial history. They are, however, still very active at Sawston, manufacturing the products mentioned earlier and aiming to serve the offices of the nation by supplying furniture, personal and furniture accessories, filing and storage equipment, office machines, stationery, pens and sundries. (Of course, Spicers do not themselves manufacture all of these lines.)

Also serving the business world and others concerned with records and documentation is the Acco Co. Ltd, a member of the Acco International Group, which has modern premises at Peterborough. This firm's office products include filing and retrieval systems, various types of binders, stapling machines, portfolios, document folders and display books.

The manufacture of wrappings, packaging and containers, another industry that has developed in a marked way in recent years, is undertaken in several parts of Cambridgeshire. Paper and plastic wrappings for bread, sweets and other products are made at Sawston and plastic shrink-wrap bags and films for food packaging at St Neots. Paper and polythene bags and sacks are produced in Cambridge and Wisbech, while corrugated and solid fibre board cases are manufactured at Burwell and Ely. With the growing interest in recycling of materials, it is encouraging to note that the Thames Waste

Paper Group and waste paper and board merchants are active in Cambridgeshire.

Although it has never been a major centre of this particular industry, the county has some clothing manufacturers. Peterborough has more of them than any other town in Cambridgeshire, one of them concentrating on weatherproof outwear, another on lingerie and corsets. Gurteens, the old-established makers of clothing for men and boys, whose main unit is at Haverhill in Suffolk, have a factory at Ely. Bought by them in 1964, it was extended nine years later and made into one of the country's most up-to-date smaller trouser factories. One realizes just how much times and industries change when, on reading the story of this family firm, one discovers that, as recently as the early years of this century, Gurteens were still making agricultural workers' smocks, with embroidery at the neck and sleeves denoting the occupation of the wearer, and sending them by horse and cart from Haverhill to Castle Camps in neighbouring Cambridgeshire. Sheepskin coats, gloves and mitts, types of clothing much in demand nowadays, are made at Sawston by the Eastern Counties Leather Co. Ltd, whose business is processing chamois and shearline leathers.

Clearly Cambridgeshire has a wide range of industrial activity within its borders and, just as clearly, it is inevitable that this will increase in variety and extent as the area itself develops as a centre of population. Already the growth of Peterborough has brought new industry into the county and with it confirmation, if this be needed, of the wealth of enterprise and initiative in our midst.

V

NATURE IN CAMBRIDGESHIRE

CAMBRIDGESHIRE is a paradise for nature and naturalist alike. One has only to visit its towns to establish this fact and one finds it abundantly confirmed in the countryside. There are areas where farming, housing, industry and other interests take priority. All the same, nature is rarely kept completely at bay, and there are very few places without some natural history interest.

In Cambridge itself I once watched a heron making its way home as I sat in a bus in a traffic jam. In the same city I observed a spotted flycatcher darting from its perch to catch insects while cars and lorries roared by. Moorhens, mallard and grey squirrels lived beside the same busy main road, most of them managing to avoid the traffic. At Cherry Hinton, on the Cambridge fringe, I heard of a man who could not use the nails in his tool shed because a blackbird had nested in the beer can containing them.

One must admit that certain habitats have been very seriously reduced over the years. Chalk grassland is a case in point. But all is not lost. Certain precious examples remain, perhaps the best surviving remnant being that on the Devil's Dyke, an ancient linear earthwork running for more than seven miles across the chalk from Reach to Stetchworth. This is still the haunt of the chalk-hill blue butterfly and its foodplant, the horseshoe vetch. It also remains the habitat of the pasque flower, whose beauty derives from the rich blue-violet of its sepals (it lacks petals). Appropriately this flower is the emblem of the Cambridgeshire and Isle of Ely Naturalists' Trust (Cambient), which watches over the part of the Devil's Dyke to the south-east of the Burwell road.

Though not so important botanically, the Fleam Dyke, another ancient linear earthwork, is nevertheless of great interest. The section running from Fulbourn almost to Balsham has chalk plants, while the stretch to the south-east of the A11 road is the East Anglian stronghold of the wild juniper, an evergreen shrub that is represented here by a few individuals. The public have rights of way along the Devil's and Fleam Dykes. They may also use the Roman Road, an ancient trackway just outside Cambridge that passes by the Gog Magog Hills golf course on its way towards Haverhill. This is another habitat of chalk plants, and even in places where hawthorn, blackthorn and coarse grasses have encroached the rock rose manages to spread and produce its bright yellow flowers.

The Dykes and the Roman Road have many attractions for bird watchers and general naturalists. Like so many parts of Cambridgeshire, they are blessed with the song of larks in summer, and later in the year with the presence of redwings and fieldfares, winter visitors which, in hard times, depend on colourful berries and fallen crab apples to keep them alive.

Between the Roman Road and the A604 road stretches the Wandlebury estate, a property of the Cambridge Preservation Society that is open to the public. With its woods and open grassy spaces, this is an area of great interest to naturalists where Cambient has established a nature trail (with guide). Unfortunately in recent years the trees have suffered badly during gales and the dry summer of 1976 did not help matters, the beeches, shallow-rooted at the best of times, being seriously affected then.

Visitors are sometimes surprised to find so many areas of woodland that have not only survived in such a highly farmed area but are managed as nature reserves. Hayley Wood and Monks Wood have been studied in such detail that books have been written about them. Hayley Wood covers 122 acres on the chalky boulder-clay plateau at Little Gransden, only ten miles from Cambridge. Since Cambient acquired this semi-natural oak-ash wood in 1962, the nature trail through it has been followed by large numbers of people. But I cannot help thinking that the greatest annual treat is enjoyed by those who visit Hayley when the oxlips bloom. The wood's oxlip population was estimated at 4 million plants in 1948. Though now less than this, it is still one of Britain's largest populations of this beautiful relative of the primrose and cowslip. One of the complications of nature is that oxlip flowers are enjoyed here by fallow deer whose browsing also affects the growth of other species. Hayley is the scene of teaching and research at university and school levels and of coppicing (cutting back to stools or stumps) of ash, field maple, hazel and hawthorn by voluntary workers.

Monks Wood is a 370-acre national nature reserve at Abbots Ripton, six miles from Huntingdon. Open only to people carrying permits issued by the Nature Conservancy Council, this ash-oak wood on clay has long been noted for rare insects, particularly the black hairstreak butterfly whose larvae feed on that common shrub blackthorn. Adjoining the reserve is Monks Wood Experimental Station, now part of the Institute of Terrestrial Ecology which, with its headquarters at Cambridge, is a component body of the Natural Environment Research Council. The Biological Records Centre, one of the units based at Monks Wood Experimental Station, houses records of many British animals and plants and acts as a link between official and voluntary bodies.

Like Hayley Wood, Knapwell Wood, a reserve of only 11 acres close to the A45 road, and Overhall Grove, a 43-acre wood on the clay slopes below Knapwell church, have spring displays of oxlips and bluebells. To add to their attractions there are tree-creepers, woodpeckers and other woodland birds and, at Overhall Grove, a colony of badgers.

There are several woodland nature reserves in that part of Cambridgeshire covered by the Bedfordshire and Huntingdonshire Naturalists' Trust (Bahnat).

In the neighbourhood of Great Raveley are three Bahnat reserves, namely Lady's, Raveley and Gamsey Woods, all probably remnants of the dense woodland that once covered the claylands of these parts. Gamsey Wood is of particular interest to tree-lovers because, like Monks Wood, it includes several well-grown examples of the service tree, a species generally thought to be a good indicator of ancient woodland.

Lady's Wood has field maples that reach a height of about fifty feet, a fact that may surprise people who are accustomed to seeing this species growing as a hedgerow or woodland shrub. Raveley Wood, with its rookery, is an important breeding area for such summer visitors as blackcap, chiffchaff and spotted flycatcher and also for a number of resident species. It is visited for educational purposes by local children for whose teachers Bahnat has prepared a guide.

Vital educational work is also carried out at Redshanks Spinney, Farcet Fen, a two-acre piece of mixed deciduous woodland on the peat of an area devoted almost entirely to intensive arable farming. Here Bahnat has encouraged local children to erect nesting boxes and to plant and protect with wire cages alder trees and sallow cuttings. Bahnat also intends to restore the old kiln and tile-making shed at its Ramsey Heights Clay Pits reserve and to convert these relics of the local brick-making industry into a field centre where children will be taught field biology and local history. Already considerable help in preparing the site has been given by volunteers, including ten-twelve-year-old children and a young bricklayer undertaking community service under the direction of the Peterborough courts. The ten-acre reserve, with its small clay pits and ponds, is rich in plants such as water violet, bladderwort, and that beautiful wild iris the yellow flag. Undoubtedly it will become a joy to nature-loving youngsters, especially those from the towns.

This is only one of a number of cases of Cambridgeshire conservationists creating nature reserves on sites modified by industrial and allied interests. At Ely the splendid co-operation of several public-spirited organizations and individuals has resulted in Cambient being allowed to establish a nature reserve (with nature trail and guide book) in the region of the Roswell Pits, a series of old and new pits used for excavating clay for building and repairing river banks since at least the seventeenth century.

Here the habitats include wet meadows, a small area of chalk grassland, scrub, woodland, reed swamp and open water. Among the abundant insect life are dragonflies and damsel flies. Wild flowers are abundant. There are bee and other orchids and an attractive spurge from eastern Europe that obviously enjoys conditions here, having spread extensively along the side of one of the pits. Some ninety species of birds occur, such striking ones as great crested grebes and kingfishers attracting much attention, visiting bearded tits adding considerably to the interest of the place in winter. Sadly, one must add that there has been a certain amount of vandalism here, those picking rare flowers being just as guilty as louts removing marker posts.

Gypsies with dogs who camped by Gray's Moor Pits in the parish of Coldham, between March and Wisbech, caused trouble but they were moved and the land embanked. This site comprises 15 acres of old gravel pits set aside by the Co-operative Wholesale Society as a wildlife reserve under Cambient management. Even during the very dry summer of 1976 water remained at a good level in the pits and large carp were seen feeding at the surface. Among the breeding birds of this reserve are kingfishers, great crested grebes, mallard and tufted duck.

In Cambridgeshire there are several other pits serving as excellent examples of the use for nature conservation of places that, having fulfilled their original purpose, might simply have become permanent rubbish tips. Several years ago, when it was decided to set aside part of it as a nature reserve, Heydon chalk pit was visited by Cambient members who collected and removed large quantities of refuse that had been dumped there over the years. This done, the site was levelled and cleared of brambles. Then there were dense growths of nettles, foodplants of larvae of red admiral, small tortoiseshell, peacock and other butterflies, and of thistles, whose flowers attract many kinds of insects. This problem was solved by cutting back those on the floor of the pit and leaving those on the sides. Many species of wild flowers appeared and these, in their turn, were visited by insects. In 1972 some examples of the Roman snail (also called edible and apple snail), the largest British land snail, were released in Heydon chalk pit. It is hoped that ecological studies carried out here will contribute to the conservation of this snail. At the same time this species of calcareous soils was introduced into two other chalk pits managed by Cambient, those at Ickleton and Stapleford.

Dumping of rubbish at this site was causing concern when the chalk pit on Coploe Hill, Ickleton, became the subject of co-operation between the parish council and Cambient early in the 1960s. The Trust provided a fence and a notice-board explaining the natural history interest of the pit and the council a stile. The result: an area which, though small, is of value for both conservation and amenity purposes. Its members also worked hard, removing scrub and rubbish, when Cambient reached agreement with the parish council over the management of Stapleford Pit on the Gog Magog Hills. Later clearance by voluntary workers was again necessary to allow harebells, thyme, perennial flax and some one hundred other species of plants to develop. Thus the chalk grassland area has been extended but in places the luxuriant growth of nettles has kept Cambient volunteers busy, and the lack of grazing rabbits has allowed some plants to grow tall, a situation that always threatens smaller, less aggressive species.

The effects of grazing by cows and horses were investigated by Cambient at their Thriplow reserve, eight miles south of Cambridge, where poorly drained streamside meadows, the haunt of snipe, lapwing and many other birds, are the habitat of large numbers of marsh orchids. Management experiments undertaken there produced the general conclusion that the best way to maintain the orchid population in a healthy state would be to ensure a regular amount of light grazing through the year. Of course, such control of sedge and other coarse vegetation benefits not only marsh orchids but other less competitive species.

Bahnat have taken care to let the grazing rights at Upwood Meadows, their fifteen-acre reserve just east of Lady's Wood. This badly drained and ancient grassland, with its tall hedges and ponds, is enlivened by 176 species of flowering plants and many birds. But its great treasure is the colony of hundreds of reddish-purple-flowered green-winged orchids, a beautiful sight when the flowers are seen as part of a rich display whose background features countless buttercups and cowslips.

On the Ouse Washes, Britain's largest inland area of regularly flooded grazed marshland, grazing by cattle, sheep and horses, and mowing in certain places, are vital factors in maintaining a sward suitable for ground-nesting birds, including black-tailed godwits and ruffs. Cambient, the Royal

Society for the Protection of Birds, and the Wildfowl Trust are collaborating in developing this land between the Old and the New Bedford Rivers in the interests of nature conservation. Since the first purchase was made in 1964, they have continued to buy land in the Washes and today they have an important and growing influence in the area.

More than sixty breeding species of birds have been recorded on the Washes. Besides those just mentioned, there are lapwing, redshank, snipe, mallard, shoveler, coot and moorhen. In winter the flooded Washes become an internationally important refuge for vast numbers of migratory wildfowl, among them Bewick's, whooper and mute swans. Hides are provided for bird watchers and at the Wildfowl Trust's Welney Wildfowl Refuge there is a spacious observatory overlooking a wide lagoon, the winter haunt of hundreds of Bewick's swans, which is floodlit at night. Botanists, who have recorded more than 260 kinds of flowering plants there, regard the Washes, with their ditches and wet patches, as a habitat for many relics from the former fens.

One must not imagine that the creation of large nature reserves on the Ouse Washes has solved all problems for conservationists or the wild creatures they are interested in safeguarding. Far from it! Management, however subtle, is necessary. This involves grazing, cutting or treating rank vegetation, or, as in the drought of 1976, pumping water from the river to maintain a few wet areas for the benefit of breeding waders, and numerous other tasks.

Many tracts of land on the Washes are still in private hands and wild birds have inevitably to travel outside protected areas. People out shooting are not always as expert or as careful as they should be and careless anglers sometimes discard tackle or leave it by the waterways. Some of the dangers to which wildfowl are exposed were revealed by Myrfyn Owen and C. J. Cadbury in their recent study of 128 swans found dead at the Ouse Washes over six winters. Forty-nine were killed by striking power lines and three Bewick's swans by colliding with other obstacles. Two of the last-named species died after heavy contamination with oil. An estimated thirty-seven swans died from poisoning from ingested lead pellets and fishing weights and, despite the fact that these birds are protected by law, several mute and Bewick's swans were probably shot and others wounded. G. J. Thomas found lead pellets in fifty-seven of 1,250 gizzards taken from waterfowl (eleven species) shot by wildfowlers at the Ouse Washes and estimated that some 400-700 birds die there each year due to lead poisoning.

Drainage and subsequent cultivation have, of course, produced a complete transformation of the fenland and very little remains that really resembles the original watery wilderness. Nevertheless there are four reserves where one can learn much about the effects of fenland drainage, the encroachment of trees and shrubs, and the work involved in maintaining a high water level. One of them, Wicken Fen, is the property of the National Trust, while the others - Chippenham, Holme and Wood Walton Fens, are national nature reserves managed by the Nature Conservancy Council.

Holme Fen, 640 acres of woodland six miles south of Peterborough, adjoins the site of Whittlesey Mere, a very large sheet of water until it was drained in 1851. Standing exposed, the famous Holme Fen post, an iron pillar which, at the end of 1851, was driven twenty-two feet through the peat until its top was level with the ground surface, shows the remarkable shrinkage of the peat resulting from drainage. Over the years the shrunken fen has been invaded by birch and other trees and shrubs and only a remnant of the acid peat vegetation of wet heath and bog survives.

At the adjacent Wood Walton Fen, a 514-acre reserve rich in animal and plant species, much attention has been given to removing invading scrub. Much work has also been involved in maintaining a high water level throughout the year, and a new mere has been excavated, giving about five acres of open water with an island left to serve as a nesting site.

The magnificent large copper butterfly, whose extinction in Britain was brought about by drainage of the fens and also by collectors who caught the last specimens at Holme Fen in 1847 or 1848, was reintroduced to Wood Walton Fen in 1927. The ground was cleared and planted with the insect's foodplant, great water-dock, and then butterflies of the large copper's

Dutch race were released. Despite winter floods, the larvae survived to produce a large number of butterflies in 1928, and the species thrived at Wood Walton until 1969 when, following the previous summer's heavy rain and flooding, the population became extinct. A reintroduction from captive Wood Walton stock held at Esher and at Monks Wood Experimental Station was undertaken in 1970 and arrangements made for the warden to breed supplementary stock on the reserve.

Managed by the National Trust and studied by scientists and naturalists for many years, Wicken Fen has been described as being almost certainly the best-documented British nature reserve. Here the original fenland vegetation has been much modified over the centuries by mowing, peat-digging, drainage of surrounding land, and other operations. Nowadays sedge and reed are cut for thatching and management is directed at maintaining a reserve where both serious researchers and ordinary visitors may find interest and satisfaction. In summer there is usually plenty to appeal to flower-lovers, and at most times of year bird-watchers find their visits well worthwhile. The construction of a mere on Adventurers' Fen, the part of Wicken Fen reserve reclaimed for agriculture during the Second World War, resulted in this and the surrounding land becoming an important area for birds, one visited by bittern, bearded tit and other scarce species.

Wicken has long provided habitats for many kinds of insects. It was here that a colony of the Dutch race of the large copper butterfly was established in 1930 after several acres had been planted with the great water-dock. But perhaps Wicken's most famous insect was the swallow-tail. I use the word 'was' because this lovely butterfly became extinct there in the early 1950s. In 1971, when the swallowtail seemed to be declining in its remaining British location, Norfolk, scientists from Monks Wood Experimental Station started studies at Wicken in an attempt to understand why efforts to re-establish it there had failed. It appeared that there were not enough suitable examples of milk parsley, the species selected by the females when they lay their eggs and that on which the larvae feed, and so several thousand plants were set out around the mere on Adventurers' Fen where the land surface is below the water level of the lodes. Grazing duck damaged many of these plants, but more were planted later. In June 1975, 228 swallowtails reared at Monks Wood from eggs collected at Hickling Broad, Norfolk, were released at Wicken and some 2,000 caterpillars are thought to have gone into pupation (the resting stage) before winter. Many swallowtails emerged in 1976. Drought conditions adversely affected the foodplant and the insect itself, but the species survived at Wicken and individuals were flying there in 1977. Future developments will be influenced greatly by the weather, the state of the fen and of the foodplant.

Chippenham Fen National Nature Reserve, three and a half miles north of Newmarket, has a greater variety of habitat than Wicken, but it is less well-known and an official permit is required to visit parts away from the public footpath. Drained, enclosed and planted after 1796, this valley fen now has areas of woodland and sedge-reed swamp communities undergoing colonization by ash and birch. There are many birds, insects and other forms of animal life, and plants, fungi, mosses, lichens and liverworts included, are well represented.

That modification, even transformation, by man cannot deprive a place of interest for naturalists is immediately obvious to people visiting Stow-cum-Quy Fen, a 108-acre common, now mainly grazing land, belonging to the three parishes of Fen Ditton, Horningsea and Stow-cum-Quy and open to the public. Ploughing destroyed the remaining true fen vegetation more than twenty years ago, but there are reed-fringed pits, nesting sites for some of the forty species of breeding birds (more than eighty species of birds have been recorded here). The Long Pond, where the phosphatic nodules known as coprolites were dug, is the habitat of dace and roach. The presence in the hedges of wayfaring trees, whose heads of white flowers give way to clusters of purplish-black berries, serves as a reminder that there is some chalky ground here, the common being at the junction of the lower chalk and the gault clay.

Fulbourn Fen, an educational nature reserve established by

St Ives: the ancient bridge over the River Ouse

A corner of St Neots

Ely Cathedral: west front

Ely Cathedral: west and south-west towers

River scene near Stretham

The Senate House, Cambridge

Market Hill, Cambridge

King's College, Cambridge

The Round Church, Cambridge

Clare College and bridge, Cambridge

Training on the river at Cambridge

Cambient in collaboration with the county education authority, is situated on the lower chalk, though in places the chalk lies beneath layers of peat. Situated near the Fleam Dyke, only five miles east of Cambridge, its sixty-seven acres include woodland, grassland, scrub and streams, wet and dry places, grazed and ungrazed areas. Earlier this century there was enough water for boating and a stream turned a water-mill, but conditions are now very much drier. Even so, the reserve remains a wonderland for true nature-lovers. One party of such people enjoyed their recent mid-September visit when in bright sunshine they saw a fine display of yellow-wort, a very attractive plant with bright cream-yellow flowers, several different butterflies, a grass snake and a number of birds, among them goldcrest, nuthatch and jay.

While continuing to acquire and manage nature reserves, conservation organizations in Cambridgeshire are paying in-creasing attention to hedges and roadside verges, marginal habitats which, in places, are subject to disturbance and even total destruction. Appropriately it was a Cambridgeshire scientist, Dr Max Hooper of Monks Wood Experimental Station, who developed a practical technique for determining the age of a hedge by counting the number of shrubby species it contains (e.g. a hedge with two or three species in a thirty yard stretch may be 200 years old, while one with ten or twelve species may be 1,000 years old).

Hedges have never been a feature of the fenland landscape, though some farmers have planted hedges of willow. Having been in the area during a 'blow', when the wind carried away vast clouds of peat and soil and gave day the appearance of night, I am surprised that more people have not followed their example.

Hedges have long divided other parts of the county and there are still some good examples on farms and certain of the nature reserves. Cambient has conducted a survey of hedges in its area with a view to selecting those of particular importance for conservation. Sad to say, it has since undertaken a survey of hedges damaged or destroyed by fire during the dry summer of 1976. Scientists from Monks Wood Experimental Station made a random survey of roadside hedges in the old county of Huntingdonshire and found that hazel, spindle, field maple and dogwood occurred much more frequently in 'woodland relic' hedges than in planted ones. Their work also shows the value of 'woodland relic' hedges as refuges for such woodland herbs as dog's mercury, bluebell, wood anemone and primrose. Much remains to be done concerning the designation and management of hedgerows as nature reserves.

Meanwhile, it is encouraging to note that both Bahnat and Cambient have surveyed roadside verges in their respective areas. Lists of those of natural history interest have been given to the local authorities concerned. Their management methods have not always met with the approval of the conservationists but they have not been slow to suggest more satisfactory ways of maintaining these important linear nature reserves. Looking down the lists, one finds that Cambridgeshire roadside verge nature reserves are the habitat of a number of scarce or otherwise interesting plants, among them crested cow-wheat, bee orchid, dyer's greenweed and spurge laurel. Undoubtedly Cambridgeshire hedges and roadside verges will become increasingly important havens for plants, birds, insects and other forms of wildlife as pressures on the land grow in intensity and as inevitable changes take effect. Likewise, the decrease in their numbers makes the conservation of outstanding hedges and verges a matter of supreme importance.

In all this, however, one must not overlook the 'swings and roundabouts' situations that so often occur. Flooding of the Diddington valley may have involved submerging twenty miles of hedges (and, of course, much else besides), but the great reservoir of Grafham Water created there has become an important area for thousands of wildfowl and other water birds in winter and a breeding site for duck, coot and waders, including the little ringed plover, in summer. The western end of the reservoir, where sailing is restricted, and part of its northern edge form a nature reserve and there is a hide for bird watchers.

The thousands of gulls using Grafham Water, the Ouse Washes and certain other places as winter roosting grounds are the subjects of another example of the complex situations involving wildlife and the land and the management and conservation of both these national assets. For the plain fact of the matter is that these gulls find much of their food on the county's rubbish tips, places often regarded as unsightly sources of pollution that involve a serious misuse of land.

It has also been suggested by ornithologists that rooks, whose population in the fenland declined with the ploughing of grassland where they fed, now depend very much on rubbish tips as a source of food. Many other kinds of birds feed on these sites, taking not only refuse but seeds, insects, snails and earthworms. Bats appear over them, attracted by insects, and owls and kestrels come to hunt small mammals. Scavenging foxes have visited tips in Cambridge and fallow deer such a fenland site. Then there are the plants. Natives, garden plants and aliens, including thorn-apple, henbane and hemp, all arrive on Cambridgeshire rubbish tips, making them botanical hunting grounds.

No less interesting are the animals and plants of Cambridgeshire gardens whose value as refuges for wildlife is indeed considerable. Some of the larger ones are outstanding in these respects. One thinks, for example, of the gardens of Anglesey Abbey. A visit to this National Trust property is a treat in store for nature-lovers who do not already know it. There is a fine collection of trees of both native and introduced species and, despite the careful attention that is always given to the grounds, there are odd corners where wild flowers abound. Colourful lichens decorate statues standing there, and spreading plants of dog lichen grow close to the ground, unharmed by the mower. In autumn the many varieties of fungi growing on tree stumps, round the bases of trees and on the ground include the honey fungus, shaggy parasol, sulphur tuft, devil's fingers and puff-balls. Throughout the year birds are present and on occasion one sees ornamental pheasants among the trees.

Birds are also attracted to Cambridge Botanic Gardens whose main purpose is to grow plants for botanical teaching and research in the university. Covering forty acres on a site enclosed by busy roads and partly surrounded by houses, this garden is an oasis of colour and interest for nature-lovers of all types. The director, Dr Max Walters, himself a distinguished

botanist and naturalist, and his staff go to considerable troubl
to assist visiting members of the public, providing explanator
leaflets in the various plant houses and a list of plants c
current interest at two of the entrances. Besides trees an
smaller plants, there are ducks and moorhens on a pond whos
water is supplied by a leat from Hobson's Brook, a sma
stream fed by the Nine Wells springs that leave the chalk jus
outside Cambridge.

Behind the scenes the staff of the University Botani
Garden play an important part in the conservation of rar
plants, growing them in case the colonies in the wild, ofte
very small, become extinct. Recent examples that come t
mind are those of the attractive crimson-flowered Fyfield pea
threatened at its Essex site by hedge clearance and infilling o
ditches, and the fen ragwort, five plants of which were foun
in a fen ditch in 1972, more than a hundred years after it wa
last seen in Britain.

The extent to which nature-lovers are indebted to th
University Botanic Garden authorities is even more eviden
when one considers that for many years they have allowe
Cambient to have an office there. Earlier the Botanical Societ
of the British Isles was encouraged to run its mapping schem
nucleus of the Biological Records Centre, now housed a
Monks Wood Experimental Station, from the Botanic Garden.

Certain of the grounds and gardens of Cambridge college
and institutions have features appealing to nature-lovers
especially those who are fond of trees, and certainly some o
the dons and undergraduates have found much to interes
them there. One thinks immediately of Charles Cardal
Babington, who became the fifth professor of botany a
Cambridge in 1861, the year following the publication of hi
Flora of Cambridgeshire. He found the fern wall-rue growin
on the steps of the Senate House in Cambridge and it was sti
there a hundred years later when, a few years after th
tercentenary of the publication by John Ray of the first flor
of Cambridgeshire, a new county flora appeared. One thinks
too, of Mr J. S. Boys Smith, Master of St John's College
Cambridge, who only ten years ago was the first observer t
describe the hedgehog's strange habit of running (walking

according to some people) in circles, an apparently aimless activity that is kept up for some time. Hedgehogs are by no means uncommon in gardens in Cambridge where on occasion they become road casualties. The old-established, somewhat neglected type of garden where bushes grow under trees appeals to the species, as indeed it does to other mammals, as well as birds, insects and other creatures.

The expression 'other creatures' refers to a vast number of invertebrate animals that are only too often neglected, even by serious naturalists. Yet they may be found in the smallest of gardens, including those in the very centres of towns. Paul Harding, the Monks Wood biologist, found eleven species of woodlice in his garden at Boxworth. One of them was new to the county list and another, a species found in nests of ants, was associated with the common black ant. I found gardens to be most productive sites during my own researches on the plant galls of Cambridgeshire. The University Botanic Garden at Cambridge alone produced several types of these peculiar growths, pustules, pouches and patches caused by the activities of insects, mites, fungi and other organisms. Alder leaves were marked by pustules caused by mites, leaflets of ash had coloured marginal roll-galls of a plant-bug, walnut leaves were disfigured by large 'blisters' caused by mites, and yew trees bore artichoke galls of a minute fly.

Understandably many gardeners prefer to devote their attention to larger creatures, such as birds and butterflies, leaving smaller forms of animal life to specialists. However, one cannot underestimate the valuable contribution these people make to nature conservation in Cambridgeshire. Many of the county's towns and villages have gardens where birds are provided with food and water and often with nesting boxes too, and there are others where trees and shrubs yield a feast of berries to hungry birds in autumn and winter. A comparatively common species like the greenfinch, though no acrobat, is seen in a new light when, visiting a town garden, it feeds on peanuts intended for those lively gymnasts the tits. And starlings noisily gorging themselves on ripe elderberries certainly enliven a garden, and so do house sparrows feasting on greenfly or winged ants. I have seen and heard all this in a

Cambridge garden. There, too, I have watched sulphur yellow brimstone butterflies in the spring and much later in the year peacock, small tortoiseshell and red admiral butterflies sipping nectar from flowers of Japanese stonecrop.

But nature-lovers, like most other people, occasionally long for a change, tiring for a time of our native species and wishing for something more exotic. Where plants are concerned there is no problem, for plants from most corners of the world can be grown in gardens and greenhouses (though heat and humidity may have to be supplied) and seen in the conservatories of great houses or in the University Botanic Garden at Cambridge. In order to appreciate in the fullest sense the interest and variety of these living plant collections one should visit them at different times of the year. Then, and only then, are the various species seen going through the interrelated processes of flowering and fruiting. Then, too, one can be sure of not missing special exhibitions that may be arranged from time to time.

Plants are, in a sense, captives. Not so birds, many of which, in any case, never leave their home ground. Fortunately there are in Cambridgeshire collections where birds of other countries and other climates can be seen.

There is one at the Wildfowl Trust's waterfowl gardens at Peakirk, an attractive area of woodland and water seven miles north of Peterborough. Here there are ducks, geese and swans of nearly one hundred kinds. The birds reared in 1975 included impressive numbers of several species, especially of Laysan teal, gadwall, Chiloe wigeon, red-crested pochard, tufted, mandarin and Carolina ducks, and North American ruddy duck.

That year Peakirk bred a few Hawaiian geese, or ne-ne. The world population of this bird, once as low as thirty-two, was substantially increased by breeding at the Wildfowl Trust's grounds several hundreds of birds, many of which have been flown back to the Island of Maui to re-establish the species in the wild. Another species that may eventually be involved in such a rescue operation is the rare white-winged wood duck from south-east Asia. It, too, has been bred at Peakirk where, in fact, the first captive-bred female to lay did so in 1973. This species has suffered badly in the wild owing to man's disturbance and destruction of the rain forest habitat, particularly in Assam where the bird is known as 'Deo Hans' or spirit duck, a name arising from its ghostly voice. There are proposals that sanctuaries be established in Asia for this and other creatures. Meanwhile, Cambridgeshire plays a part in rearing individuals of this endangered species, thus helping to ward off its extinction.

Two miles from Peakirk is Borough Fen Decoy (not normally open to visitors) where the Wildfowl Trust operates a ringing scheme as part of its research into the biology of wildfowl. Formerly several thousand duck were caught here each year and sent to market in wicker crates made from osiers growing at Peakirk. Now the birds are caught, ringed and released, careful records being kept of species and ring numbers so that data on movements, age and other factors can be built up as ringed duck are subsequently caught, killed or found dead. In 1975, 1,505 ducks were ringed at Borough Fen, this number being made up of 932 mallard, 559 teal, twelve shoveler and two pintail.

The decoy pond, which has eight curved catching 'pipes' radiating off it, has a roosting population of up to 1,500 duck in autumn, but this number falls in winter and few of the duck stay to nest. Covering about two and a half acres, the pond lies in 14½ acres of mixed woodland, the haunt of nearly 130 species of wild birds.

Like Borough Fen Decoy, the Wildfowl Trust's grounds at Peakirk act as a refuge for wildlife in an area where agriculture takes priority over large stretches of the countryside. Within their 17 acres one may enjoy the spring songs of willow warbler, blackcap and whitethroat, and watch migrating birds passing through. Water attracts the heron and spinneys of ash and hawthorn form an ideal habitat for woodpeckers and tree-creepers. Grey squirrels, those agile but harmful aliens, are seen there, as are water voles, gentle creatures often called water rats and persecuted by the ignorant. Wood mice and voles occur, and stoats venture into the grounds on occasion, only to be evicted immediately they are detected. The many trees, shrubs and wild flowers are a great attraction to insects, orange-tip and brimstone butterflies being among the most colourful.

Margaret Palmer's study of the invertebrate community of Borough Fen Decoy pond, a shallow stretch of water more than three hundred years old, revealed the presence of some fifty species of invertebrates (animals without backbones), half of them pond skaters, water beetles and other insects. In addition three-spined and ten-spined sticklebacks were present. These fish act as hosts for the parasitic larvae of the swan mussel whose shells measured up to $5\frac{1}{2}$ inches in length at Borough Fen.

Neglected by many nature-lovers, fish form an important element in the fauna of Cambridgeshire, one that brings considerable pleasure to anglers and food to herons, kingfishers and other fish-eaters. Eels, wriggling at night across wet grass, reach dykes, ponds and the moats of old houses. The indigenous pike, long known as tyrant of the rivers, lies in wait for smaller fish, young waterbirds, small mammals, frogs and newts, while another 'freshwater wolf', the introduced pike-perch or zander, is also present in Cambridgeshire waters. Carp and tench feed on invertebrates and plants in rich weedy lakes and slow-flowing rivers and are perfectly at home in parts of the county.

Barbel, whose name refers to the barbels (little beards) with which they explore for food, frequent parts of the Ouse and, being strong fighters, their capture involves all of an angler's skill. Chub and dace abound in Cambridgeshire rivers. 'The fearfullest of fishes', the chub eats a great variety of animal and plant food, insects, spiders, berries, seeds and small fishes all being taken. The dace's old name, dart, gives a good impression of this lively fish, seen in summer darting at flies on the surface. Parts of the Ouse hold great shoals of bream, roach and bleak. Much more widespread than the silver bream, the common or bronze bream feeds at the bottom, gorging itself upon almost anything eatable, rising on sunny summer days to the surface to enjoy the warmth. On hot sunny days the roach will rise to the top and take flies, but as a rule it lives near the bottom. Despite their name, bleak are bright and silvery, pretty and lively, well deserving to be called freshwater sprat, dear old Izaak Walton's name for them. Another Cambridge-shire fish, the rudd, is handsome with gold and crimson. Like bleak, it will nibble at dry bread crusts floating on the water.

Trout are found in the higher reaches of the Cam and the form known as sea trout is taken in parts of the Ouse. The introduced rainbow trout occurs in several places, notably at Grafham Water. But perhaps the fish that has caused most excitement in recent years is that very local and rare species the burbot. The discovery of this species, the only British freshwater fish of the cod family, in the county came at a time when many people believed it to be extinct in Britain. The burbot's retiring disposition obviously helps it to remain undetected. We must hope that it will continue to breed in Cambridgeshire, for, though it is rarely seen, it is nevertheless truly part of our national heritage of wildlife.

VI

CULTURAL AND LEISURE ACTIVITIES

A COUNTY with numerous rich historical associations, Cambridgeshire is inevitably the home of several organizations
actively concerned with the past, with the study, conservation
and enjoyment of records, buildings and other relics of former
times. There are, for example, Cambridge Antiquarian Society,
Cambridge Society for Industrial Archaeology and Cambridgeshire Family History Society. Members of these bodies may,
like other interested people, visit the great collections of books
and records held by the County Council at Cambridge
Central Library, the County Record Office at the Shire Hall,
also in Cambridge, and elsewhere. Exhibitions are arranged
from time to time in the department devoted to the Cambridgeshire collection at Cambridge Central Library and the
County Council's archaeological officer holds occasional
'workshops' there to identify objects found in the neighbourhood. Such events enable people to see for themselves the types
of material that are likely to be of interest to others now or in
the future and at times they encourage visitors to produce
things of historical value from their own collections.

Nowadays few individuals are able to amass large and
important archaeological and historical collections or to afford
the cost of maintaining buildings of archaeological or historical
value and not everyone has the means of visiting outlying
places of interest that may be open to the public. But,
fortunately for those living in the area, the Cambridge Centre
of the National Trust, a voluntary association formed and run
by National Trust supporters, enables members to enjoy visits
to houses and collections whose owners include private
individuals, the National Trust and other organizations, in
Cambridgeshire and adjoining counties.

Several members of the university take prominent parts in

running the centre with the result that lectures and social gatherings are often held in certain of the colleges, affording people opportunities of seeing parts of these historic buildings that are not generally open to the public. Speaking personally, I have the happiest memories of visits to St John's and Corpus Christi Colleges when those energetic and able young men John Pritchard (who was, I believe, known affectionately to his friends as 'the great pilchard') and Nicholas Rock ran the centre. And the interesting people one met at meetings! Who could ever forget Miss Doris Shillington Scales, a keen member of the Cambridge Centre, who was still riding a bicycle and playing the harp at an age when many people are only too content to surrender completely to their television sets. As an octogenarian she had the great pleasure of hearing people recall with gratitude her father, the first radiologist in Cambridge, who died in 1927.

For those interested in literature and the world of books Cambridgeshire is also something of a wonderland. The county library service operates throughout the area, there are many bookshops, particularly in Cambridge, and large numbers of books are written, printed and published there. Lord Butler, until recently Master of Trinity, makes a quiet distinguished contribution as President of the Royal Society of Literature of the United Kingdom, a body founded in 1825 by King George IV, and the contributions of members of the university faculty of English, whose lectures are often open to all who are interested, are no less valuable. People who are not content merely to read and enjoy the works of others, however eminent or capable, and wish to see their own poems or stories, articles or novels, in print find companionship and encouragement as members of the Cambridge Writers' Circle. This friendly group has an active President in Miss Gillian Edwards, novelist and writer on the history of words, and hospitable members allow certain meetings to be held in their homes.

Cambridgeshire is also a great centre for music-lovers of all types, Cambridge, as mentioned in another chapter, being especially well-known for its musical activity. One very pleasing aspect of the county's music-making is the encouragement given to young musicians Young people may, for example, become members of Cambridgeshire Schools Holiday Orchestra and even those who have no intention of becoming professional musicians derive considerable enjoyment from the experience. The Arbury, Cambridge Concert, Phoenix and other orchestras are active in Cambridgeshire and there are many groups and societies that tend to cater for specialist interests, ones that are not necessarily esoteric.

The Susato Consort, with its concern for Renaissance and medieval music, is typical of those groups fostering interest in an important living link with the past (for music, like literature and other forms of art, certainly fulfils that vital function). There is a society interested in the works of Gilbert and Sullivan and several whose members devote their leisure to amateur operatics. The county, with two cathedrals and many churches within its bounds, also has much to offer church-music enthusiasts, and what lover of the sights and sounds of the English countryside has not had good cause to thank the church bell ringers who, by the way, have their own associations in Cambridgeshire.

The sense of sharing experiences with others, fellow players and audience alike, permeates the activities of all concerned with the theatre, amateur no less than professional. Cambridge has its ADC and Arts Theatres and Peterborough its Key Theatre and there are in various parts of the county amateur dramatic societies, some associated with large businesses such as Pye of Cambridge, some with village colleges and other educational institutions, and a number with churches and certain localities. These groups do not always advertise themselves or their performances very widely, but there are times when public recognition is made of their contribution to the cultural life of the county. Such an occasion was the celebration in 1973 of the thirteenth centenary of Queen Etheldreda's foundation of her religious community. At that time amateur dramatic societies of the diocese presented the Wakefield Towneley Cycle of Mystery Plays in Ely Cathedral.

Ely Art Society, whose annual exhibition formed part of the thirteenth-centenary celebrations, is one of a number of such bodies in Cambridgeshire where Cambridge Drawing Society and Cambridge Society of Painters and Sculptors are well known. Pictures and other works by members are exhibited by the societies, while those of other artists may be seen in places such as Ely, where the Old Fire Engine House has a gallery and a restaurant, and Cambridge where public libraries, museums and galleries usually have something on show to arouse interest, delight or amusement. Remarks made by visitors to a certain Cambridge gallery showed most effectively that 'modern' works of art may also have the effect of horrifying viewers.

Certainly no one should complain that artists are not given opportunities of displaying their work in Cambridgeshire. Even the East of England Show at Peterborough, an annual event firmly based on agriculture, includes an impressive art exhibition.

Those who maintain, not without good reason, that the best gardeners have something of the artist in them will be pleased to hear that Cambridgeshire has its share of men and women who seek to beautify and enliven their surroundings by planting trees, shrubs and smaller plants. Gardening clubs bring together like-minded people in several parts of the county and those who wish to develop an interest in some special group of plants are provided for by specialist bodies such as Cambridge Orchid Society and Cambridge and District Branch of the National Cactus and Succulent Society.

Allotments societies existing in certain parts of Cambridgeshire serve their members and remind us that here, as in so many other parts of the country, there is a growing interest in self-sufficiency regarding vegetables and other produce. This development has encouraged gardeners to think of honey production and a beekeepers' course for beginners run by the Cambridge Beekeepers' Association was well supported, eighty-five people attending the first session, twice as many as at any previous course. Beekeepers' associations are active in other parts of the county, that covering Peterborough, Oundle and district holding exhibitions at the East of England Show.

Gardening, beekeeping and many allied activities have long been among the numerous and varied interests of the Women's Institute movement, which is well represented in

Cambridgeshire. In 1945 the district had played a special part in the founding of Denman College, where Women's Institute members attend residential courses, for that year the annual general meeting of the National Federation decided to establish it at the suggestion of the County Federations for Cambridgeshire and Oxfordshire. Nowadays the Women's Institutes of Cambridgeshire are concerned not only with handcrafts and home economics but matters of local, national and international importance and there is no doubt that, besides bringing warmth and friendship into the lives of many people who might otherwise feel isolated, they provide opportunities for members to serve both their own movement and the wider community.

Even a casual glance at lists of voluntary organizations and specialist groups appearing in the *Citizens' Guide*, a *Cambridge Evening News* supplement, and similar publications will show that there are plenty of people in Cambridgeshire who are prepared to give such service to others. They work through local branches of national organizations (Amnesty International, the Royal National Institute for the Blind, and many more), or local bodies like the Cambridgeshire Society for the Blind, Ely Diocesan Association for the Deaf, and various community associations.

Some people devote part of their leisure to outdoor pursuits, which in Cambridgeshire may take many different forms. Although the town of Newmarket, the home of English racing, is in Suffolk, the two Newmarket racecourses, the July course and Rowley Mile course, are almost entirely within the East Cambridgeshire District Council area and so county residents may follow 'the sport of kings' on their own home ground. One of the world-famous races run at Newmarket, the Cambridgeshire, an event founded in 1839, the year the Cesarewitch was also introduced there, must have done much to keep the county's name in the public eye and to attract racing people to the autumn meetings.

It was, by the way, an interest in racing and a wish to be near Newmarket and his property the Barton Stud that led Huttleston Broughton, later Lord Fairhaven, to buy Anglesey Abbey, now one of the National Trust's most interesting houses in this part of England, and to develop its beautiful gardens. And let us not forget that at Wandlebury on the Gog Magog Hills, just beyond the Cambridge boundary, is the grave of the Godolphin Arabian, one of the original Arabian stallions brought to England. This famous ancestor of many of the racehorses of today died in 1753 at the age of twenty-nine.

Like the Wandlebury area, several parts of Cambridgeshire have green lanes and bridleways that attract people who prefer to ride horses rather than watch others do so, even though the circumstances and atmosphere may be less exciting than at the races. These rural by-ways are also of interest to ramblers, naturalists and other countrygoers who may locate them with the help of official maps of the Ordnance Survey or guides available from local bookshops.

Golfers, whose game enables them to enjoy exercise in the open air in pleasant surroundings, are well provided for in the county. Girton Golf Club's course at Girton and the Gog Magog Golf Club's course near Wandlebury are comparatively close to the centre of Cambridge. At Ely is the City Golf Club's course, with fine views of the cathedral, and also within East Cambridgeshire is the Links Golf Club whose moorland course is opposite the racecourse just outside Newmarket. Peterborough has its Milton and Thorpe Wood courses, the last-named having been opened only a few years ago as the city's first public golf course.

In due season cricket occupies much of the leisure of those Cambridgeshire people who are drawn to this most English of all summer games and matches are played on carefully tended grounds in Cambridge, Ely, Peterborough and other towns and on village greens in many parts of the county. In recent years there has been some concern that players do not always know, let alone understand, all of the laws governing cricket and, in the hope of improving matters, Cambridgeshire Association of Cricket Umpires has held weekly sessions to explain them and their implications to captains of local clubs. Undoubtedly there would have been some interesting reactions to this situation from the undergraduates of Cambridge University who, early this century, founded the Pagans' Cricket Club. For, although they admired and supported cricket on the village green, the Pagans were opposed to those in the university who took sport, and especially cricket, seriously.

Having no captain or officials, they picked a 'leader in the field'. The batting order was settled by the drawing of playing cards, he who drew the knave becoming wicket-keeper, and for many years the score was kept by the notching of a piece of willow. Pagans were required to aim at a tie, and so strong was their rule that they should never win a match that there was some consternation when, in 1950, it was announced that they had defeated the University Women's Cricket Club by four runs. Honour was, however, saved when the ladies signed a document stating that the unwanted four runs had been scored from the seventh ball of an over.

Bowls is another game enjoyed in Cambridgeshire by people using greens laid out and maintained by local authorities and clubs in most of the towns and some of the villages. Often regarded as being merely a summer pastime for elderly men, bowling is supported throughout the county by men and women, many of whom are young in spirit if not in years, and membership of an indoor club, of which there are several here, has obvious advantages. Ten-pin bowling, a much older game than many people think (it is said to have been taken to the U.S.A. by Dutch settlers in the seventeenth century), does not seem to have found as much popularity in Cambridgeshire as in some other parts of Britain, though Peterborough took to it with enthusiasm some years ago.

Croquet has its devotees here and facilities, complete with the necessary equipment, are provided for full-scale games on at least one public recreation ground (Christ's Pieces in Cambridge). This open-air game, in which two or more players use mallets to drive balls through a series of hoops leading to the winning peg, was largely superseded about 1875 by lawn tennis, for which there are clubs and public and private courts in many parts of the county.

Table tennis, the indoor game developed in Britain late last century, possibly from real tennis, is popular in Cambridgeshire, though early in the present century, when it was still known as ping-pong (it became known officially as table tennis in 1926), certain people in Cambridge regarded it as a subject for derision. Sent to report a tournament arranged by the Cambridge Conservative Club, a local journalist wrote in 1902: ". . . are we not going just a wee bit mad over such an inane piece of nonsense? Ping pong! Just think of it! Why, the very name suggests something weak and childish!" There are still people who look down their noses at table tennis and those who play this game, but there are few social and youth clubs where enthusiasts are not to be seen in action.

Many people are devoted to badminton in Cambridgeshire and there are plenty of clubs, some associated with evening and community centres, schools and churches. The keenest and most energetic players are not always in the ranks of the young. Squash has its supporters, too, Cambridge being a stronghold of the game, one that seems to attract the ladies.

Unlike some of the activities mentioned so far, archery, once an aid to survival in both peace and war, is almost as old as the human race. The City of Cambridge Bowmen and others who enjoy the sport are therefore safeguarding an ancient tradition. Historical records of Cambridgeshire contain many references to butts, where archery was practised, including land between Maids Causeway and the river, part of Midsummer Common, in Cambridge, where a man called Martin, who owned an archery ground on the outskirts of the town, was still making bows and arrows until late last century. Although there were times in past centuries when they had to deal with Cambridge undergraduates who caused trouble by illegal use of bows and arrows in the streets, those in authority, the learned and the powerful, were seriously interested in archery. One of their number, Roger Ascham, classical scholar and leading educational theorist, wrote a treatise on the subject, *Toxophilus* (1545), that recommended him to Henry VIII, so that a few years later he became tutor to the Princess Elizabeth, the future Queen Elizabeth·I.

It is clear from diaries and other old records that forms of football were played in Cambridgeshire hundreds of years ago and that, even when played by Cambridge undergraduates, they could become very rough. Now there are many village greens and other open spaces where keen youngsters, whose only thought is to enjoy themselves, may be seen using heaps of clothing to mark the goals just like long-forgotten players of camp ball, the ancient game in which the ball was the size of a cricket ball (the game was known as kicking camp when a large football was used and savage camp when played with shoes on).

Two professional soccer clubs, Cambridge United and Peterborough United (known as the Posh), play in the Football League and there are amateur soccer clubs in most parts of the county. Cambridge, Ely and Peterborough and certain of the schools are the main centres where Rugby Union football is played and enjoyed. One wonders whether it is this game's association with the public schools that has led many people in these parts to regard it as being beyond them. The issues involved are difficult, if not impossible, to define, but were perhaps hinted at by the man whose son left a public school without having acquired a single educational qualification. "At least," he said, "the boy was taught to play rugger and he's the only one in his unit's team who isn't an officer!"

Whatever may be said about the superiority, real or imaginary, of other pursuits, there is little doubt that rowing interests many people in Cambridgeshire. At Cambridge it is still often regarded as taking pride of place in university sport and this is fitting, for the city owes much to its river and the county to its many waterways, both natural and artificial. Organized rowing began at Cambridge in 1827, the year the University Boat Club was established, and was obviously well supported, so much so, in fact, that the historians of Jesus College felt that there was little doubt that the late nineteenth-century decline in the undergraduate population of the college was due to over-emphasis on rowing, many of whose adherents were rowdy and idle where academic work was concerned.

Today Cambridge men practise for the famous boat race against Oxford at Ely, the trial eights using the stretch of river between Prickwillow and Adelaide Bridge. It was on the challenge of Cambridge that the first Oxford and Cambridge Boat Race was rowed at Henley in 1829. Ten years later the second race was rowed from Westminster to Putney and in 1856 the contest became an annual one. Many of those who have followed the Boat Race (as this great event has come to be known) on radio and television do not always realize that crews from Cambridge have secured victories in other major events. Jesus Boat Club, for example, has won the Putney Head of the River Race against eights from all over Britain and the Grand Challenge Cup at Henley.

On the river at Cambridge itself the colleges compete against one another during the May Races (The Mays), now held in June, and the Lent Races (The Lents) at the end of the Lent term. As the Cam is a comparatively narrow river, these events take the form of bumping races, each boat of the line having to catch up with the one in front, bumper and bumped, victor and victim, changing places in the starting order next day. Even those who do not watch from the towpath or from the riverside at Fen Ditton may keep in touch with the progress of the Bumps by following tables published in the *Cambridge Evening News*, a lively and informative daily newspaper.

Some outstanding personalities have been associated with rowing in Cambridge and there are many impressive stories about them. There was Steve Fairbairn who as an undergraduate captained Jesus Boat Club and rowed for Cambridge and later, having spent twenty years as a grazier in his native Australia, returned to Cambridge to coach the boats of his old college. Forty years after his death he is remembered as the brilliant teacher of rowing who instituted the Head of the River race, Putney–Mortlake, in 1925, whose enthusiasm was tempered by the belief that rowing should be enjoyed, win or lose.

Charles Hose, Fairbairn's junior in Jesus College by a year, left Cambridge without having resided there long enough to get a degree and he does not appear to have shone as a rowing man. But he is remembered not only for his distinguished service in Sarawak, contributions as ethnologist and naturalist and successful investigation of the principal cause of the disease beri-beri but for his success in getting the Borneans to abandon warfare in favour of boat racing as a means of settling tribal disputes. Lambert Charles Shepherd, who did make his mark as a rowing man at Cambridge, twice rowed a small boat all alone across the Strait of Dover at the time of Dunkirk, each time bringing back several British soldiers from the evacuation beaches. And so one could continue.

Besides the university boat clubs there are in Cambridge several rowing clubs with members from the city and surrounding area, which take part in bumping races each July, and there is sufficient interest in rowing to support clubs in other Cambridgeshire towns, notably in Peterborough, and, of course, many people take to the oars in a much more leisurely way than the serious rowing types.

The punt, a flat-bottomed boat propelled by a pole, is a striking feature of pleasure boating on the Cam at Cambridge, where this and other types of boats and canoes can be hired for trips along the Backs or to Grantchester. Many a novice has discovered that punting is no pastime for fools, certainly not for fools who cannot swim. The punter has to know, among other things, how to handle the pole so that the punt does not move on without him.

Motor boats can be operated on many stretches of the Cambridgeshire waterways and in recent years there has been a great increase in holiday cruising. Throughout the area boatyards provide hire craft and offer facilities for fuel, fresh water and other services, and certain of the riverside towns, river authorities and others provide moorings. Sailing is also enjoyed on Cambridgeshire waterways, including the Roswell Pits at Ely and Grafham Water, and clubs exist in many places.

With its abundant coarse fish, Cambridgeshire has attracted anglers for countless generations and not surprisingly there are many fish preservation and angling clubs and societies and several specimen hunters groups. There is some free fishing (for example, that controlled by the local authority on the southern side of Ely), but most fishing rights are leased to private clubs and organizations, some of which issue day and season tickets to visitors. A good rule for those in doubt is always to enquire in advance from local tackle shops or council offices where they will receive information as to any licences or permits required. Despite the fact that one often sees long lines of anglers stationed at intervals along the river banks, there are places where fishermen who value true solitude feel perfectly happy. There is trout fishing on the higher reaches of certain Cambridgeshire rivers, but all the beats are strictly controlled by private syndicates. Trout fishing by the general public is available at Grafham Water where thousands of rainbow trout and brown trout are landed during the season.

During really hard winters, mercifully few and far between in recent times, Cambridgeshire waterways become natural skating rinks and there are always plenty of people eager to venture on to the ice. This enthusiasm may have led to the tradition that the fens were the birthplace of skating in England. Be that as it may, Cambridgeshire people have undoubtedly long enjoyed skating and have shown remarkable proficiency at it. Skating contests were popular here in the eighteenth century, when village blacksmiths made skates and local farmers offered purses of money, barrels of beer, sides of beef and red flannel petticoats as prizes, and during the following century some of the Cambridgeshire skating champions became known well beyond the county boundaries. William ('Turkey') Smart, supreme champion of the Cambridgeshire fens for ten years, continued to compete on the ice while in his sixties, as did William See, whose nickname Gutta-Percha referred to his toughness.

To keep in practice during the summer and at other times when it was not possible to use ice skates, some of the Cambridgeshire skaters trained on roller skates on the roads near their homes. Roller skating itself became popular in the county at the end of last century, the sport having a particularly large following in Cambridge, where several rinks opened and carnivals were held, with many of the roller skaters in fancy dress, until well into the present century. Roller skating has certainly not died out in Cambridgeshire, but skateboarding seems to have overtaken it in popularity among the young. As I write there is talk of local authorities being pressed to set aside areas away from traffic and pedestrians where skate-boarders (and, one would hope, roller skaters) can enjoy themselves without endangering their own lives and those of other people. One hopes that something will be done along these lines, for it is surely desirable that young people should be encouraged to let off steam in harmless ways.

At a time when medical experts are urging able-bodied people not to surrender to sedentary ways of life, it is encouraging to find the authorities at Peterborough deciding to provide an extensive cycleway system. Cycling has long been a popular pursuit there, Peterborough Cycling Club having been founded more than a hundred years ago. In Cambridge where, as in Peterborough, the bicycle is an important means of transport, there are a number of cycling clubs.

Cycling as a sport became popular there with members of the university in the 1880s when members of the Bicycle Club enjoyed the use of a riding path in a field along the Backs. Then, as is often the case even now, certain dons did not consider it to be beneath their dignity to ride bicycles. Arthur Christopher Benson, Master of Magdalene College, enjoyed cycling in the Cambridgeshire countryside and was doing so in the 1920s, well after the age of sixty. One realizes that conditions have changed in recent times but, even so, one cannot help feeling that there are many people today who would benefit by cycling in a leisurely way for pure enjoyment.

In Cambridgeshire, as elsewhere, large numbers of people find pleasure in motoring and motor cycling and some become members of the various clubs concerned with these activities. Hard things may be said of motorists and motor cyclists who drive their vehicles along green lanes and trackways, which were never intended for such traffic and are indeed quite unsuitable for it, and similar remarks may be made about those who drive noisily or carelessly or behave in other ways that endanger others or cause them unnecessary disturbance. But, on balance, there is no doubt that the use of motor vehicles had enlivened the leisure of countless people, especially those living in remote areas such as still exist in parts of the fenland, opening up vast new areas of interest for them. For people living in Cambridgeshire it is something of a blessing to possess a motor cycle or a car and thus be able to travel independently once in a while to the coast at, say, Hunstanton in Norfolk or to venture into hilly or mountainous parts of the country.

Some people, having no form of transport of their own, go on coach trips operating from centres such as Cambridge and Peterborough, especially during the summer. As one who has enjoyed such outings from Cambridge, I recall a trip to the Wye Valley, one made memorable by the obvious enjoyment of so many of my travelling companions, and another to Whipsnade when the sight of this beautiful place on a perfect summer's day made me wish that there were more spacious zoological parks like it.

There is a great interest in animals of all types in Cambridgeshire and many people devote a significant part of their leisure to keeping certain kinds at home and to visiting places where various species may be observed. Dogs are popular as pets, but unfortunately for the poor animals concerned some people keep them as 'company' without realizing that companionship requires, as in the case of close relationships between people, giving as well as receiving. The dog needs to be exercised or kept where it can enjoy a reasonable amount of freedom, but sadly many owners are unable or unwilling to provide these conditions. Worse still perhaps are those who keep dogs purely as status symbols or as fashionable objects and I have known such people in Cambridge.

Perhaps I had better bite my tongue and be thankful that in Cambridge and other centres there are thoughtful people who organize dog-training classes and sessions where dog handling is combined with road safety. There are others who spare time to support the R.S.P.C.A., the Blue Cross, and Cambridgeshire Homeless Dogs, all worthy of our gratitude and respect.

There are those in the county whose admiration goes to cats and some at least would agree with the late Sir Compton Mackenzie's opinion that cats are more civilized creatures than dogs and ones whose friendship is less easily gained. That great cat-lover was also convinced that cats reward best those who spoil them. Perhaps it is their inability to pay this price that leads people to lose cats when, on occasion, they stray or go wild.

In the list of Cambridgeshire animal societies, which also includes societies for those interested in cage birds, horses, ponies and many more, it is pleasing to find the name of the

Cambridge Cavy Club, for cavies, often better known as guinea pigs, make delightful pets for children and when carefully groomed the different varieties look most attractive. Besides I must confess a fondness for these little animals whose particular charms I discovered more than forty years ago when I bought a pair from a Norwich grocer who, in the belief that they discouraged rats, kept a large number in the cellar under his shop.

Not everyone has the facilities for keeping pets and many have no inclination to do so. There are, however, collections of living animals within reasonable travelling distance of most parts of Cambridgeshire (one thinks of such places as Whipsnade and Kilverstone Wildlife Park), but unfortunately very few within the county itself. The zoo at Linton near Cambridge, which is being developed by the Simmons family as an educational and conservation centre, is becoming increasingly popular with local people and others from outside the county. With large and small species of mammals, reptiles, amphibians and birds, the collection is interesting and representative. Within the space of only a few years Linton Zoo has established something of a reputation for its breeding successes, a pleasing state of affairs enabling visitors to enjoy the sight of baby animals, so often playful and full of fun, and other collections to receive examples of species that cannot or should not be obtained from the wild.

Linton is believed to be the first zoo in this country to breed the Indian eagle owl in captivity. By the end of 1977 sixteen of these birds had been hatched and reared there and sent to other British collections where many of them are now reproducing. Another very unusual occurrence was the breeding and rearing at Linton of a binturong, a long-haired, fruit-eating Asian mammal, in 1976, an event repeated in 1977 when the second kitten of the litter died after a few days.

Many other species breed at Linton and not unnaturally the young attract much attention from visitors. Lion, puma and leopards have produced cubs, some of which have had to be hand-reared, a task involving considerable time and attention. Small-spotted genets, crested porcupines, Nigerian dwarf goats, degus, red foxes and other species have also increased their numbers there. A project that attracted great interest was the opening of a new enclosure to house a pair of young pumas. One of them, an escaped pet, had avoided destruction on the intervention of a Suffolk businessman who provided the cost of the new building. Its mate, a male, was born at Linton in 1975.

Formed in 1976 to encourage and assist in the aims of the zoo and to foster public interest both in the collection and wildlife generally, Linton Zoological Society holds meetings, including illustrated lectures on such subjects as the mountain gorillas of Rwanda and Asian elephants. The Friends of Linton Zoo, a separate group whose energies are devoted to raising funds, has given valuable support to the zoo's Himalayan bear project whose object is to breed this animal, one seen in comparatively few collections, which is declining in the wild largely due to the destruction of forests forming its natural habitat.

At a time when it is fashionable to jump on the conservation band wagon and talk, as always, is cheap, it is pleasing to find a small zoo and its supporters, including children who raise funds by holding jumble sales in their back gardens, actually doing something in the interests of wildlife and, what is more, enjoying it all.

Voluntary workers who devote part of their leisure to the practical tasks of conserving wildlife also assist the Cambridgeshire and Isle of Ely Naturalists' Trust and the Bedfordshire and Huntingdonshire Naturalists' Trust, two bodies that, between them, cover the modern county of Cambridgeshire. Indeed it is true to say that without such help these trusts could not hope to achieve much and would certainly not be managing nature reserves in the way they now do. But even willing horses require a break now and again and fresh volunteers are always needed.

Not everyone realizes that there is much more to nature conservation than acquiring, say, a piece of heathland and putting up a notice board. One is dealing with a constantly changing situation with living organisms, including the potentially most dangerous and destructive of all, man. Birds and insects fly in and out of the reserve and animals of other types come and go. People arrive and on occasion damage vegetation and land surfaces, cause fires and interfere with wildlife. Seeds of birches and pines and of other trees and shrubs arrive, carried by the wind and other agencies, and before long the open heath begins to resemble a scrubby kind of wood. Nature conservation volunteers play a vital part in dealing with such situations, wardening reserves at weekends and other busy times, removing invading saplings and cutting back scrub, recording the presence of the various species of wildlife, and, an absolutely vital activity, arousing the interest and enlisting the support of members of the public. Cambridge Conservation Corps runs work parties, mainly on Sundays, when anyone aged twelve or over is welcome. Tasks undertaken have included coppicing in Hayley Wood and other nature reserves, felling dead elms at Wandlebury and clearing scrub on the Devil's Ditch.

In Cambridgeshire, as in so many other places, there are large numbers of people who would never think of themselves as serious nature conservationists but who do, in fact, help the cause by putting out food and water for wild birds and by providing shelter and nest boxes for them. This may take up a very small part of their leisure, but it is time well spent.

Several organizations concerned with birds and bird watching are active in the county. Mention has been made of the Wildfowl Trust and the Royal Society for the Protection of Birds, which has local groups in Cambridgeshire and its headquarters at Sandy in neighbouring Bedfordshire, but there are others. Perhaps the most outstanding of them is the Cambridge Bird Club whose members are drawn mainly from Cambridgeshire, including Cambridge University. Committed to promoting the study of birds and to collecting and publishing information about Cambridgeshire species, it provides a meeting place for those interested in various aspects of the subject. As well as indoor meetings at which well-known ornithologists speak, there are informal gatherings when members report on bird-watching trips and talk about their interests, and visits, usually on Saturdays and Sundays, to bird haunts in Cambridgeshire and neighbouring counties. Through its work of co-ordinating local contributions to national studies and organizing local bird surveys, the club provides members with constructive ways of occupying at least part of their leisure.

Cambridge Natural History Society also attracts people from both city and university. Having celebrated its centenary in 1957, it is a well-established member of the increasing group of cultural and leisure organizations in the county. During the inter-war years the society played a useful part in encouraging naturalists to observe and photograph wild organisms and not to collect them. Nowadays there are section meetings for entomology, botany, zoology, geology, cell biology and applied biology, and less specialized general meetings. A conversazione is held towards the end of the Lent term, exhibits being provided by the sections, local schools and research establishments.

Peterborough has a flourishing natural-history society and the Fauna and Flora Society formed in Huntingdonshire before that county was embodied in modern Cambridgeshire continues to study the wildlife of its area and to co-operate with the Bedfordshire and Huntingdonshire Naturalists' Trust and other bodies.

There are individuals in Cambridgeshire who spend their leisure involving themselves in other aspects of conservation. Much of their activity amounts to little more than theorizing and some of them waste a considerable amount of other people's time and energy. Personally I have far more respect for people who, realizing the great practical difficulties involved in so many situations, are content to operate in small ways in their own immediate neighbourhoods. For example, the villagers who club together and plant a few trees on the village green are, it seems to me, making a far more effective contribution than those who use thousands of sheets of paper to propagate theories about the world's dwindling forest resources that few will ever read.

Happily there are in the county people who, with a wide variety of knowledge and experience, spend substantial parts of their leisure serving as members of local authorities, representing their colleagues on local committees of trade unions and on trades councils, business associations and similar bodies.

These men and women play a far more important part than many of us realize, for they do indeed form the very basis of our democracy, dealing with matters of local concern and conveying opinions and information, protests and requests, to county, regional and national levels. On occasion it is alleged that certain local bodies are politically, socially or otherwise unbalanced. The answer is very simple: more people of all types must be prepared to come forward and serve on them. To some readers this may seem a strange note on which to end this chapter. However, as one who served as secretary of the Cambridge branch of a great trade union, N.A.L.G.O., and represented it at district and national levels, I am convinced that many men and women would enrich their leisure by becoming more involved in the affairs of organizations connected with their daily lives and neighbourhoods. There is far more to all this than power or power-sharing or, to use another modern cliché, decision-making. For one thing, there is considerable interest to be derived from seeing people in surroundings and situations that are unfamiliar to many and listening to them in debate.

Armed with a copy of Dr Desmond Morris's book *Manwatching*, an illustrated field-guide to human behaviour, one might develop a completely new view of life and leisure. But what of those who simply want to stand and stare? To be quite honest, one must admit that there are excellent opportunities for this activity (Or should it be called non-activity?) in Cambridgeshire. How could it be otherwise in a county of waterways and bridges, colleges and churches, busy markets and quiet by-ways?

VII

CAMBRIDGE

CAMBRIDGE means many things to many people. For some it is sufficient to think of this city with a population of 104,000 as the seat of an ancient university. For others Cambridge means a centre of research, the home of world-famous bookshops, electronics and printing industries, or the River Cam, haunt of rowing and boating enthusiasts. For many others the city means beautiful buildings, fine open spaces, historical, literary and scientific associations, music, museums or festivals. In actual fact it means all this and much more.

Inevitably Cambridge produces reactions in long-term residents very different from those of undergraduates who may leave the place after a few years, never to return. One finds it almost impossible even to hazard a guess at the effects it has on tourists who, in their thousands, undertake quick conducted tours of colleges and chapels. But there is no doubt that the presence of these visitors, American and German, Japanese and French, and many others, adds to the special atmosphere of Cambridge, home, albeit often only a temporary one, of people of almost every race, religion and nationality.

In the streets, some narrow and congested, eminent scholars and scientists go about their daily business, only those who have appeared on television, a small minority, being recognized in public. Undergraduates, many on bicycles, surge about, their jeans and other informal attire a somewhat curious element in a background of ancient courts and buildings and carefully tended, well-established lawns. The townsfolk take all this in their stride, though many of them are not slow to air their views on student behaviour and many another matter concerning the university.

For some years students at Cambridge, like those in other places, have been enmeshed by the confusion surrounding universities, their organization, aims and activities. There are those who feel that the university should, in the national interest, produce more scientists, more educated women, more people with an interest in industry, and so on. At the other extreme there are those who consider that young people should pass their years at university sheltered from the harsher realities of life, all thought of earning a living and such practical matters being left until much later. Added to all this are the effects of those twin evils, snobbery and the determination to maintain class divisions, still so very much alive in Cambridge, as indeed they are in many other parts of Britain.

Much of this stems from the simple fact that Cambridge University, like all other universities, is simply a body of people. And people, including those most able to pass examinations and those who can make the right impression when it suits them, are blessed with varying degrees of character, courtesy and commonsense, those invaluable 'three Cs' which, together with the 'three Rs', have led men and women to achievement and distinction at national and international levels. Moreover, one must not lose sight of the fact that students (and indeed teachers) reach Cambridge from widely different backgrounds. The extent to which a student widens his horizons while at Cambridge depends on such factors as the part he plays in college life, the subjects he is reading, his activities outside the lecture room and library, and many more.

At Cambridge an individual becomes a member of the university after satisfying its entrance requirements and gaining admittance to a college, complying with any additional requirements it may lay down. Each college is a separate, self-governing body, generally founded, as we saw in an earlier chapter, by a ruler or some other wealthy or important patron. The college is provided with chapel, library, dining-hall, common rooms and other accommodation for the use of members. Under the Head (usually called the Master), the college forms a community whose senior members, many of them holders of university appointments, guide and teach the student members, such help and encouragement supplementing university lectures. Members may represent their college on the sports field or on the river, or take part in other inter-college activities.

The colleges, their histories and architecture, are dealt with in considerable detail in several other books.* Many colleges allow visitors to walk round the courts and to visit the chapels and on occasion certain other parts. Information as to the availability of private guides (any time of year) and the operation of guided tours (daily in the summer) is gladly given by Cambridge City Council's Tourist Information Centre, which is situated in the city centre and clearly signposted.

Conveniently, many of the colleges are in, or close to, the very centre of Cambridge. Thus, armed with a street map, one can plan walking tours to suit one's mood or athletic ability. Visitors to the more outlying colleges, such as Girton and Churchill, would probably prefer to travel by car or bus.

Cambridge university itself, the body concerned with promoting research, teaching, holding examinations and con-ferring degrees, is governed by a Regent House composed of all office-holders in the university and the colleges. During the course of his tours of the colleges the visitor will pass several of the buildings provided by the university to house lecture rooms, libraries and laboratories for its many faculties and departments. But to reach the real and ancient heart of the university (the university as opposed to the colleges) he must visit the Old Schools, opposite Great St Mary's, as the univer-sity Church of St Mary the Great is usually called.

The first part of the Old Schools site between King's Parade and Trinity Lane was given to the university by Nigel de Thornton about 1278. Work on the north range, part of a block of four ranges round a court, was begun about the middle of the fourteenth century. Said to have been completed in 1400, it is held to be the first university building erected specially for teaching purposes, having housed the Divinity School, with the Senate House (Regent House) and chapel above. The west range (built c. 1435–55) contained the Canon Law School with a library above. The south range, whose two lower storeys date from 1457 to c. 1470, housed the Civil Law School with a library above (the third storey was not added

*Notably in C. R. Benstead, *Portrait of Cambridge* (Robert Hale).

until 1864–7). The east range was built during the second half of the fifteenth century but replaced during the eighteenth century.

Changes in the use of these buildings have been made from time to time. Early in the eighteenth century, when the library was growing at an impressive rate, books were housed in the north range and a new Senate House was therefore needed. The university acquired more land, demolished houses in the area, and called in the architect James Gibbs, who had studied under Fontana at Rome. As a result the present Senate House, standing not far from the Old Schools, was built in 1722–30. Used for the conferment of degrees and other ceremonies, this distinguished classical building cost a total of £16,386 (including the cost of the site and incidental expenses). Gibbs, who was paid £151 for his work, had originally proposed a symmetrical arrangement with the Senate House balanced by a similar building on the south, but his scheme was not completed.

Two hundred years after the completion of Gibbs's Senate House the university's growing collection of books was still causing problems, having outgrown the space available in the Old Schools and a nineteenth-century extension (now the Squire Law Library and Seeley Historical Library). Finally, in 1934, the entire library, together with a number of seventeenth- and eighteenth-century bookcases, was moved to the new university library between Queens' Road and Grange Road. This "cathedral of intellectual life" was designed by Sir Giles Gilbert Scott and built between 1931 and 1934. "It has administered a violent shock to the Cambridge centre of gravity", exclaimed one writer in 1940, but the controversy surrounding its erection appears to have evaporated. Now the university library, comprising Sir Giles's building and a large recent extension, houses several millions of volumes and, as one of the great copyright libraries, may claim a copy of every work published in Britain.

The library is mainly intended for the use of members of the university, but other people are shown round parts of it at certain times. Members of the public are also allowed to visit other university collections whose hours of admission will be found in current guides. The Fitzwilliam Museum and the University Botanic Garden are mentioned elsewhere in this book, and visitors should certainly allow time for their enjoyment.

In Lensfield Road the Scott Polar Research Institute, a memorial to Captain Scott and his companions, has a museum with relics and souvenirs of expeditions and exhibits relating to current polar research. In Downing Street are the Museum of Archaeology and Ethnology, including Cambridgeshire material from excavations and chance finds, the Sedgwick Museum of Geology, and the University Museum of Zoology. The Museum of Classical Archaeology, containing many casts of Greek and Roman sculpture, is in Little St Mary's Lane, and the Whipple Science Museum, with large collections of sixteenth-eighteenth century scientific instruments and books, in Free School Lane. Kettles Yard Art Gallery in Castle Street, with its collection of modern art and exhibitions of modern art and craft, is another university property open to the public. Clearly the people of Cambridge and the city's vast numbers of visitors owe an enormous debt of gratitude to the university.

They are indebted, too, to those who run the Folk Museum (Castle Street), among whose treasures are many items illustrating the history of Cambridge, including the standard weights and measures used by the university to check the honesty of the town's traders. The industrial archaeologists who are creating the Cambridge Museum of Technology at the old pumping station at Cheddars Lane are also worthy of public support. Their aim is to build the collection round the two late nineteenth-century Hathorn Davey 80 h.p. steam pumping engines, the only surviving examples of a once common type. Intended to display items illustrating industrial activity in Cambridgeshire from 1800 to the present day, this new museum numbered among its earliest exhibits a fine 1860 Headly horizontal steam engine and the university's Titan computer of 1963.

With this wealth of collections already available in Cambridge, the local authorities have not felt it necessary to open museums of their own. Over the years they have, however, paid careful attention to building up there the Cambridgeshire collection at the Central Library and the county archives at the Shire Hall, valuable sources of material on the history of the area.

Cambridge itself is a great place for those interested in history and historical associations. Although there have been some startling changes in recent years, most parts of the city now containing at least a few new elements, one simply cannot escape the past there. This is nowhere more evident than in the area around Market Hill, not far from the Old Schools and the Senate House. The west side of this busy centre is bounded by the Church of St Mary the Great, a fine structure produced by a general rebuilding begun on the site of an earlier church late in the fifteenth century. Nowadays people come on Sunday evenings during university terms to hear outstanding people of all denominations speak on important topics of the day. Many others come to ascend the tower whose building, begun in 1491, was not finished until 1608 (the projected spire was never built).

On the opposite side of Market Hill, set among shops and restaurants, is the International Biographical Centre whose publications, *The International Who's Who in Poetry* and other dictionaries of biography, may well be invaluable to those who, in future generations, undertake research into the history and personalities of our own times. If only we now knew more about the skilled craftsmen and even the labourers who built the castles, churches and houses that have survived the centuries. As it is, there are many with which we cannot associate a single name!

Happily the Market Hill fountain has an interesting history involving at least one real character, for it is fed by Hobson's Conduit, also known as Hobson's River, a stream built early in the seventeenth century to conduct water from Nine Wells near Trumpington for drinking, street cleansing and scouring the drains in Cambridge. The name commemorates the Cambridge man whose custom of letting his horses in strict rotation led to the saying 'Hobson's choice'. The cost of the scheme was shared between university and town, Thomas Hobson and Samuel Potto leaving properties as endowments for its upkeep. The fountain that supplied drinking water from the new stream, now standing at the conduit-head at the Trumpington Road end of Lensfield Road, bears inscriptions reading: "Thomas Hobson Carrier between Cambridge and London a great Benefactore to this University Town. Died January 1st 1630 in the 86th yeare of his age. This structure stood upon the Market Hill and served as a Conduit from 1614 to 1856 in which year it was re-erected on this spot by Public Subscription." Standing on the south side of Market Hill, is the Guildhall, a building of quiet dignity and pleasing proportions. Dating from 1936-7 and provided with council chamber, committee rooms, offices and meeting halls, it no longer has sufficient accommodation for the entire staff of Cambridge City Council, some of whom work elsewhere. Itself a relic of times when Englishmen were less beset by laws and regulations and bureaucrats of all types, the Guildhall houses the Corporation insignia and plate and a great oak chest, probably that made in 1531 at a total cost of £10 10s 4d, which included carriage to London and back and £1 9s 4d for three hundredweight of iron, eleven iron plates and a thousand nails. Set in the wall on the first floor of the east wing is the foundation stone of the Town Hall erected here by James Essex junior in 1782, two years before he died aged sixty-two.

The 'ingenious Mr Essex', as he was known, was born and educated in Cambridge and originally worked as a practical builder. After studying architecture under Sir James Burrough, a well-known Cambridge advocate of the classical style, he carried out much important work, including designing and building the west front of Emmanuel College, Cambridge, restorations and alterations in Ely Cathedral, and putting up the four spires and battlement of the central tower at Lincoln.

On the north side of Market Hill town and gown meet, the ground floor of the building erected in 1934 to provide extra accommodation for Caius College being occupied by shops. To the north of this, "the best modern building of its date at Cambridge" (to quote Pevsner), St Michael's Court (1903), another part of Caius College, follows Rose Crescent round to Trinity Street, partly surrounding as it does so the medieval Church of St Michael.

Visitors to this and other places of worship here will discover many fascinating details of the long history of religion in Cambridge and of the development of the city. Eleven of the seventeen churches (excluding those of the nine religious foundations) mentioned in the description of Cambridge in the Hundred Rolls of 1279 survive, altered or restored to varying extents over the years, and three of the nineteenth-century churches – St Andrew the Great, St Giles and All Saints – are rebuildings of medieval ones, the last-named having been erected on a new site opposite Jesus College, only the churchyard of the old building surviving opposite St John's College.

Seven of these churches – St Peter, St Giles, St Clement, Holy Sepulchre ('the round church'), All Saints, Holy Trinity, and St Andrew the Great – stand along or close to the old road from the north-west that passes the site of the castle, crosses the river by Magdalene Bridge (the Great Bridge), and proceeds through the town by way of Bridge, Sidney and St Andrew's Streets. Six more of these churches – St Michael, St Mary the Great, St Edward, St Bene't, St Botolph and St Mary the Less (formerly St Peter) – are by the old High Street, another main arm of the medieval street system, now consisting of St John's Street, Trinity Street, King's Parade and Trumpington Street.

The medieval Church of St Andrew the Less ('the abbey church'), a survivor of the ancient suburb of Barnwell, stands on the Newmarket Road, and to this and others mentioned so far must be added the medieval churches of Cherry Hinton, Chesterton and Trumpington, villages now within the boundaries of Cambridge.

One has only to consult the Royal Commission's *An Inventory of the Historical Monuments in the City of Cambridge* (1959), with its two large parts and container of maps and plans, to begin to appreciate what a vast wealth of interest there is in each of these churches.

As one of England's most important surviving round churches, the parish church of Holy Sepulchre is of particular interest. Built on the east side of Bridge Street on land granted to the Fraternity of the Holy Sepulchre by Reinald, Abbot of

Ramsey, early in the twelfth century, the church was much altered in the fifteenth century. Part of the aisle-vault collapsed in 1841, and restoration, involving the destruction of the fifteenth-century belfry and other alterations, was carried out by the Cambridge Camden Society in 1841-3. A stone altar and credence-table were erected and this led to a lawsuit and the closing of the church from 1843 to 1845 when, the Court of Arches having declared them illegal, the offending objects were removed.

Holy Trinity, standing on the west side of Sidney Street, was the centre of the Cambridge evangelical revival associated with the name of the Rev. Charles Simeon (1759-1836), Fellow of King's College, perpetual curate and lecturer here from 1783 to 1836, who established a trust for acquiring church patronage and was a founder of the Church Missionary Society. Early in his ministry Simeon was persecuted on account of his Calvinistic views and, according to Henry Gunning's *Reminiscences* (1854), "for many years Trinity church and the streets leading to it were the scenes of the most disgraceful tumults". But there came a time when certain people, thinking he had forsaken his earlier views, deserted him and took to attending the Old Green Street Meeting House, an independent chapel. Much to his credit, Simeon did not neglect them: he made the minister at Green Street, John Stittle, a permanent quarterly allowance "for shepherding my stray sheep".

The Church of St Andrew the Great, formerly known as St Andrew-without-Barnwell Gate, stands on the west side of St Andrew's Street, marooned at one end of the modern Lion Yard complex with its shops and new central library. It holds one great surprise in the form of a wall monument to Captain James Cook, R.N., "one of the most celebrated navigators that this or former ages can boast of", his wife, and their six children. The gallant captain was killed by natives of Owybbe in the Pacific Ocean in 1779, three children died very young, two sons, Nathaniel, a midshipman, and Hugh, a scholar of Christ's College (immediately opposite the church), died in their teens, and another, James, a commander in the Royal Navy, was drowned in a high sea. Mrs Cook, who survived them all, lived alone for forty-one years. When she died at the age of ninety-four in 1835 she was buried in Great St Andew's where originally Hugh and later James had been laid to rest.

Several of the churches by the Old High Street have been mentioned already, but that of St Edward King and Martyr, between King's Parade and Peas Hill, must not be overlooked. The many wall-tablets and floorslabs are of great interest and there is an early sixteenth-century pulpit associated with Bishop Hugh Latimer, Fellow of Clare Hall, Cambridge, who preached in this church, and was condemned as a heretic and burnt at Oxford in 1555.

Away from the historic town centre new churches began to appear towards the end of the first half of the nineteenth century. For some years Cambridge had been growing towards the east and south-east. There was an added stimulus to development when the first trains reached Cambridge and the Eastern Counties Railway Station was opened in 1845, though the railway was not at first allowed to disturb the Sabbath, for on Sundays trains could not take up or set down passengers at Cambridge or within three miles of it between 10 a.m. and 5 p.m., unless the morning train was unavoidably delayed. With the population of the parish of St Andrew the Less, Barnwell, increased from 252 in 1801 to nearly 10,000 in 1841, the church was no longer adequate and two others were built in the Tudor style, Christ Church on the south side of New-market Road near Maid's Causeway (1837-9) and St Paul's on the east side of Hills Road (1841).

During the second half of the nineteenth century the growth of Cambridge continued, all sides, particularly those to the east and south-east, being affected, part of the demand for housing coming from Fellows of colleges who, in 1882, were permitted to marry. New churches appeared, including St Matthew, Geldart Street, with its octagonal nave, the yellow brick St Barnabas, Mill Road, a church without a tower, and St Luke, Victoria Road, with its spire and polygonal apse, and St John Evangelist, a towerless brick building on Hills Road.

Since 1900 more and more areas have become built-up, especially to the north, east and south-east of the old town centre. Several more churches have been built, but there has been talk recently of certain old ones being made redundant. It is to be hoped that some satisfactory use will be found for them. Colchester and Norwich, where old churches now house museums, have done much to show that such problems can often be solved in ways that benefit both church and community.

In Cambridge, as elsewhere, churches, active and redundant, new and old, are reminders of the long years of intolerance during which men and women were persecuted and victimized, tortured and murdered, often because of conscientious objections to a form of words, an act of ritual, or some other situation created by mere men. Be this as it may, they did not succeed in suppressing those of other persuasions, though it was not until last century that Acts of Parliament removed many outstanding disabilities of Roman Catholics, Jews and Nonconformists and freed university admissions, degrees and lay posts from religious tests.

It was late in the nineteenth century that the imposing Roman Catholic Church of Our Lady of the Assumption and the English Martyrs was built at the expense of Mrs Lyne-Stephens, formerly Yolande Duvernay, an operatic dancer, at the corner of Hills Road and Lensfield Road on a site given by the Duke of Norfolk. Among the heads on the hoods of the south aisle windows is Christopher Scott, parish priest for many years. Early in the present century this kind and hospitable man was assisted for a time by Robert Hugh Benson. This son of Edward White Benson, Archbishop of Canterbury, was educated at Trinity College, Cambridge, and received into the Roman Catholic Church nine years after taking anglican orders. His popularity as a preacher was such that his elder brother, Arthur Christopher Benson, fellow (and later master) of Magdalene College, Cambridge, was asked to use his influence with Hugh that he should leave the town. Much to his credit, this fine writer, himself an anglican, refused to do anything of the kind, and Hugh Benson remained in Cambridge for several years, though he is said to have felt himself suspected of vague designs on the spiritual life of the place.

Nonconformists (the dissenters of earlier years) must often have experienced such feelings in Cambridge. George Fox, the shoemaker who founded the Society of Friends (Quakers) got a rough reception from the students when he visited Cambridge in 1655, and just before the end of the century a recantation was extracted from Roger Kelsall, an undergraduate of Jesus College, who had attended Quaker meetings at a shoemaker's house nearby. Less than three weeks after it was entered in the college register and duly signed, however, Kelsall secretly withdrew from college, joined the Quakers, publicly professed "their insane doctrines", and was pronounced expelled. It seems probable that the shoemaker's house stood on the site of the present Friends Meeting House in Jesus Lane, a building of 1777 that was remodelled earlier this century.

The seventeenth-century Independent Chapel has long since disappeared from Green Street (between Trinity Street and Sidney Street), but a tablet removed from it, commemorating John Stittle, minister from 1781 until his death in 1813, is now at Eden Chapel (Baptist), Fitzroy Street, a building of 1874 that replaced the original Calvinistic Baptist chapel of 1825. St Andrew's Street Baptist Church also has strong links with the past, the present building of 1903 having replaced that of 1836 which itself replaced one of 1764. It contains a chair used by the Rev. William Carey, D.D., who died in 1834 aged seventy-three and who, as the inscription plate records, was the pioneer of modern foreign missions who inspired the founding of the Baptist Missionary Society. The son of a Northamptonshire schoolmaster, Carey was a shoemaker who joined the baptists in 1783 (he was then twenty-two) and became a pastor. He went to India, where he made a living as foreman of an indigo factory and preached in Bengali. Then he became professor of Sanskrit, opened a mission chapel, compiled grammars and dictionaries of several native languages, and issued translations of the scriptures.

Cambridge has more places of worship from the last century, including Zion Chapel (Baptist), East Road, and Emmanuel Congregational Church, Trumpington Street (containing certain fittings from the former Congregational Chapel in Downing Place, a late eighteenth-century building that became part of the university music school). Others have been built this century and now the Christian Spiritualist Church, the Church of Jesus Christ of Latter Day Saints, the First Church of Christ Scientist, the German Lutheran Church, the Hebrew Congregation, Jehovah's Witnesses, the Salvation Army, and other groups have a presence in the city.

Those who go in search of church and chapel, taking time and going on foot (the only way to see the city and to enjoy its many aspects and varied moods), will quickly appreciate the wealth of grassy open spaces with which Cambridge is blessed. Seen from the air they appear to dominate parts of the city, forming a background against whose greenness buildings gain considerably in attractiveness. For the pedestrian they provide a means of escape from busy streets, though nowadays not always from the noise of traffic.

Parker's Piece, behind Regent Street, one of the main shopping streets, is one such oasis where on sunny days many people rest, relax and sunbathe. The town acquired this important public open space, previously part of the common fields, from Trinity in 1613, in exchange for land on both sides of the river at the back of the college. Taking its name from Edward Parker, the college cook, who held a lease of the property at the time of the exchange, Parker's Piece was the setting for county and university cricket matches until the middle of last century when the 'cherry orchard' to the south-east was opened as a cricket ground.

Fenner's, as it is called after its original owner, is now the university cricket ground, but local clubs and youngsters still play games on Parker's Piece. Hobbs's Pavilion, erected there in 1928, commemorates Sir John ('Jack') Hobbs, the famous cricketer who was born in Cambridge in 1882, the son of a professional cricketer on the ground staff at Fenner's. He scored his first century at the age of nineteen when playing against Cambridge Liberals, and went on to play for England (1907–30) and Surrey (1905–35), achieving 197 centuries and more than 61,000 runs in first-class cricket.

Adjoining Drummer Street bus station, only a comparatively short distance from Market Hill, is the open space known as Christ's Pieces where there are trees and flower beds and areas set aside for bowls, croquet and tennis. Just beyond its northern edge is the great area bounded by the River Cam, comprising Jesus Green and Midsummer Common. There are facilities for informal games, bowls, football, hockey, putting and tennis at Jesus Green and a swimming pool is open there during the summer months.

Midsummer Common is the scene of much activity and revelry when it serves as fairground. Midsummer Fair takes place there in June when, at noon on the first day, it is proclaimed by the Mayor, who is attended by the Town Clerk and the Sergeant-at-Mace. After the reading of the traditional proclamation, relating mainly to the maintenance of order during the fair, new coins are thrown to the crowd and the fun of the fair begins. The fair's long history began early in the thirteenth century when the king granted it to the priors and canons of Barnwell. Their priory stood to the north of the Newmarket Road, immediately north of St Andrew the Less, the church they built and served until the Dissolution.

In former years Midsummer Fair, commonly called Pot Fair on account of the china sold there, was well patronized by local gentry and the university, including some of its senior members. Nowadays the eminent are not so much in evidence but, having had one such learned doctor introduce me to the delights of the iced lolly, I should never be surprised to find some distinguished scholar tucking into a hot dog there. By the way, those who venture into this part of Cambridge will discover pleasant riverside walks and enjoy the opportunity of refreshing themselves at the Fort St George in England, a sixteenth-century inn standing on the south bank of the Cam on Midsummer Common.

Further along the river, as it approaches the city's eastern boundary, is Stourbridge Common, the very mention of whose name recalls the great fair held thereabouts from at least the time of King John. With river traffic a vital factor, the Vice-Chancellor and Heads of colleges in the university and the aldermen of Cambridge in 1650 pointed out that any interruption of the navigation would cause considerable damage. "A great prejudice will," they declared, "thereby befall to a great part of this whole nation by the stoppage of the general commerce at Stourbridge Fair." But times change and by the eighteenth century a decline in trading set in. This continued and the ancient fair was ended by royal decree and proclaimed for the last time in 1933. The chapel of the Leper Hospital at Stourbridge, to which King John granted the fair about 1211, stands on the north side of Newmarket Road. Dedicated to St Mary Magdalene, it was restored in 1867 and is now in the care of Cambridge Preservation Society.

On the western side of Cambridge, close to the city centre, Coe Fen and Sheep's Green, areas of common grazing land, extend south from Silver Street. There is much here to interest the nature-lover, a fact recognized by both the Commons Committee of Cambridge City Council and the Cambridge-shire and Isle of Ely Naturalists' Trust when they co-operated over the publication of a guide to a nature trail. This runs through the meadowland of Coe Fen, beside the river to Robinson Crusoe's Island, where a rare purple-flowered plant is parasitic on the roots of willow trees, and back over Sheep's Green. An area for swimming has been set aside at Sheep's Green, but it is no longer considered necessary, as it was just before the First World War, to advise ladies to dispose of the "slight drawback" of passing the bathing-place by "a deft wielding of the parasol". Nearby there is a footpath leading across the meadows to Grantchester, and a recreation ground, Lammas Land, where one may play bowls and tennis.

In this place one is reminded (if reminder is needed) that nowhere in Cambridge is one very far from field or river, that the city is very much part of the surrounding countryside. True the Corn Exchange no longer serves its original purpose. Opened in 1875, this great glass-roofed building behind the Guildhall once housed 130 stands, but now it is a centre where roller skating, dances and meetings are held. Marochetti's statue of Jonas Webb, a leading nineteenth-century stock-breeder and exhibitor of Southdown sheep and shorthorn cattle, who farmed at Babraham, was removed from the building several years ago. It now stands in the open on Hills Road, not too far from the Cattle Market where, between the railway and Cherry Hinton Road, livestock are still bought and sold.

Very few Cambridge people work on the land, though

some are employed in and around the city on research into various aspects of agriculture. Many more work in research establishments of other kinds or make equipment and instruments for use in laboratories and hospitals. Firms concerned with the manufacture of electronic equipment, printing, building and retail distribution also provide much employment. Some residents are involved with official administration. There are a number of government offices in the city. One complex in Brooklands Avenue is known locally as 'the holiday camp', and there are tales of a well-known and much-photographed Cambridge character, who is usually seen with a bottle at his lips, arriving by taxi to collect his social security payments.

The varied activities of local government involve the services of another section of the population, Cambridgeshire County Council, Cambridge City Council and South Cambridgeshire District Council all having offices here. Concerned as it is with the past, present and future of Cambridge, whose ancient centre was firmly established long before the age of the infernal combustion engine, the City Council shoulders a difficult and complex task. Active in encouraging interest in the city, a major attraction for visitors to Britain, it is one of several bodies helping the Cambridge Festival Association to promote the Cambridge Festival, a two-week programme of concerts, recitals and other events held in July. Towards the end of the same month thousands, many of them coming specially from abroad, make for the grounds of Cherry Hinton Hall to attend the City Council's annual Folk Festival. Even people who are not enthusiastic about folk music usually derive some interest from the event, particularly from the antics of the colourful characters it brings to the city.

This constant influx of visitors, some staying for a few years, others for a few days or even just an hour or two, is a fascinating feature of life in modern Cambridge. Added to the university's contribution to the regular ebb and flow of population are those of the many schools of English and the Cambridgeshire College of Arts and Technology. The Technical College, or Tech, to use the name by which the last-named institution is so well known, provides courses for nearly 8,000 full, part-time and sandwich-course students, having greatly expanded since 1948 when the number of full-time students was only 300. Students are prepared for examinations at GCE 'A' level, National Diploma and degree levels in a wide range of subjects, including art, printing, languages, catering and hotel administration, engineering and building, management and business studies, and science. In addition to laboratories, workshops and many other facilities, the college has a well-equipped theatre where works by Chekhov, Euripides, Shakespeare, Verdi and others have been produced.

This is one of three theatres where people from Cambridge and the surrounding district may see a wide range of plays. Another is the ADC Theatre, headquarters of the University Amateur Dramatic Club, whose facilities are also used by other amateur groups. The third is the Arts Theatre on Peas Hill.

Held by a Trust, the Arts was built just before the Second World War and financed by the eminent economist Lord Keynes who played a leading part at the Bretton Woods conference of 1944 and became first British governor on the two great institutions that emerged from it: the International Monetary Fund and the International Bank. As a result of his marriage to the dancer Lydia Lopokova, John Maynard Keynes, as he then was, had become interested in ballet and was for a time Chairman of C.E.M.A., later the Arts Council. His foundation, the Cambridge Arts Theatre Trust, endeavours to entertain the city and university by providing throughout the year a varied programme of drama, ballet, opera, music and cinema (the Arts Cinema is in Market Passage).

At the Arts Theatre there are productions of the Cambridge Theatre Company, touring companies and Cambridge amateurs. The Ballet Rambert, the London Contemporary Dance Company, and other groups perform there, and on occasion there is opera from the English Opera Group and others. There is a traditional Christmas pantomime, an event associated for many years with that original and delightful entertainer Cyril Fletcher, and, of course, presentations by such university groups as the Footlights Dramatic Club and the Marlowe Dramatic Society.

Founded in 1883, the Footlights produces its May Week Revue at the Arts Theatre each year. Once described as "admirable home-made revue", it has served as nursery of many who later achieved fame. The name of Jack Hulbert, the comedian celebrated in musical comedy and revue, springs to mind, as do those of his brother Claude, another well-known comedian, Richard Murdoch, and Jimmy Edwards. The Marlowe has made a useful contribution by performing many of the more difficult and lesser-known Elizabethan plays.

Music is another strong element in the life of Cambridge. Indeed many people would be surprised at the amount of musical activity whose extent becomes apparent only when one studies the useful "What's On" brochures issued by the Information Service of Cambridgeshire Libraries. During a recent month, one quite outside the festival season, there was hardly a single day without at least one concert or recital open to the public. One day, a Sunday, six musical events were held, an organ recital in St John's College chapel at six o'clock and, later that evening, a celebrity recital in the Guildhall, the Medici String Quartet at Selwyn College, the annual choral and orchestral concert at Girton College, and concerts by Clare Choral Society and King's College Music Society in their respective colleges.

The choir of King's College, admired by countless visitors to the chapel and even more who listen to its broadcasts and recordings, has done much to maintain the outstanding musical tradition of Cambridge and to bring the city's name into prominence throughout the world. Naturally music-making is an essential activity at King's College School where, since the seventeenth century, the choristers have been educated with other children. With its origin going back to Henry VI's statutes for King's College with their provision for sixteen choristers who were to be members of the foundation, the school has among its old boys men of great distinction.

Orlando Gibbons, remembered for his madrigals and motets and other compositions, entered the choir of King's College in 1596 and, dying twenty-nine years later at the age of forty-two, was buried in Canterbury Cathedral. A much later composer, William Sterndale Bennett, later to be knighted, was in the same choir in 1824-6. Having attracted the attention of the German composer Mendelssohn by his first concerto in 1832, when he was just sixteen, Bennett went on to become professor of music at Cambridge and principal of the Royal Academy of Music, appointments sometimes thought to have stifled his original gifts.

Cambridge has two more schools whose foundations are rooted firmly in the city's historic past. The Perse School for Boys was founded in 1615 by the will of Dr Stephen Perse, a great local benefactor, who also provided a safe and dry raised path, a "sufficient Causey", from the further end of Jesus Lane to the hither end of Barnwell. Sited in Free School Lane for over 250 years, the Perse moved out a bit to Gonville Place in 1890 and even further out, to its fine grounds on Hills Road, in 1960. Included in its long list of scholars are the names of Jeremy Taylor, the seventeenth-century Bishop of Down and Connor, to whom Charles I, shortly to be executed, sent his watch and some jewels, and Edward Henry Palmer, the nineteenth-century orientalist who was murdered by Arab robbers while negotiating with tribes beyond Suez.

St John's College School was founded as a choir school in 1660 by Dr Peter Gunning, Master of the college, who became Bishop of Chichester and later Bishop of Ely.

After the seventeeth century other schools, mainly church schools, were provided by voluntary effort in Cambridge and they received no aid from public funds until 1883. Now the city has many schools of all types, some in modern premises, others in buildings that have been adapted or improved with varying degrees of success. One can only hope that more and more of those who attend them will benefit from the facilities and resources now available and eventually go into the wider world determined to maintain high standards in everything, in the interest not only of their city and county but of the country as a whole.

VIII

THE CATHEDRAL CITIES

THE MODERN county of Cambridgeshire includes within its
borders two cathedral cities, those of Ely and Peterborough,
the former on its eastern side, the other in its north-western
corner.

Ely is a small market town with a population of some
11,000. Over the centuries drainage of the fens has resulted in
the loss of much of its ancient island character, but 'eel island',
as one of its old names puts it, still owes much to its position
on the River Ouse. Like a large stretch of the surrounding
fenland, Ely is dominated by its great cathedral. This
magnificent building is ashlar-faced, much of the stone having
come from Barnack whose quarries north-west of Peterborough were exhausted in the eighteenth century. Once
described as a "great Gothic wedding cake", it has many
interesting features, only a few of which can be mentioned
here.

The Norman nave, twelve bays long, is particularly impressive. Its painted roof was started by Henry L'Estrange Style-
man Le Strange and completed after his death in 1862 by
Thomas Gambier Parry, a recognized authority on decorative
painting who invented the 'spirit fresco' process. With a
picture for each bay painted on wood, it introduces red, gold,
green and blue as elements of a rich but delicate colouring.

A large slab in the floor of the nave is said to mark the
entombment of Alan de Walsingham who, early in the fourteenth century, was a monk at Ely. He became sacrist and
later had his election as bishop-elect twice set aside by the
Pope. As sacrist, Alan was, it appears, responsible for the idea
of erecting an enlarged octagon in place of the Norman
crossing tower that fell down in February 1322. Often
regarded as Ely's crowning glory, the stone octagon with timber

144

Riverside scene at Ely

The Maltings, Ely

Peterborough: the cathedral from the gardens

Peterborough: gateway to the cathedral

Wisbech: the North Brink

Riverside scene at Godmanchester

March: the Church of St Wendreda

The Old Nene passes through March

Ye Olde Ferry Boat Inn, Holywell (foreground: rushes being dried)

Potato clamps in fenland farm country

The village college at Linton

Typical fenland farm country

A corner of Hinxton

An ancient house at Houghton

Landbeach: All Saints' Church

Grantchester: thatch among the trees

lantern is both a marvel of engineering and a structure of considerable beauty.

One of the country's finest examples of its style, the retro-choir or presbytery dates from the thirteenth century and includes some delightful features, the group of lancets at the east end being truly beautiful. This part of the cathedral was built by Hugh of Northwold, Bishop of Ely from 1220 to 1254, a man of character and conscience who offended Henry III by refusing the benefice of Dereham to the King's half-brother. Bishop Northwold's fine canopied tomb in the north chancel aisle bears three figures. Illustrating the story of St Edmund, they serve to remind us that, in his younger days, Hugh of Northwold was a monk of the Benedictine abbey of Bury St Edmunds where, despite opposition of the King's party, he became Abbot.

If one has to single out another part of Ely Cathedral for special mention it must surely be the mid-fourteenth-century Lady Chapel. This large chapel is unusual in that it was not erected in the customary position at the eastern end of the cathedral but as a separate building to the north of the choir. Sadly much of its former beauty disappeared after the Reformation when carving and stained glass were mutilated or completely destroyed.

Man and the centuries have also taken their toll of the monastic precinct, but patient and observant visitors will nevertheless find much to interest them and to remind them of times when the Bishops of Ely were powerful figures in the land and the Benedictine priory rich in lands and manors. Begun in 1397, Ely Porta, or Walpole Gate, was the great main gatehouse of the priory. The chambers beside the gate-way housed the porter's lodge and guardroom, while that above was the meeting-place of the prior's court and the courts of the manor of the priory.

The Bishop's Palace stands on a site near the cathedral selected late in the fifteenth century by Bishop Alcock. Much of his palace was pulled down by Bishop Laney, who altered the building during the seventeenth century, but his east tower and the lower parts of his west tower survive in the present structure. The palace, now a school for physically handicapped children, was the official residence of the Bishop until early in the Second World War when it became a convalescent home for servicemen.

The first Bishop of Ely who did not live in the medieval palace was Edward Wynn who took a smaller medieval house, the former deanery, now called simply the Bishop's House. Bishop Wynn was a man with a deep sense not only of tradition but of history. In 1941 he chose 7th August, the festival of the Name of Jesus, for his enthronement at Ely because of his triple connection with Jesus College, Cambridge, where he had been scholar and later chaplain and was, as Bishop of Ely, its Visitor. Throughout the enthronement ceremonies he carried the crozier which had belonged to Matthew Wren, the Bishop of Ely who three hundred years before had been imprisoned in the Tower of London for a long period.

A number of buildings of the original monastery are occupied by the King's School, one of the oldest public schools in Britain, whose millennium was celebrated in 1970. One building used by the King's School contains the remains of the Prior's House. On its south-west side Prior Crauden's chapel, often described as a jewel of the Decorated style, is now the school chapel. By the way, John de Crauden, prior from 1321 to 1341, was succeeded in office by his friend Alan de Walsingham, already mentioned in connection with Ely Cathedral's incomparable octagon. The house of the headmaster of the King's School was originally the Queen's Hall, named thus after the visit to Prior Crauden of Philippa of Hainault, queen of Edward III, who deserves to be remembered if only for the way in which she interceded for the six principal burgesses when Calais surrendered in 1347. The fifteenth-century monks' granary, standing close to the Ely Porta, has been converted into a dining-hall and the cellarer's house is also used by the King's School.

Close to the ancient monastic centre of Ely is the Church of St Mary. There is a reference to the original building in a charter of Hervey who, as first governor of the diocese, was Bishop of Ely from 1109 until his death twenty-two years later. However, the present church was begun during the time of Eustace, the Bishop of Ely who died in 1215. A window in memory of the men who fell in the Great War has figures of St George, who is fighting the dragon with the princess looking on, the Archangel Michael, and Earldorman Brihtnoth as a warrior. Below Brihtnoth, who was fatally wounded when fighting the Norsemen in 991, is a picture of the boat bringing his body to Ely, rowed by nuns, candles burning by the bier.

Adjoining St Mary's churchyard is the vicarage, a half-timbered house named after Oliver Cromwell who lived here from 1636 to 1647, during which time he became governor of the Isle of Ely. Incidentally, Cromwell was related on his mother's side to Robert Steward who, as last Prior, surrendered the monastery and later became first Dean of Ely.

The Church of St Peter was built as a chapel of ease to Holy Trinity parish and as a memorial to the Rev. Edward Bowyer Sparke, Canon of Ely and son of the then Bishop of Ely. The canon's widow, Catharine Maria Sparke, who laid the foundation stone on St Peter's Day, 1889, bequeathed funds to supply an assistant priest. Designed by John St Aubyn, the church contains a fine rood screen and some attractive stained glass.

There is further evidence of the development of religious activity in Ely in the form of the Roman Catholic Church of St Etheldreda (successor to the tin mission church that served the area from 1890 to 1903), the late Georgian Congregational Church (Countess of Huntingdon's Connexion), the Methodist, Baptist and Seventh-Day Adventist churches, and the Railway Mission and Gospel Halls.

Turning to economic and industrial aspects of the life of Ely, visitors will discover that the market place was, in earlier times, one of many sites devoted to the activities of St Etheldreda's Fair, an event marking the anniversary of the saint's death that brought merchants to Ely from all parts of the country. Now it is the scene of a weekly Thursday market and of amusement fairs in May and October. Just before the middle of the nineteenth century a corn exchange was built here but, having outlived its usefulness, it has been replaced by a shopping centre.

A permanent reminder of the long association between Ely and the brewing industry was established a few years ago when, after a fire and the owners' decision to close the local brewery, the local council acquired the Maltings for a nominal sum and converted it into a public hall. Thus, after serving its original purpose for almost a century, the building erected for the brewery of Ebenezer William Harlock in 1868 is now used for stage shows, meetings, receptions and other functions. Adjudged third out of 157 entries in the public sector competition in the Royal Institution of Chartered Surveyors/*The Times* Conservation Awards in 1974, the Maltings is a striking feature of Ely's pleasant riverside. This area, including Waterside and Quayside, was once an important centre of trade, a busy loading and unloading point for shipping, but nowadays it deals almost entirely with leisure craft.

Industry, much of it concentrated on the Broad Street Industrial Estate, hardly affects the country market-town atmosphere of Ely, and certainly does not spoil its attraction for those interested in angling and many other forms of sport and recreation. Ely City Golf Club's eighteen-hole parkland course on the southern side of Cambridge Road is a valuable asset to the district, as is the town's open-air swimming pool.

Ely being a place where educational facilities were first made available many centuries ago, it is most appropriate that the city should have within its borders schools forming part of the county educational system. The City of Ely College accommodates a comprehensive secondary school and also a central sixth form for pupils from a large area and, as one of the village colleges of Cambridgeshire, offers further education, adult and youth activities.

Ely branch of the county library maintains a close relationship with the schools. The design of the building on Palace Green, close to the cathedral, earned the county council a commendation in the 1968 Civic Trust awards. Besides housing lending and reference sections, children's department and a special lecture and study room containing a local-history collection, the library serves as an information centre for tourists.

Ely welcomes visitors from all parts of the world. It has a

friendly association with Ribe in West Jutland, Denmark, which shares its status of ancient cathedral city and small market town. Since the councils of both 'friendship cities' resolved to foster goodwill and understanding between one another there have been contacts between organizations in the two places. As evidence of the link, Ely now has a block of flats for elderly people called Ribe Court and a road named St Catherine's after the Danish town's parish church. The historical aspects of the association were not lost on a twentieth-century borgmester of Ribe who, after visiting Ely, wrote: "As you have reminded me, the last time you had Danish visitors to Ely more than a thousand years ago, they burnt down your city, and I am glad that we have not added to your insurance problems."

Like Ely, Peterborough survived the visit of destructive Danes in the ninth century and the attentions of later vandals too. Unlike Ely, it has long been an area of considerable industrial development and is one of Britain's fastest growing cities.

Peterborough, situated in the archaeologically important Nene valley, has at Fengate a site where remains have been found of human occupation from Neolithic (New Stone Age) to Roman times. This area on a gravel promontory beside the river was, in prehistoric times, at the edge of the swampy fenland. Before the industrial complex was built there in recent years the site was fully excavated, items discovered by archaeologists being preserved in the museum in Priestgate, Peterborough.

Evidence of the earliest settlements, revealed by aerial photographs and excavations, continues to accumulate, much of it due to the activities of the Nene Valley Research Committee which, since its formation in 1957, has looked after the interests of local archaeology. Supported financially by the Development Corporation, the Department of the Environment and the local authorities, the Research Committee examines many sites before development and construction work begins.

In addition to that at Fengate, already mentioned, there is an interesting site at Lynch Farm in the Ferry Meadows area of Nene Park.

Occupied by man from Neolithic to Roman times, the Lynch Farm complex was fortified by linear ditches during the late Iron Age. The Romans built a villa (farm) there and traces of outbuildings have been preserved. Just across the river was a Roman fortress, a 27-acre site manned on occasion by 2,500 or more soldiers. Part of the site was excavated before the construction of Thorpe Wood Golf Course. Other archaeological digs have been carried out in the neighbourhood and information concerning them is recorded in the Nene Valley Research Committee's annual publication *Durobrivae*.

The history of modern Peterborough is often regarded as having started with the foundation in the seventh century of the monastery called Medeshamstede. After more than 200 years, during which the place increased in importance, it being claimed that many miracles were worked there, the monastery was sacked by the Danes in 870. About a hundred years passed and then, with the support of King Eadgar, St Ethelwold, Bishop of Winchester, rebuilt the monastery. Cenwulf (or Kenulf), Abbot in 992 (he later became Bishop of Winchester), built a wall round the place and about this time the monastery was known as Burgh, the town or borough, later becoming Peterborough from the dedication of the abbey.

In 1070 the monastery was again sacked, this time by Hereward. Angered by William the Conqueror's decision to appoint a Norman abbot and to give certain of the abbey lands to Norman knights, he assured the monks that his removal of treasures was "from affection to the monastery". Less than fifty years later a great fire completed Hereward's work, destroying the monastery and much of the town that had grown up around it. Rebuilding began in 1118 under Abbot John de Séez and continued for many years. Built of Barnack stone, the great church remained that of a Benedictine monastery until the Dissolution and then, in 1541, Henry VIII raised it to cathedral status and created the township of Peterborough a city under the lordship of the Dean and Chapter.

There have been countless changes in Peterborough since

those days but the cathedral survives, the major (but not the sole) remains of the Benedictine monastic house that had sixty/sixty-five monks before the Black Death broke out in the middle of the fourteenth century. Although it lacks Ely Cathedral's power to dominate its surroundings, Peterborough Cathedral leaves no doubt in the mind as to its true and unchanging purpose. The west front, magnificent as it is, impresses by its quiet dignity, while the medieval painted wooden ceiling of the nave, with its pictures of kings, queens, saints and other figures, seems, like the cathedral's many monuments, to give the past a quiet presence here.

One such silent reminder is the marble slab in the north choir aisle marking the last resting place of Catherine of Aragon, Henry VIII's first queen. Abandoned by her royal husband in 1531, she was removed to the country. Catherine was virtually a prisoner there when, in March 1534, the Pope pronounced the validity of her marriage to Henry VIII who had already taken Anne Boleyn as his second queen. With many of her supporters being executed and she herself living in fear of poison, Catherine developed a serious illness. She died early in 1536 and was buried here, in what was then the abbey church.

There is also a memorial in the cathedral marking the spot where the body of Mary Queen of Scots was buried for twenty-five years after her execution at Fotheringhay, nine miles south-west of Peterborough. The letter from King James I of England ordering the removal of his mother's remains to Westminster Abbey in 1612 is in the cathedral library.

Not far from the cathedral, in the very heart of the city, is St John the Baptist's, the ancient parish church of Peterborough. Until the beginning of the fifteenth century the church stood to the east of the cathedral (then the abbey church), but flooding made access difficult in winter and it was rebuilt on its present site, next to the Guildhall. Completed in 1407, this spacious building in the Perpendicular style contains some fifteenth-century English embroidery and a large octagonal font with quatrefoil panels.

The seventeenth-century Old Guildhall, now scheduled as an ancient monument and regarded as one of the finest British market crosses of the period, is another strong link with the city's past. The coats of arms on the eastern front include those of Joseph Henshaw, Bishop of Peterborough 1663–79, James Duport, who became Dean of Peterborough in 1664 and was a benefactor of Peterborough Grammar School, and Sir Humphrey Orme, an active seventeenth-century participant in the local government of the city, whose family monument in the cathedral was defaced by Cromwell's troops. In 1874, when Peterborough was incorporated as a municipal borough, the historic building became the Town Hall, the room over the Cross being used as the council chamber.

For Peterborough the nineteenth century was a period of active growth. The coming of the railways brought industry to the city, a fact which must not be overlooked now that they have, as in so many other places, declined. East Station was built in the Tudor style in 1845, the Great Northern Hotel was erected near the North Station in 1852 and extended three years later, and in 1854–66 the New England estate was developed to provide 226 cottages for railway workers. Brick-making was occupying many workers and engineering was growing in importance here.

With the increase of population more churches were needed. St Mark's was built with tower and spire and half-timbered dormer in 1856. St Mary's dates from 1859 and St Paul's, with several stained-glass windows by Cakebread, from 1868. Later in the century came the Methodist church in Wentworth Street, a yellow and red brick building of 1874–5. The Church of All Saints in Park Road was built to an original design in 1894, and two years later the Church of All Souls was opened by the Roman Catholics. The century ended with the erection of St Barnabas's Church, a towerless brick building, in 1900.

During the early years of the present century Peterborough began to settle down after the busy Victorian years of building and development. Then came the First World War. Two engineering companies, controlled establishments under the Munitions Act, co-operated in a way that led to their amalgamation in 1920 and to the formation of one of Peterborough's largest employers, Baker Perkins Limited, part of a great international organization which has always regarded the world as its market.

One of the companies concerned was Werner, Pfleiderer and Perkins (later Perkins Engineers Ltd). In 1903 they had bought for £3,040 a ten-acre site on the west side of Peterborough where they soon started to build their Westwood Works, now a very important centre of production and also the headquarters of Baker Perkins Holdings Ltd. The second company involved was Joseph Baker and Sons Ltd whose factory at Willesden was dismantled in 1933 when the entire production was concentrated at Peterborough. By producing war material in 1914-18 both companies probably helped to prevent the Great War dragging on for a much longer period. But it was their co-operation over the production of the Baker Perkins Standard Army Bread Plant that led to developments so vital to the future industrial progress of Peterborough. Perkins, founded by Jacob Perkins who came to England from the U.S.A. in 1819, made the mixing machines, final moulders and draw-plate ovens, while Bakers, founded by Joseph Baker who arrived here from Canada in 1876, produced the dividers, the first moulders and provers.

The decision to move to the Westwood site at Peterborough was taken by a remarkable man, an engineer named Frederick Charles Ihlee, who was successively Works Manager and Managing Director at the Regent Square, London, works of Werner, Pfleiderer and Perkins. One of a family who had left Germany to escape the effects of Bismarck's despotism, the young Ihlee was forced into the wool firm which his father had helped Dr Jaeger, a German scientist, to establish. On his father's death Ihlee left Jaeger and worked for Werner, Pfleiderer and Perkins. After undergoing thorough training at their works in Germany he returned to the firm's London works where, as a member of the technical staff, he displayed the ruthless driving force and concern for efficiency that marked his distinguished career.

By the time he died in 1938 Ihlee had been vice-chairman of Baker Perkins Ltd and chairman of the Board of Management for eighteen years. The one real failure of his career appears to have been brought about by his fanatical interest in the motor-car. Three of his Mercials were built at Peterborough but there was little interest in them as cars or as delivery vans when they were later adapted. When Ihlee died his fellow directors paid tribute not only to his devoted work for the company but to his humanity, loyalty and sympathy. There is no doubt that he greatly supported the British cause in the First World War and that he did much to advance the development of Peterborough as we now know it.

Another of Peterborough's larger employers, the firm of Peter Brotherhood Ltd, specialist engineers, made an important contribution to the war effort in 1914–18, more than 3,000 people being employed to make high and low pressure air compressors, steam engines and turbines driving generators, deck and submerged torpedo tubes, torpedo engines, submarine mines and depth charges, and many other things. This company had come to Peterborough from London in 1907, only a few years after Perkins, just mentioned, had moved there from the capital. In deciding to exercise their powers to acquire the land occupied by Peter Brotherhood and others, for the erection of the new County Hall, London County Council certainly did Peterborough a good turn!

An historic event for Peterborough occurred in 1932 with the formation in the city of F. Perkins Ltd, a private company whose original prospectus announced its intention of specializing in engineering products and particularly in diesel engines. With F. A. Perkins as chairman and managing director, the company produced its first prototype diesel engine, the Vixen, at the end of the year. In 1933 thirty-five of its second engine, the Fox, were produced, one being installed in a Hillman car and another in a Commer truck. Two years later six world diesel speed records were set by Reg Munday driving a Parry Thomas racing car fitted with a Perkins Wolf engine. By 1937 a complete range of Wolf, Lynx and Leopard Perkins diesels was available for vehicles, industrial, agricultural and marine applications, and in 1939 production exceeded a thousand engines for the first time. Now Perkins Engines is a member of the world-wide Massey-Ferguson Organization and, with a workforce in the 8,000–12,000 range, is Peterborough's largest employer.

Before the outbreak of the Second World War the city centre had been reconstructed and the new Town Hall of brick with stone dressings was designed by E. Berry Webber as something English and civic that would nevertheless not rival or challenge the cathedral. Professor Sir Nikolaus Pevsner appears to recognize the architect's attempts to make the building fit into the city's street architecture, though he obviously has reservations as to the choice of the Neo-Georgian style at so late a date.

The outbreak of hostilities in September 1939 found the engineering firms of Peterborough making war materials or preparing to do so. Baker Perkins adapted machinery for making cordite, made apparatus for the manufacture of detonators and, still before war was declared, produced parts and machined carriage bodies for anti-aircraft guns. They became the country's chief producer of the top carriage of the 40-mm Bofors gun, making over 10,000 of them at Peterborough, and manufactured various weapons, 25-pounder guns and 6-pounder anti-tank guns among them, and mobile bakeries that helped to feed not only British and American forces but civilians in bombed areas.

Brotherhoods were busy throughout the Second World War, producing torpedos, guns, armaments for naval purposes, air compressors, pumps and turbines and diesel engines for submarines. In addition to war work they built prototype nylon-spinning machines, completing the first major contract in this field at Pontypool in 1946. Perkins Engines was also engaged on war work, its diesels being used by the armed forces in midget submarines and as auxiliary power in air-sea rescue launches.

The cessation of hostilities left many difficulties and these, like the shortages of the time, were still causing severe problems in many places, Peterborough included, when 1950 ended.

After the middle of the century came the government's dramatic decision to expand the city to help relieve population pressures in London and the South-East. In 1967 16,000 acres of Peterborough and the surrounding area were designated as a new town and the following year Peterborough Development

Corporation was appointed under the New Towns Act 1965 to plan and carry out the expansion in partnership with the county and city councils.

Approved by the Secretary of State for the Environment in 1971, the master plan, the blueprint for expansion, provides for the three new townships of Bretton, Orton and Castor, each with several distinct neighbourhoods, local shops and schools, west of the old city, and the extension to the north-east of the residential areas of Paston and Werrington. Building work began in April 1970 and from 81,000 (July 1967) the population of the new town area had expanded by June 1977 to an estimated 108,000, about sixty-seven per cent of the expansion programme target of 160,000. To think that Peterborough had only 3,580 inhabitants in 1801!

The rapid scale of development becomes even more apparent when, considering other figures relating to progress at 30 June 1977, one finds 10,000 new houses, some 11,500 extra jobs and eighty-five newly arrived industrial firms.

Eventually some 17,000 people will live in Bretton, the first of the new townships, some in the Development Corporation housing neighbourhoods, others in private housing. Corporation homes have central heating by gas or electricity, but what is claimed to be Britain's most extensive low-rise district heating scheme provides, by means of its two natural gas boilers, central heating and domestic hot water from some 4,000 rented and private houses, shops, offices and other buildings. At Bretton Centre, heart of the new township, there are shops, banks, a health centre, offices and a public house. New schools, community centres and surgeries for doctors and dentists have opened, and the Cresset acts as a large social, recreation and church centre. A fifty-acre park has been laid out in Bretton and this includes children's play areas. In this part of Peterborough industry is confined to an area between the township and the railway where the average area of industrial units on Development Corporation land tends to be about 51,000 square feet.

Also west of the old city, but south of the River Nene, is Orton, a township for nearly 24,000 people. Shopping and community facilities are provided here and special 'bus only' roads are intended to speed buses and link housing areas with other parts of the township and the city centre. Between Orton township and the A1 (Great North Road) is the new employment area of Orton Southgate. Here the Development Corporation leases sites of up to 100 acres for individual firms to develop and also advance factories in units or multiples of 3,000, 10,000 and 20,000 square feet. Clad in green-coloured aluminium, the factories are provided with offices, services and ample car-parking space.

Five miles of disused British Rail track running from Orton to Wansford were bought by the Development Corporation and leased to Peterborough Railway Society. In 1977 this group of local enthusiasts began running the Nene Valley Railway, a steam passenger service, along this stretch of line. Passengers travelling from Wansford to Orton Mere, the new station built beneath Peterborough's new river bridge, enjoy splendid views of Nene Park whose many amenities include facilities for walking, riding, sailing, boating, fishing and other outdoor pursuits. Undoubtedly the Nene Valley Railway will attract railway enthusiasts in increasing numbers. Certainly its locomotives (steam and diesel, British and foreign) and passenger coaches make an impressive collection, another interesting feature being its booking office, formerly the village railway station at Barnwell.

Eventually Castor, north of the river and north-west of Orton, will become the third township of the growing city of Peterborough. The Development Corporation's 80-acre nursery, with its 500,000 gallon reservoir and irrigation system, was established there in 1971. Hundreds of thousands of shrubs and trees are grown there for use in shelterbelts and for landscaping the new areas. In one year alone the staff of the Forestry and Landscape Service planted 74 acres of new shelterbelts and used trees and shrubs to landscape more than 1,000 new houses, 50 acres of sports fields, 2 miles of parkways and 5 miles of distributor road. In order that planting may be done in summer (outside the normal season) and thus keep pace with Peterborough's expansion, thousands of shrubs and trees are grown in containers and many others are put into cold store in December and left there until early summer.

Besides the opening of new ones at Bretton and Orton Southgate, already mentioned, three industrial areas—Eastern, Woodston and North Westwood—have been extended. Another feature of the development of Peterborough is the modernization of certain parts of the old city. Three such renewal areas were named in the approved City Centre Plan, namely North Minster (for offices and car parks), Rivergate (for public buildings and car parks) and Queensgate (for shops of various types and sizes, restaurants, new bus station and tiered car parking).

In addition to office sites in the heart of Peterborough and the centres of its new townships the Development Corporation is making available a number of 'office parks', large sites for major new developments. The first of these is Thorpe Wood near the village of Longthorpe, site of Longthorpe Tower with its fourteenth-century wall paintings and of the Church of St Botolph with reminders of the thirteenth century. In the parkland setting of Thorpe Wood close to Ferry Meadows, the central part of Nene Park, where three lakes have been excavated for sailing, boating and fishing, are the national computer centre of Pearl Assurance, a divisional headquarters of Cambridgeshire Constabulary, and the world travel headquarters of the Thomas Cook Group. Over a thousand people work in Cook's four-storey office block whose 20-acre site includes sports pitches for the use of the staff. Replacing the Berkeley Street, London, headquarters, Thorpe Wood administers the activities of 160 Thomas Cook offices in the United Kingdom and over 700 overseas offices. This is an attractive part of the new Peterborough and one where many people may enjoy themselves, quietly or more actively, in the open air. A nature trail has been created in Thorpe Wood itself and nearby are an eighteen-hole public golf course and a nine-hole pitch and putt course.

Another important area for recreational facilities is the Embankment, an 80-acre site bounded in the south by the River Nene and in the west by Bridge Street. Pleasure-boat cruises are run from the old Customs House, a building probably dating from about 1700 that was originally concerned with waterborne trade but is now scheduled as an

ancient monument and used as headquarters by the local Sea
Cadets and Royal Marine Cadets.

To the east of the old Customs House and with pleasant
river views overlooking the Embankment, the Key Theatre is
a centre for the performing arts. Opened in 1973, it seats 390.
Swimming enthusiasts are well catered for in this part of the
city. An outdoor public pool built here in 1936 has been
extensively refitted and Peterborough's new indoor pool stands
not far away, providing main, diving and teaching pools,
solarium, bar, restaurant, club rooms and seating for up to 600
spectators. Between the outdoor and indoor pools is the
Wirrina Stadium whose ballroom, sports hall and sauna suite
provide for a wide range of activities, boxing, dancing and
roller skating among them.

On the other side of the river is the City Leisure Centre
where people may enjoy tenpin bowling and such other
amenities as the late-night cafeteria and club bar. Nearby is
Peterborough United Football Club's ground where supporters
of 'the Posh' have enjoyed some good football in recent years.

The large number of people visiting Peterborough to take
advantage of its leisure facilities, to shop or to engage in
business of one kind and another has led to much thought
being given to ways of ensuring the free flow of traffic and of
reducing congestion. Peterborough's second river bridge, an
eleven-span, 240-yard structure near Orton Staunch, was
opened in 1974, and an integrated system of new roads,
including thirty-four miles of parkways built to urban
motorway standards, is under construction. Eventually a
72-mile cycleway system will serve the townships, connecting
them to industrial areas, the 6-mile stretch of Nene Park and
the city centre. An experimental cycle route through older
parts of Peterborough has aroused considerable interest not
only in this country but overseas.

Contacts with other parts of the world have long been
developed at civic, business and personal levels. For more than
twenty years Peterborough has been twinned with the historic
French cathedral city after which Bourges Boulevard (between
Bridge Street and Taverners Road) has been named. Until
1972 the link between the English and French cities was

maintained at local authority level through civic exchanges, but then Peterborough City Council decided that wider contacts should be encouraged so as to involve far more members of the community. Twinning officers appointed by the two cities have since arranged regular visits between schools and organizations concerned with various sports and cultural activities.

Peterborough owes much to people and companies who have come not only from other parts of Britain but from overseas. Like many another English city, Peterborough is now very much a multi-racial society. This development has led to the introduction of new customs and to the appearance of places where members of the various Asian groups may worship in their own ways. It would be idle to pretend that there have not been problems of integration, a process that has its difficulties even in situations of the utmost goodwill. But Peterborough is fortunate in its Council for Community Relations, a representative body whose aims include the elimination of racial discrimination and the promotion of equal opportunities. Prepared to assist individuals or groups, the Council is helped in its work of fostering good race and community relations by volunteers who, as a member of the council put it, must accept the fact that "this isn't a cosy, comfortable job; one can't expect to be patted on the back for it". Come to think of it, the long and continuing development of Peterborough has not been a cosy, comfortable job, but the modern cathedral city-new town is a living, growing monument to all those who, over the centuries, have lived and worked there.

IX

CAMBRIDGESHIRE WORTHIES

OVER the centuries many individuals have helped to develop the county and to bring Cambridgeshire and certain of its towns and institutions into prominence. At the risk of being invidious, I propose to give pride of place to Peada, under-king of the South Mercians, who in A.D. 655 founded the first monastery at Peterborough.

The eldest son of Penda, King of Mercia, who had championed heathenism against Christianity, Peada was baptized on his marriage with Alchfled, daughter of Oswiu, King of Bernicia, in 653. At Peterborough he may have followed the example of his father-in-law who had himself erected a monastery. Little is known of Peada who was killed in 656, the year after his father-in-law had slain Penda.

At least one Abbot of Peterborough rose to a position of great distinction in the land, John de Caux (or Caleto) becoming Treasurer of England under Henry III in 1260. He was born in Normandy, was a monk and later Prior at St Swithun's, Winchester, and served as Justice Itinerant. The last abbot, John Chambers, became first Bishop of Peterborough in 1541, when Henry VIII raised the former Benedictine monastery to cathedral rank. He held the see for the best part of fifteen years, but the second Bishop of Peterborough, David Pole, Fellow of All Souls and doctor of canon law, lasted only about two years, being deprived for refusing to take the oath of supremacy on Elizabeth I's accession.

As third Bishop of Peterborough, Edmund Scambler assisted in the translation of the 'Bishops' Bible' of 1568, work commissioned by Archbishop Parker whom he had served as chaplain ten years earlier. Like his friend Archbishop John Whitgift, Richard Howland, Bishop of Peterborough 1585–1600, was attacked in anonymous tracts published by

John Penry and others under the pseudonym of "Martin Mar-Prelate". The tracts led to a severe act against the puritans and another against seditious writings.

As her chaplain, Thomas Dove, fifth Bishop of Peterborough, impressed Queen Elizabeth I, but during the reign of James I he was twice charged with remissness for allowing silenced ministers to preach. Even so, the eloquent and scholarly bishop held the see for twenty-nine years until his death in 1630. William Piers became Dean of Peterborough in 1622 and was consecrated Bishop in 1630. His two years as Bishop of Peterborough appear to have been uneventful, which is more than can be said of his later period as Bishop of Bath and Wells when he ran into serious trouble as a follower of Archbishop Laud.

Francis Dee, eighth Bishop of Peterborough, was concerned with the foundation of Sion College, London, in 1630, and is remembered as a benefactor of St John's College, Cambridge. His successor, John Towers, a supporter of the royal prerogative, signed the bishops' protest and was imprisoned by Parliament during the reign of Charles I. William Lloyd was translated from Peterborough, where he was twelfth Bishop, to the diocese of Norwich of which he was deprived for refusing the oath of allegiance to William III. For the same reason, his successor at Peterborough, Thomas White, was deprived of the see less than two years after he, one of the 'seven bishops', had challenged James II on a number of issues.

He was followed as Bishop of Peterborough by Richard Cumberland, who held the see for twenty-seven years, during which he attracted some attention on account of his opposition to the views of Thomas Hobbes, the philosopher. White Kennett, Dean of Peterborough in 1708 and fifteenth Bishop ten years later, was one of the original members of the Society for Propagating the Gospel in Foreign Parts, author (he published a *Compleat History of England*), historian, antiquarian, topographer and philologist.

Richard Terrick, at Peterborough as eighteenth Bishop for seven years, was perhaps more worldly than his two immediate predecessors, Robert Clavering and John Thomas. A follower of the powerful Earl of Bute, father figure to George

III and close friend of his possessive mother, Terrick became Bishop of London and privy councillor. John Hinchcliffe, Bishop of Peterborough 1769–94, who earlier in his career was assistant master at Westminster School, offended the government by his liberal speeches in the House of Lords and in 1788 was made Dean of Durham on condition that he resigned the mastership of Trinity College, Cambridge, a post he had held for twenty years.

Spencer Madan followed Hinchcliffe as Bishop of Peterborough. He attracted much less attention than his elder brother Martin whose book in favour of polygamy upset many people. The next Bishop of Peterborough, John Parsons, was obviously a man of principle and conscience. He should be remembered, if for nothing else, as one who helped strengthen the examination system at Oxford University so that honours were awarded for real merit. His successor at Peterborough, Herbert Marsh, Bishop for twenty years from 1819, was an active and controversial preacher, writer and pamphleteer who introduced German methods of research into biblical study.

George Davys, formerly tutor to Princess (later Queen) Victoria, held the see of Peterborough for twenty-five years from 1839. The twenty-sixth Bishop, William Connor Magee, "one of the greatest orators and most brilliant controversialists of his day", held the see of Peterborough for twenty-three years before becoming Archbishop of York a few months before he died in 1891. Since his day the Bishops of Peterborough have come and gone, certain of his successors having been translated to London, Winchester and elsewhere.

The name of St Etheldreda, who began the Minster at Ely in 673, must also appear early on this roll of honour of the county. Daughter of Anna, King of the East Angles, Etheldreda, "a wife only in name", was first married to Tonbert, chieftain of the Southern Gyrwe ("prince of the fenmen"), becoming possessed of the Isle of Ely either by way of dower from her husband or in her own right. Tonbert died soon after the marriage and within a few years Etheldreda was married to Egfrid, late King of Northumbria. Determined upon a religious life, she disowned her marriage duties and was separated after being Egfrid's consort for twelve years.

A year after becoming a nun and entering the convent of Coldingham, Etheldreda retired to her property, the Isle of Ely, to found a monastery of her own for both monks and nuns on the hill top where Ely and its cathedral now stand. Having been consecrated as first Abbess, Etheldreda led a life of great austerity and devotion, gaining the love and admiration of all who came into contact with her. She died in 679 and is still remembered nearly 1,300 years later, particularly on 17th October, the day her festival is kept.

It was on this date in the year 1106 that the body of St Etheldreda was translated from the old Saxon church of the abbey of Ely and laid in a stone shrine behind the high altar of the new church, the present cathedral church of the Holy and Undivided Trinity. The shrine did not escape the destructive attentions of the iconoclasts and only a few fragments have survived. Since 1953 St Etheldreda's Catholic church in Ely has housed the only remaining relic of St Etheldreda. This, the left hand, is contained in a shrine at the end of the north aisle.

St Etheldreda, whose sister St Withburga was a nun at Ely, was succeeded as Abbess in turn by her other sister St Sexburga, widow of the King of Kent, her niece St Ermenhilda, widow of the King of Mercia, and her great niece St Werburga.

After 1109, when 'the island in the fens' was made the see of a bishop and the abbey became a priory with the Bishop as titular abbot, the dignitaries of Ely often held high office or otherwise rose to prominence. The very first Bishop of Ely, Hervey (or Hervaeus), who earlier had been driven from the diocese of Bangor by the Welsh, was confessor to Henry I. After twenty-two years he was succeeded by Nigel. Remaining Bishop of Ely for thirty-six years, and serving as the King's Treasurer and presiding Justiciar in the *curia regis*, he lived a far from sheltered life. Having raised the suspicions of Henry I's successor Stephen and fortified Ely, which was taken by the King, Nigel fled to Matilda who had earlier been recognized by the bishops and barons as successor to her father Henry I. When Matilda's cause failed, he submitted to the King and was restored. Later, accused of connivance in Geoffrey de Mandeville's revolt, he was obliged to purchase his peace.

Geoffrey Ridel, third Bishop of Ely, had served as Henry II's Chancellor and shared with two other bishops the office of Chief Justiciar. His memorial is the massive west tower of Ely Cathedral, completed about 1189, the year he died. William Longchamp, fourth Bishop of Ely, was a faithful servant to Richard I, serving him as intermediary at home and on the Continent and as Chancellor, and joining the King while he was in prison in Germany following his attempt to travel through that country in disguise. Eustace, Longchamp's successor at Ely, became Richard I's Chancellor and Keeper of the Seal, and was sent by the King to remonstrate with Philip Augustus of France on alleged infringements of the five years' peace. During the reign of Richard I's successor, Eustace was one of three prelates commissioned by Pope Innocent III to urge King John to recognize Stephen Langton as Archbishop of Canterbury. John's refusal to do so and his clash with the Pope resulted in an interdict being laid on England (all church services were suspended) and to his excommunication. Later Eustace was associated with Langton in procuring from Rome threat of deposition on the King. Eventually, as the history books show, Archbishop Langton supported the barons in securing Magna Carta, 'the first great step on the constitutional road', from King John, while the Pope, now supporting the King, declared Magna Carta null and void!

William of Kilkenny, who died just over a year after his consecration as Bishop of Ely, had been Henry III's Controller of the Wardrobe and at one time was styled Chancellor. Hugh de Balsham, whose election by the monks as Bishop of Ely displeased Henry III but was confirmed by the Pope, made his mark by founding Peterhouse, the first college foundation at Cambridge. John Hotham, Bishop of Ely for the twenty-one years 1316–37, served as Chancellor of England under Edward II and Edward III and as Treasurer under Edward II. In 1326 he appears to have joined Queen Isabella when the 'she-wolf of France' (as she was known) sailed with her son, the future King Edward III, and her lover Roger Mortimer to invade her husband Edward II's kingdom. Perhaps we should forget this period, ending as it did with Edward II being brutally murdered, Mortimer being hanged, drawn and quartered, and

Isabella retiring to a life of quiet and seclusion, and allow the magnificent octagon tower at Ely Cathedral, successor to the Norman crossing tower which collapsed in 1322, to be John Hotham's memorial.

Simon Langham, Bishop of Ely from 1362 to 1366, held the great English offices of state of Chancellor and Treasurer under Edward III. He was Archbishop of Canterbury from 1366 to 1368 when he was created Cardinal-priest. Five years later he was made Cardinal-bishop of Praeneste, as the ancient Italian town of Palestrina was formerly known. Curiously he was the first to deliver speeches in Parliament in English. Bishop John Barnet, Langham's successor at Ely, served as Edward III's Treasurer. He was followed by Thomas Arundel, who was Bishop of Ely for fifteen years before becoming Archbishop of York and later Archbishop of Canterbury. Arundel served both Richard II and Henry IV as Chancellor of England. His period of office at Canterbury was interrupted in 1397 when, impeached by the House of Commons for assisting the commission of regency in derogation of Richard II's authority, he was banished. Returning to England in 1399 with Henry IV, whom he crowned, Arundel again took up his duties at Canterbury, visiting Cambridge two years later to clamp down on Lollardism.

John Fordham, who had served Richard II as treasurer, succeeded Arundel as Bishop of Ely and occupied the see for thirty-seven years. His life was comparatively quiet and uneventful. Thomas Bourchier, translated to Ely in 1443, was a much more active man of affairs. Brother of Henry Bourchier, first Earl of Essex, who married Edwards IV's aunt Isabel, he had been Prebendary of Lichfield, Chancellor of Oxford University, and Bishop of Worcester before becoming Bishop of Ely. Later, as Archbishop of Canterbury, Bourchier was Henry VI's Chancellor. When Henry was deposed in 1461 Bourchier crowned Edward IV. He raised troops for Edward's restoration to the throne when in 1470 the King fled to the Netherlands and Henry regained the throne for a few months. Bourchier survived to crown Richard III and in 1486, the last year of his life, to marry Henry VII to Elizabeth of York. There is some doubt over his date of birth, but he appears to have been over eighty when he died.

Dr William Grey, an Oxford man, who followed Bourchier as Bishop of Ely in 1454, had earlier been Prebendary of St Paul's, Lincoln, Lichfield and York, Chancellor of Oxford, and Proctor of Henry VI at Rome. After his translation to Ely he was Edward IV's Lord High Treasurer and head of the commission that negotiated with Scotland in 1471–2.

When Grey died in 1478 John Morton became Bishop of Ely. Before his election to this office he had practised as a canon lawyer in the Court of Arches and, having followed the Lancastrian party, was attainted. His attainder being reversed when he submitted after the Yorkist victory at the Battle of Tewkesbury, Morton became Prebendary of St Paul's Cathedral and Master of the Rolls, and undertook certain diplomatic missions, before becoming Bishop. As Bishop of Ely, he was present at the death and funeral of Edward IV in 1483. That year he himself was arrested and imprisoned in the Tower of London and later at Brecknock Castle, where he encouraged the powerful Duke of Buckingham to revolt against Richard III. Escaping, Morton made first for Ely and then Flanders. Summoned home by Henry VII in 1485, Morton became Archbishop of Canterbury the following year, holding office until his death in 1500. Only scholarly works record his subsequent appointments as Privy Councillor, Lord Chancellor and Chancellor of Oxford and his elevation to Cardinal. But those concerned with the fens remember him for Morton's Leam, the waterway he constructed from Peterborough to Wisbech in an attempt to improve drainage.

John Alcock, whose chantry chapel is an interesting feature of Ely Cathedral, followed John Morton as Bishop of Ely and died the same year as him (1500). A doctor of laws in the university of Cambridge, he had held a number of important church offices, including the bishoprics of Rochester and Worcester, had served as Chancellor of England under Edward IV and Henry VII, and was a member of several royal commissions during the reigns of Richard III and Henry VII. He was tutor to Edward V, one of the young princes in the Tower whose deaths form one of the saddest episodes in the history of England. Sir Thomas More who, as a boy had been placed in the household of Archbishop Morton, former Bishop of Ely, put the responsibility for the murder of the twelve-year-old Edward V and the even younger Duke of York firmly on the shoulders of the Duke of Gloucester and Richard III.

John Alcock was succeeded as Bishop of Ely by Richard Redman, restorer of the cathedral of St Asaph. Then came James Stanley who is remembered in Cambridge for his part in the foundation of St John's and Christ's Colleges and for compiling statutes for Jesus College. Denounced by Protestants for 'loose morals', he nevertheless died in office. The next Bishop of Ely was Nicholas West, Fellow of King's at Cambridge, diplomatist, chaplain to Henry VIII's Queen Catherine of Aragon, and builder (he added to buildings of St George's, Windsor, King's College, Cambridge, Putney parish church, and Ely Cathedral, where his chantry chapel remains).

Bishop West was followed at Ely by Thomas Goodrich, chaplain of Henry VIII and ecclesiastical commissioner under him. When the young Edward VI succeeded his father Goodrich continued as commissioner, later acting as ambassador to Henry II of France and as Lord Chancellor. He was commissioner for the trial of Stephen Gardiner, Bishop of Winchester, who suffered imprisonment and was deprived of his see because of his opposition to doctrinal changes. Like Goodrich, once a Fellow of Jesus College, Gardiner had associations with Cambridge, having been educated at Trinity Hall, becoming its Master and also Chancellor of the university.

Also educated at Trinity Hall, Cambridge, Thomas Thirlby, the next Bishop of Ely, played his part in affairs of state and church, appearing to have been something of a 'survivor'. Commended by Archbishop Cranmer to the 'pope-king' Henry VIII, he was by 1534 Archdeacon of Ely and member of the convocation which recognized the King's ecclesiastical supremacy. Six years later, as prolocutor of Canterbury convocation, he signed the decree annulling Henry's marriage with Anne of Cleves. Made Bishop of Ely by Queen Mary, whose chief purpose was to restore papal authority in England, Thirlby presided at the trial of John Hooper, Bishop of Worcester and Gloucester, who was burned for heresy. Then he assisted at the degradation of his old sponsor Thomas Cranmer who, like the good Bishop Hooper, was burned. Thirlby refused to take the oath of supremacy to Elizabeth I, under whom the breach with Rome was renewed, and was deposed.

Richard Cox held several posts of distinction before becoming Thirlby's successor as Bishop of Ely in 1559, including that of tutor to "God's Imp" Prince Edward, later the boy-king Edward VI. As Vice-Chancellor of Oxford during most of Edward VI's short reign, he destroyed 'popish' pictures, statues and books, and not surprisingly was a prisoner and later an exile during Mary's reign. Cox alienated much property of the see of Ely to court favourites, while his successor, Martin Heton, alienated to the Crown the richest manors of Ely.

While Bishop of Ely (he was eventually translated to Winchester), Lancelot Andrewes was first on the list of scholars appointed to make the authorized version of the Bible (1611), having seven years earlier attended the Hampton Court conference which gave rise to this translation. The next Bishop of Ely, Nicholas Felton, helped to translate the Epistles for the authorized verson.

For some time very few bishops had been appointed to the great English offices of state, but the Bishops of Ely continued to go about their business, most of them dying in office. Some led more disturbed lives than others. Matthew Wren, Bishop of Ely during the years 1638–67, was imprisoned in the Tower of London for several years after the impeachment of high treason of Archbishop William Laud, who had suppressed the activities of puritans who, in their turn, considered that Laud and his supporters were destroying the Protestant character of the Anglican church.

Before succeeding Wren at Ely, Benjamin Laney, chaplain to Charles I, suffered as a royalist and high churchman, being deprived of his preferments and ejected from his mastership at Cambridge, waiting until the Restoration of 1660 to recover them. Francis Turner, Bishop of Ely 1684–90, was one of the seven bishops who petitioned James II against the order requiring clergy to read from their pulpits his Declaration of Indulgence, suspending the laws against Roman Catholics and dissenters and admitting them to civil and military posts. Taken to the Tower and put on trial for publishing a seditious libel, they were acquitted by a jury. Bishop Turner refused the oath of allegiance to William and Mary, who acceded after James II fled the country, and was deprived of the see of Ely in 1690. During the remaining ten years of his life he corresponded with the exiled James II and was frequently arrested.

Simon Patrick, Bishop of Ely from 1691 until his death sixteen years later, led what may be called a quiet and sheltered life. Yet he took an active part in reviving church life, founding with four others the Society for the Promotion of Christian Knowledge. His successor as Bishop of Ely, John Moore, was famous throughout Europe for his great library, which George I bought and presented to Cambridge University. Author of many religious works, William Fleetwood, next to occupy the see in 1714, had a preface to some of his sermons attacking Tory principles condemned by Parliament to be burnt (it was, however, published in *The Spectator*). He seems to have been the last Bishop of Ely to fall foul of any part of the establishment!

William Fleetwood, bishop for nine years before dying in office, was followed over the next thirty-one years by three bishops translated from Norwich. One of them, Thomas Greene, was called upon to deal with Richard Bentley who ruled Trinity College, Cambridge, with almost despotic power from 1700 until 1742. Having upset the fellows by encroaching on their privileges, Bentley appeared before John Moore, the Bishop of Ely mentioned earlier, who died soon after, leaving a draft judgment against him. Nineteen years later Bishop Greene came to the same conclusion and deprived Bentley of his mastership, a sentence never executed by those with the necessary power. Loathed and feared, dictatorial, insolent and unconstitutional, as he was regarded by many, Bentley, "the greatest classical scholar of his day", continued to rule until his death.

Matthias Mawson, Bishop of Ely for sixteen years from 1754, founded twelve scholarships at Corpus Christi College, Cambridge. His successors over the next one hundred years were, in the main, men who made little impression on the world outside church and university. Thomas Turton, Bishop of Ely

1845–64, found time to produce controversial writings and compose church music, and Edward Harold Browne, who was translated from Ely to Winchester after nine years, published religious writings.

The period during which James Russell Woodford was Bishop of Ely (1873–85) was marked by the appointment of a reforming royal commission. One result of its enquiries was the production of statutes for Jesus College, Cambridge, granting the Master and fellows the unrestricted right of election to all fellowships without reference to the Bishop of Ely, who had been known to place his relations in them, and the fellows the right to elect the Master, who until then had been appointed by the bishop. The Bishop of Ely remained as Visitor to the college, being empowered to act if the Master or fellows failed to observe the statutes.

Since those times the Bishops of Ely, no longer such powerful figures as many of their predecessors, have carried on the work of a diocese at the heart of which is Ely Cathedral whose restoration, repair and maintenance now involve such very great expense that the State should, in the opinion of informed people, accept responsibility for its preservation.

The royal commission mentioned earlier was regarded in Cambridge as having brought to a head the academical revolution started earlier that century. In 1874 the foundation of the Cavendish Laboratory in Cambridge by the seventh Duke of Devonshire, Chancellor of the university, started a scientific revolution which is still proceeding. After Eton, the Duke, himself a Cavendish, was educated at Trinity College, Cambridge, where the young Isaac Newton, later to become Sir Isaac, had matriculated as a sub-sizar in 1661.

Successive Cavendish professors of experimental physics and their colleagues have maintained a tradition of research that has made Cambridge known in and well beyond academic and scientific circles throughout the world. James Clerk-Maxwell, first Cavendish professor, dealt with electricity and magnetism, contributing to the kinetic theory of heat and developing the electromagnetic theory of light, which stimulated Heinrich Hertz to the discovery of wireless waves. His successor, John William Strutt, third Baron Rayleigh, author of 446 scientific papers, directed research on redetermination of electrical units in absolute measure and later retired to Terling Place, Essex, to work in his private laboratory. A Nobel prize-winner, he is remembered as the scientist who, with Sir William Ramsay, isolated argon, a rare gas that exists in small quantities in the air.

The Nobel prize-winner Sir Joseph John Thomson was Lord Rayleigh's successor as Cavendish professor of experimental physics, holding office from 1884 until 1919, during which time the Cavendish laboratory became the greatest research school in experimental physics, and one where vital investigations were made into the structure of the atom.

Ernest (later Lord) Rutherford, another Nobel prize-winner, followed his old Master, Sir J. J. Thomson, in the Cavendish professorship, having left his native New Zealand to come to Trinity College, Cambridge, to work under him almost a quarter of a century earlier. A great pioneer in atomic physics, Rutherford and his associates made a series of discoveries fundamental to all recent developments in the atomic field. After Rutherford's death in 1937 the Cavendish professorship went to Sir Lawrence Bragg. In 1915, at the age of twenty-five, he shared with his father Sir William Bragg a Nobel prize for physics for research work on X-rays and crystal structure. Their technique of the X-ray analysis of crystals was to prove invaluable in the investigation of the atomic structure of solid substances.

In 1954 Nevill (later Sir Nevill) Mott followed as Cavendish professor. He had been professor of theoretical physics in the University of Bristol and worked on wave mechanics, the theory of atomic collisions, electronic processes in ionic crystals, atomic structure and the strength of metals, and allied matters. In 1971 Sir Nevill who also served as Master of Gonville and Caius College, handed over the Cavendish professorship to Sir Brian Pippard who is known as the author of works on classical thermodynamics, the dynamics of conduction electrons, and on forces and particles.

In addition to those just mentioned, Nobel science prizes have been awarded to other scientists educated at, or otherwise connected with, Cambridge University. A recent survey showed that twelve of the British recipients who were still living were educated at Cambridge, seven at Trinity College, two at St John's College, and one each at Gonville and Caius College, Peterhouse, and Emmanuel College.

The oldest of these Cambridge recipients, Professor Archibald Hill, was awarded a Nobel prize in 1922 for his discovery relating to the production of heat in the muscle. He was a member of the war cabinet scientific advisory committee from 1940 to 1946 and for most of that period was M.P. for Cambridge University. His Nobel award came in the category 'physiology or medicine', as did that received by Lord Adrian in 1932 for discoveries regarding the functions of neurons. Lord Adrian, who died in his eighty-eighth year while this chapter was being written, became Master of his college, Trinity, in 1951, and served as Chancellor of Cambridge university till 1975. He has been appointed professor of physiology at Cambridge in 1937.

In 1963 two of Lord Adrian's former students, Sir Alan Hodgkin, professor of biophysics at Cambridge since 1970, and Sir Andrew Huxley, Royal Society research professor in the department of physiology at University College, London, since 1969, shared with Sir John Eccles, the Australian physiologist, the Nobel prize for physiology or medicine. Also under this category, an award was made in 1962 to Professor Maurice Wilkins who, after being up at St John's College, Cambridge, made discoveries concerning the molecular structure of nucleic acids.

A Nobel physics prize went to Professor Brian Josephson in 1973 for his theoretical predictions of the properties of a supercurrent through a tunnel barrier. He studied at Trinity College and since 1974 has been professor of physics at Cambridge. In 1974 a Nobel physics prize was awarded to Professor Antony Hewish, professor of radio astronomy at Cambridge since 1971, for pioneering research into radio astrophysics and his decisive role in the discovery of pulsars, oscillating radio stars sending out regular radio pulses.

The other five Cambridge-trained Nobel prize-winners received their awards for work in chemistry. In 1952 Professor Archer Martin, who was up at Peterhouse as a young man, shared a Nobel prize with Professor Richard Synge who was at Trinity College, Cambridge. The award was in recognition of their invention of partition chromatography, a refined method of chemical analysis. Dr Frederick Sanger, who received a Nobel prize in 1958 for his work on the molecular structure of proteins, particularly that of insulin, went from St John's College, Cambridge, to research in biochemistry at Cambridge, later becoming a staff member of the Medical Research Council. Sir John Kendrew, recipient of a Nobel prize in 1962, was educated at Trinity College, Cambridge, after which he became the authority on the structures of globular proteins. Ronald Norrish, whose Nobel award for studies of extremely fast chemical reactions came in 1967, his seventieth year, was born in Cambridge and educated there at Emmanuel College. Professor emeritus, he was Director of the department of physical chemistry at Cambridge for twenty-eight years.

At least eight other Nobel prize-winners who were alive at the time of the recent survey have connections with Cambridge, though they were originally educated elsewhere. Since 1962, the year he became a Nobel prize-winner, Dr Max Perutz has been chairman of the Medical Research Council laboratory of molecular biology at Cambridge, where Dr Francis Crick, who shared a Nobel prize with Professor Maurice Wilkins, mentioned earlier, and John Watson in 1962, has worked since 1949. The Astronomer Royal, Sir Martin Ryle, honoured with a Nobel prize for pioneering research in radio astrophysics, directs the Mullard Radio-astronomy Observatory at Cambridge where he also holds a professorship. Lord Todd, a Nobel prize-winner for his work on nucleotides and nucleotide co-enzymes, was professor of organic chemistry at Cambridge from 1944 to 1971, and has been Master of Christ's College there since 1963. Sir Ernst Boris Chain (discovery of penicillin and its curative effect in various infectious diseases), Sir Hans Krebs (discovery of the citric acid cycle), Professor Paul Dirac (discovery of new productive forms of atomic theory), and Sir George Porter (studies of extremely fast chemical reactions), all Nobel prize-winners, have carried out research or held posts at Cambridge.

Although the rules governing the award of Nobel prizes have on occasion been interpreted somewhat liberally, there are scientists who are, strictly speaking, not eligible, as Alfred Nobel's will provided three annual prizes for science – one each for chemistry, for physics, and for physiology or medicine. The kinds of scientists who are not normally eligible for Nobel awards may receive recognition from the Royal Society, the Linnean Society of London, the British Trust for Ornithology, or one of a number of other bodies, many men and women associated with Cambridgeshire having been honoured in this way.

The efforts and achievements of workers in many other fields have been acknowledged by the award of honours, including ones of such great distinction as the Nobel prize for literature and the Order of Merit. One immediately thinks of Bertrand Russell, who succeeded his brother as third Earl in 1931. At Trinity College, Cambridge, he specialized in mathematics and became a lecturer, losing this position during the First World War when his pacifist views brought him trouble and imprisonment. Author of works on mathematics, philosophy, marriage and morals, and other topics, he was awarded the Order of Merit in 1949 and the Nobel prize for literature the following year. A leading advocate of nuclear disarmament, he died at the age of ninety-eight. E. M. Forster, who also died in 1970 at a great age, was another distinguished man long associated with Cambridge, where he was educated at King's College. Author of the famous book *A Passage to India* and other works, he was awarded the Order of Merit and became a Companion of Honour and a Companion of Literature. His assertion that he would always support his friend if forced to decide between being loyal to him or to his country tells us much of Forster's character and his deep sense of personal integrity. G. M. Trevelyan, who received the Order of Merit and became a Companion of Literature, was educated at Trinity College, Cambridge, where he became Master in 1940, thirteen years after being appointed Regius professor of modern history at Cambridge. Great-nephew of Lord Macaulay and son of the distinguished historian Sir George Otto Trevelyan, he produced his first book, *England in the Age of Wycliffe,* at the early age of twenty-three. First published when he was fifty, his *History of England* has gone through several editions and remains a lively and useful work.

Many more scholars and writers could be added to this roll of honour, but we must not forget the printers who give their work some form of permanency and who help to disseminate their ideas and information. Printing was begun at Cambridge in 1521 by the German Johann Lair of Siegburg who was known as John Siberch. His first book was the *Oratio* of Henry Bullock, a speech made when Cardinal Wolsey visited the university in 1520. Also in 1521, Siberch printed *Cuiusdam fidelis Christiani epistola,* a sermon by Augustine, whose title-page bears the first Greek printing in metal type in England. Thomas Thomas, author of a Latin dictionary which went through many editions, was appointed first official printer to the University of Cambridge in 1583. His press was seized by the Stationers' Company, but Lord Burghley, Chancellor, who had been at St John's College, Cambridge, upheld his rights. Thomas died at the tragically early age of thirty-five in 1588 and was succeeded by John Legate, who, in 1591, printed the first Cambridge Bible, an octavo edition of the Geneva version. Printer to the university since 1625, Thomas Buck, "a quarrelsome man but a good printer", printed in 1629 the first edition of the authorized version of the Bible to be produced outside London. The University of Cambridge assumed direct control of its printing press in 1698, a syndicate being appointed to supervise its management and working.

Meanwhile, in 1638, Cambridge, England, made an important contribution to the development of the English-speaking world when one of its natives, Stephen Daye, set up the first press in North America at Cambridge, Massachusetts. Daye was employed by Henry Dunster, M.A. of Magdalene College, Cambridge, England, president of the college, now the senior university and oldest educational institution in the U.S.A., named after its principal founder, John Harvard, M.A. of Emmanuel College, Cambridge, England.

Back home in seventeenth-century Cambridgeshire renewed efforts were being made to drain and improve the fenland and this brought more men of energy and enterprise to the fore.

Early that century Sir John Popham, Lord Chief Justice, led a group of wealthy businessmen who agreed to drain land around Upwell in Cambridgeshire and Norfolk in return for stretches of the newly drained land. He and his associates ran into trouble of one kind and another, but some land was reclaimed. Sir John, whose distinguished career included service as M.P. for Bristol, speaker of the House of Commons, and attorney-general, died in 1607. The cut or channel still known as Popham's Eau remains as his memorial in the fens.

Sir John Peyton bought land at Littleport in 1602 and within a few years 1,490 acres had been embanked and divided into meadows. When he acquired his fenland estate Sir John was Lieutenant of the Tower of London, a post he relinquished in 1603 to become Governor of Jersey. His only son, another Sir John Peyton, who was educated at Queen's College, Cambridge, became Lieutenant-governor of Jersey in 1628 and Governor when old Sir John died in 1630.

Sir Cornelius Vermuyden assisted Francis Russell, fourth Earl of Bedford, owner of some 20,000 acres of fenland, his son William Russell, first Duke of Bedford, and their associates with their great project for the draining of the fens. Vermuyden, the brilliant Dutch drainage engineer, had earlier repaired sections of the Thames embankments. He was so interested in the fenland project that he worked on his plans during the civil war, when drainage work stopped, returning afterwards to direct once again the labours of thousands of men. Surprisingly, we do not appear to be certain about Vermuyden's dates of birth and death. We do know, however, that he was knighted in 1629 and that twenty-four years later Cromwell gave him the important task of soliciting a close alliance with his native country, Holland. As far as England is concerned, his monument must surely be the Bedford River (now known as the Old Bedford River), a straight channel seventy feet wide and twenty-one miles long which carried the waters of the River Ouse from Earith to Denver.

Francis Russell, fourth Earl of Bedford, leader of the adventurers, wealthy businessmen who adventured their capital on the vast drainage scheme, succeeded his cousin, the third Earl, in 1627. He was privy councillor in 1641 and made his appearance on the wider, national stage when he endeavoured to mediate between Charles I and Parliament. The fourth Earl's son William, who took his place when he died at the age of forty-eight in 1641, was something of a turncoat who served as a General of Horse in the Parliamentary army, abandoned the Parliamentary cause and was pardoned by Charles I, and finally returned to the Parliamentarians. He survived to continue his father's fenland drainage project and to reach the age of eighty-seven.

With the benefit of hindsight, it is now known that the Russells and their engineer Vermuyden had apparently overlooked the fact that drying fen peat shrinks, causing land levels to fall and rivers to overflow their banks. In due time, all this began to happen. Nevertheless their results, achieved without the aid of equipment that is available today, remain impressive, and certainly these adventurers brought great changes to the fenland scene. One is reminded of them and also of others who supported projects that turned a watery wilderness into a rich farming district by names still in use – Adventurers' Fen at Burwell and Adventurers' Ground at Swaffham Bulbeck, to mention but two. Somehow their endeavours seem to stir the imagination in ways those of their successors of the nineteenth century, the engineer John Rennie the elder and others, fail to do, important as these have been.

Cambridgeshire also owes much to the undertakers, those who undertook the actual work of fenland drainage and reclamation for which the adventurers supplied the money. The names of many of them are long forgotten, but here and there one is commemorated in the name of a hamlet or drainage channel. For example, Edmund Welch is remembered from Welches Dam, a small hamlet beside the Old Bedford River. In the middle of the seventeenth century he was responsible for building a sluice gate at this place where the Forty Foot Drain discharged into the Old Bedford River. A practical man, with his feet planted firmly on the ground, he made a real and effective contribution to the solution of the fenland problem. What a great pity that so little is known of him. What a great pity, too, that so many other hard-working people, whose labours transformed this part of England, are completely unknown.

These nameless workers and millions like them deserve to be commemorated by a national memorial, for, even in our own day and age, John Donne's assertion that "No man is an iland intire of itselfe" still rings true. Indeed without the presence and support of 'lesser mortals' few people would achieve greatness or even have it thrust upon them.

X

SOME CAMBRIDGESHIRE VILLAGES

MANY villages are mentioned in other chapters of this book, but I want to give readers a more complete idea of the wealth of historical and other interest in which the county abounds. I have therefore selected Peterborough, March, Huntingdon, Ely and Cambridge as centres from which to explore a number of Cambridgeshire villages. Armchair travellers will find that this fills several gaps in our survey, while readers who decide to travel to some of these places will discover others on the way.

North-west of Peterborough is St Martin's Without (otherwise Stamford Baron), the Cambridgeshire portion of the beautiful stone-built town of Stamford, whose greater part lies north of the river in Lincolnshire. Standing there in acres of rolling parkland is Burghley House, the large Elizabethan mansion that has been the home of the Cecil family for over 400 years. Early in the sixteenth century the manor of Burghley had been bought by a wealthy squire whose only son, William Cecil, Lord Burghley, reached high office in the land and spent some thirty years enlarging and remodelling the family house. William Cecil was greatly influenced by Edward Seymour, Duke of Somerset, builder of Somerset House in the Strand, whom he served as secretary.

Mostly of stone from the neighbouring parish of Barnack, Burghley House has numerous attractive features, among which must surely be numbered its short square towers and chimney-shafts in the form of tall Tuscan columns, its ogee-capped turrets and frilled balustrade, all contributing to the considerable interest of the skyline. The interiors were executed in the latter part of the seventeenth century, while the grounds were remodelled during the second half of the eighteenth century when Capability Brown created what has been described as "one of the most perfect landscape settings in England".

Also in the county's north-western corner is Maxey, lying away from which is the broad grey Church of St Peter whose tower is Norman. Here, in an area where Iron Age and Romano-British finds have also been made, is the site of Saxon timber-framed long houses, hearths and rubbish pits. At Castle End a moat marks the site of Maxey Castle. The building has disappeared, but we know that in 1374 a licence authorizing the addition of battlements was granted to Sir William de Thorpe, and that later Henry VII's mother, Margaret Beaufort, Countess of Richmond, lived there.

The adjoining parish of Northborough has a church dedicated to St Andrew. Small and towerless, it is the last resting place of two people closely connected with Oliver Cromwell: his widow and John Claypole, his second daughter Elizabeth's husband. Elizabeth, who is said to have interceded for royalist prisoners, died at the early age of twenty-nine in 1658, the year of her father's death, and was buried in Westminster Abbey. Her remains seem to have been treated with more respect than those of her father, which, it may be remembered, were disinterred and hung on the gallows at Tyburn in 1661. John Claypole married Elizabeth in 1646, the year after he took up arms for Parliament. Five years later he raised a troop of horse and became master of the horse to his father-in-law, the Protector, and one of his peers. Imprisoned as a suspect in 1678, he survived another ten years, dying in 1688, thirty years after Elizabeth and her father. John Claypole's manor house, whose fourteenth-century structure was greatly altered three centuries later, still stands in Northborough.

John Clare, 'the peasant poet', lived for ten years in a cottage only a few hundred yards from Northborough church and the manor house. His sad life was punctuated by a period (1837–41) in the private asylum of Matthew Allen, a pioneer in the humane treatment of mental illnesses, at High Beach in Epping Forest. Clare wrote many poems there and his condition improved, but the pull of home became too much for him and he set out, without a penny in his pocket, for Northborough, walking the 80 miles in three days. He found himself "homeless at home", as he wrote in his journal, and some months later was, on the ground of having spent "years addicted to poetical prosings", placed in the county asylum, where he spent the last twenty-two years of his life.

Today in Helpston, the village south-west of Northborough where he was born and buried, there is a memorial to John Clare by the crossroads, almost opposite the ancient village cross. In many places people still turn to his poems of rural life. Only the other day I found the professor of agrarian history at the University of Kent at Canterbury quoting "the poor demented village poet of Helpston" (to use the learned man's expression) on the subject of the enclosure of open fields, commons and waste lands, something which John Clare obviously disliked.

This part of Cambridgeshire has associations with the family of Daniel Defoe, the journalist and novelist whose best-known work, *Robinson Crusoe*, appeared in 1719. His parents lived at Etton, east of Helpston, before moving to London, Daniel's birthplace. St Stephen's at Etton is a fine example of an Early English church and the manor house to the east of it is Elizabethan.

Set among cedars, St Mary's Church in the adjoining village of Marholm has its short Norman tower and low thirteenth-century nave somewhat dwarfed by the large and ambitious chancel rebuilt by Sir William Fitzwilliam, who died in 1534 and was buried in the place he had "lately edified". Sir William, who became Sheriff of Northampton ten years before he died, had been Sheriff of London and Warden, and later Master, of Merchant Taylors' Company. There is a monument in Marholm church to his grandson, another Sir William Fitzwilliam, who died in 1599. This grandson served in Ireland for many years, becoming Lord Deputy there, and was governor of Fotheringhay Castle, just across the county border in Northamptonshire, when Mary Queen of Scots was executed. Mary gave him a portrait of her son James, and one concludes that Sir William must have given her courteous and considerate treatment such as his grandfather had extended to Cardinal Wolsey, whom he entertained at the time of the eminent statesman's disgrace.

Sir William Fitzwilliam, the Yorkshireman who, as already

mentioned, died in 1534, bought Milton, a property south of Marholm, in 1502, twenty years before he was knighted. Early work survives there in the north front of the house (*c.* 1600), but the interior is mostly Georgian. The work of the eighteenth-century architect Henry Flitcroft is represented, 'Burlington Harry' (as he was called from the name of his patron) having designed, among other parts, the south front, Palladian in style. Sir William Chambers, who studied architecture in Italy and Paris and went on to design Somerset House, did much work here in the latter part of the eighteenth century, and later still John Carr was involved with the library and other features. Repton, who had become a professional landscape gardener after losing his fortune, remodelled the garden in 1791.

Unlike those in the north-western corner of the county, the parishes around the fenland town of March, on the eastern side of Cambridgeshire, are large and 'empty' and few in number. Doddington, south-west of March, once derived considerable importance from the presence of the palace of the Bishops of Ely. Reputed to have been the biggest parish in the county and the wealthiest rectory in the country, it attracted some outstanding personalities. Christopher Tye, the musician, obtained the living here in the sixteenth century. He is said to have replied to Elizabeth I's criticism of his playing by telling her that the royal ears were out of tune. One hesitates to believe such a story, but one thing is certain, namely that he did write Masses and compose hymns and has indeed been called "the father of the anthem".

Parts of St Mary's Church at Doddington date from the thirteenth century and there is much of the following century too. From the nineteenth century there is stained glass made by William Morris's manufacturing and decorating firm for Langton Green, Kent, and given to this Cambridgeshire church in 1923 in memory of a rector who had come there from the East End of London for his health's sake. The dedication of the window containing this glass was the last public act of Sir Charles Townshend, 'the hero of Kut', who in September 1915 defeated the Turks and captured Kut al Amara, where he was later besieged and forced to surrender following the failure of Sir John Nixon's attempt to relieve him.

The division of Doddington, "the richest living in England", created seven rectories—Doddington itself, four in March, Benwick and Wimblington. Benwick, which does not seem to have been mentioned until 1221, has a brown stone church, St Mary's, of 1850, while Wimblington's church of St Peter was built of grey coursed rubble with stripes of buff stone in 1874.

There are far more parishes around Huntingdon than in the neighbourhood of March. Though mostly smaller than those in the fenland, they are usually more densely populated and often have much more of a past. Robert Hutchinson, the nineteenth-century restorer, was obviously alive to the history of the place and at St Martin's Church, Little Stukeley, he made effective use of earlier remains, incorporating them in the fabric of the building. There are Norman column-shafts in the wall of the tower, a length of Norman corbel-table in the north aisle wall, and much else besides.

One is reminded of the less distant past in St Mary's Church, Brampton, where the stalls have splendid misericords whose carvings include representations of a knight and lady with a shield, a woman gleaning, a man reaping and a woman with a sickle. Here too is a monument to Mrs Paulina Jackson, "last of ye family of ye Peps in this parish 1689". She was the sister of Samuel Pepys, author of the famous diary which, written in cypher, still arouses considerable interest. A house, north-east of the church, was owned by the Pepys family but it appears that, despite information in certain guidebooks, Samuel was not born there, though he certainly knew Brampton well, as readers of the diary will appreciate.

He went there on 6th July 1661, following the death of his Uncle Robert. What with the smelly corpse, which he had moved into the yard and watched by two men, his aunt's condition ("a most nasty ugly pickle"), and trouble over his uncle's will ("his estate appears nothing as we expected"), this was hardly a visit to enjoy. But there were to be other journeys from London to Brampton, where Pepys's parents settled after leaving London, and visits to nearby Hinchingbrooke, the great house of his father's first cousin, Sir Edward Montagu, first Earl of Sandwich, who has been described as "the key to Samuel Pepys's career". In September 1663 Pepys and his wife enjoyed gathering nuts in Brampton Woods and the diarist himself supped with his relatives at Hinching-brooke. Just over four years later, while visiting his father in Brampton, Pepys confided to his diary that "I bless God that I am like to have such a pretty place to retire to". But things turned out very differently, for in retirement he lived mainly in Clapham, where he died, aged seventy, in 1703. Since Pepys's time Brampton has developed considerably and Hinchingbrooke now houses a school.

Buckden, south of Brampton, was formerly not only an important stage on the Great North Road but the site of the moated palace of the Bishops of Lincoln. Much of the palace was destroyed after it passed into secular hands in 1837, only the great tower, the inner gatehouse, the outer gateway and some walling, all of the fifteenth century and in red brick with diapers of dark blue bricks, surviving. A red-brick house was built on the site in 1875 by Sir Arthur Marshall, the Huntingdon brewer, and later restoration work was started by the Edleston family, one of whom intended to establish there a museum dedicated to the Emperor Napoleon III. In the 1960s the great tower was restored and re-roofed by the Claretian Fathers and a church, now serving a Catholic parish, was built between it and the house.

The fifteenth-century tower of the Anglican parish church of St Mary stands close to the great tower, so close, in fact, that in earlier times it had to be buttressed to prevent it falling into the palace moat. There are monuments in the church to several Bishops of Lincoln. One, Thomas Barlow, who died in 1691 at the age of eighty-four, was obviously a survivor, having accommodated himself to circumstances on a number of occasions. Another, John Green, an eighteenth-century Bishop of Lincoln, had held posts at Cambridge and published anonymously pamphlets on university reform. Yet another who is commemorated in Buckden church, the nineteenth-century Bishop George Pelham, was "notorious for his greed of lucrative office" (His father, Thomas Pelham, first Earl of

Chichester, held several lucrative sinecures!).

Buckden has several other interesting buildings, including the almshouses of 1840, with their inscription "Industry rewarded, Age protected", reminding us that lesser mortals have also lived and worked there.

Alconbury has evidence of its past in the shape of the old Wheatsheaf Inn, now used as two houses, standing near the former junction of the A1 and the Old North Road. Also to be seen are a fifteenth-century four-arched bridge on the green, a medieval platform bridge in the hamlet of Alconbury Weston, a sixteenth-century manor house with exposed timbers and a few seventeenth-century houses. Those who know the fine Early English Church of St Peter and St Paul delight in explaining how in 1877 the tower was rebuilt while the spire was held up on great timbers, and how, when the work was completed and the props removed, the spire settled safely upon its new base. People who disbelieve them are invited to consult the brass in the church showing how the task was accomplished.

A few miles north-west of Alconbury the parish of Upton and Coppingford, a comparatively small area with few buildings, is full of signs of past occupation. There are ponds and moats showing where Coppingford manor house and other habitations once stood and in Coppingford wood the foundations of a hermitage whose position is shown on an early seventeenth-century map. Coppingford church was destroyed some 300 years ago and quite recently the farmhouse where Charles I lodged in 1646 met the same fate. Even Upton's small Church of St Margaret, with its Norman font, now appears to belong mainly to the past.

Sawtry, the much larger parish to the north, has acquired new houses and a village college and is no longer the quiet place it was, though it too has evidence of former inhabitants. Ditches, excavations and fishponds mark the site of the Abbey of St Mary where Cistercian monks lived for nearly 400 years (1147–1536). One of their properties was Monks Wood, Abbots Ripton, now a National Nature Reserve. There are materials from the abbey in the Church of All Saints, Sawtry, which was virtually rebuilt in 1880 by Sir Arthur Blomfield, the bishop's son who became an architect and is remembered for the important restorations he made in the cathedrals of Salisbury, Canterbury, Lincoln and Chichester. An outstanding brass to Sir William de Moyne (died 1404) and his wife has survived in the church.

Conington, the former royal manor on the edge of the fenland north of Sawtry, was for several centuries a seat of the Cotton family. Sir Robert Bruce Cotton, the antiquary who died aged sixty in 1631, rebuilt the family mansion, Conington Castle, now demolished. A collector of manuscripts, he gave free use of his library to many scholars of the day and after his death the collection was presented to the nation. Sir Robert was knighted by James I in 1603 and created baronet in 1611 after he had advised the King, then badly in need of funds, to revise the so-called order of baronets, anyone seeking the honour having to pay a lump sum and establish that he was a gentleman born and one who possessed a good estate. He was imprisoned in 1615 for trying to screen the Earl of Somerset by altering dates of letters. Later, as a Member of Parliament, he supported Sir John Eliot (the patriot who opposed the King and died in prison) and the parliamentary party and, as a result, was openly insulted by Charles I.

Sir Thomas Cotton, who succeeded his father as second baronet, started draining Conington Fen in 1639 and served as M.P. for Huntingdon in the Short Parliament of 1640. He died in 1662. The sixth and last baronet, Sir John Cotton, died in 1752, 141 years after the creation of the baronetcy. Now, with both the family and their home gone, Conington is left with a rich series of Cotton monuments in the Church of All Saints. Dating from about 1500, this large building, with its octagonal Norman font, has a magnificent tower, tall and pinnacled, a landmark visible for miles.

Cambridgeshire's second Conington, where Cottons also lived, is south-east of Huntingdon. On one side it adjoins Fenstanton, a village whose old features are now surrounded by the very new. The Church of St Peter and St Paul has a large fine chancel built by the fourteenth-century rector William de Longthorne, whose memorial stone is in the floor. Against the north wall is the tomb of Lancelot 'Capability'

Brown, the celebrated eighteenth-century landscape gardener, who came to live here when, in 1768, he was given the manor of Fenstanton-cum-Hilton by the Earl of Northampton in payment of a debt. Capability was accused of being too destructive of lime and elm avenues, of lacking genius, and so on. But let us forget the criticism and remember the verdict of Miles Hadfield who some ten years ago, while serving as chairman of the Arboricultural Committee of the Royal Forestry Society, wrote: "He [Brown] had added more superb trees to our landscape and ornamental woodlands, as distinct from our forests, than any man before, or any man is likely to do in future." Certainly Capability Brown is still remembered, whereas the names of many of his critics mean nothing in the modern world.

Hilton, part of Brown's manor, has a beautiful village green, an ancient earth-cut maze, some fine houses, and a church dedicated to St Mary Magdalene whose tower dates from the fourteenth century. The neighbouring village of Papworth St Agnes was the home of the Mallory family, who are said to have been descendants of Sir Thomas Malory of *Morte d'Arthur*, the eastern part of Manor Farm having been built for them towards the end of the sixteenth century. A few miles away is Toseland Hall, a fine dark red-brick house, whose attractive clustered chimneystacks were saved from reduction (which would have amounted to destruction) when, following protests, the direction of one of the runways of a nearby airfield was altered. Today the manor house of about 1600 stands with its contemporary barn, an aisled and thatched building, but the airfield no longer exists.

To the north-east of Huntingdon there are two villages of particular interest to specialists. Old Hurst which, according to some experts, should really be Wold Hurst, the wood on the wold, has a small church whose nave and chancel form a single rectangular chamber. Humble as it is, though, St Peter's has a Norman pillar piscina with decorated stem (a great rarity) and an octagonal font of about 1300. Woodhurst, Old Hurst's larger neighbour, is considered to be one of the best examples of an English ring village, the type of settlement made by clearing a stretch of woodland and surrounding the open space created by a road and then a strong fence or stockade. Today, as any detailed road map will show, it is still possible to enter Woodhurst from either side and to travel right round the village without leaving it. The small Church of St John Baptist has a weather-boarded bell turret. The brick manor house has a hipped roof (with sloped instead of vertical ends), as has a late seventeenth-century brick house at the east end of South Street.

Ely, headquarters of the district's local government, is a convenient centre from which to explore some of the villages of East Cambridgeshire. Like Littleport, mentioned in the Waterways chapter, Little Downham is a large fenland village. Lying to the north-west of the cathedral city, it was well-known to the medieval Bishops of Ely who spent much time there at the palace, their favourite country residence, according to all accounts. Today there remains but little of the magnificent house where, it is said, five of the bishops died. St Leonard's Church, its south doorway and part of the small tower Norman, is, however, still very much part of the village. The yellow brick rectory dates from the late eighteenth century when the present village hall was in use as a school established by a village charity. If further evidence of Downham's earlier history is needed, one has only to remember that it lies alongside the New Bedford River or Hundred Foot Drain. Such names as Westmoor Fen, Fodder Fen, Byall Fen and West Fen, all found within the parish, tell their own story.

Also beside the New Bedford River is Downham's neighbour, Coveney. The jewel of this small village is the little thirteenth-century church, which, like the chapel in the Tower of London, is dedicated to St Peter-ad-Vincula (St Peter in Chains). One seems almost surprised to find it housing a fifteenth-sixteenth-century German reredos with painted carvings of the Passion and an eighteenth-century Danish pulpit with painted figures of Christ and the Evangelists. Coveney Mansion, timber-framed and thatched, adds to the charm of the place. Mepal, a small parish for these parts, straddles the Bedford Rivers. Its small church, twice renewed last century and again in 1905, has a tablet to James

Fortrey, a refugee from Brabant, who was groom to James II
and apparently came to the fenland when the King, his royal
master, went into exile. Witcham, a little village, clusters
round St Martin's Church, a small much-repaired thirteenth-
fourteenth-century building whose very rare feature is its
Perpendicular stone pulpit with its steps.

At Witchford, a busier place with some newer houses, St
Andrew's Church has a thirteenth-century tower and work of
the following century. It was here that the monks of Ely made
their peace (at a price) with William the Conqueror. As the
Liber Eliensis puts it:

> Afterwards, as the king was leaving, the said Gilbert de Clare
> came in to see the monastery, and after looking everywhere,
> found the monks at dinner in the refectory. "Oh wretched and
> foolish men," he said, "to sit here stuffing yourselves at this of all
> times, when the king is here and in your church." And there-
> upon they forsook the tables and rushed to the church, but could
> not find the king. Much perturbed, and having little hope save in
> God's Providence, they besought Gilbert to intercede for them
> with the king lest ill befall. This he agreed to do and was able
> with some difficulty to obtain them an audience with a view to
> averting the royal wrath by prayers or presents. And being
> brought before the king at Witchford, where he then was,
> through the mediation of Gilbert and other nobles, they were
> received back into favour at the price of 700 marks of silver.

South of Mepal, Sutton stands on a ridge above the fens,
along the ancient route from Ely to Huntingdon, and not
surprisingly its large fourteenth-century Church of St Andrew,
whose magnificent tower has been described as unforgettable,
forms a conspicuous landmark. Off the road from Sutton to
Ely is the quiet village of Wentworth where the church has at
least three Norman features, namely the south and north
doorways and a piece of sculpture of a robed figure with a
book.

South-east of Ely is a group of villages bordering on to
Suffolk. Soham, usually thought of as a small town rather than
a big village, is a busy residential, shopping and business centre
on the Ely to Newmarket road. Early in the seventh century it
became a cradle of Christianity when a monastery, later

destroyed and never rebuilt, was founded there by Bishop Felix of Burgundy (Saint Felix), who had established a missionary base at Dunwich on the Suffolk coast. Opposite the place where the monastery is supposed to have stood the Church of St Andrew displays its splendid tower topped with battlements and pinnacles and rising above the fenland like, as one old writer put it, a symbol of faith that many waters cannot quench. Dating from the late twelfth century, it has many attractive features, one of the most beautiful being the roof of the nave. In the churchyard is the grave of Oliver Cromwell's great-granddaughter, Elizabeth D'Aye. Her mother, Elizabeth Cromwell, married an army officer who died before his creditors caught up with him, and she, in her turn, married a Soham man who went through a fortune and died in the workhouse. Happily Elizabeth D'Aye's daughter, another Elizabeth, married the village shoemaker of Soham, an honest and sensible man who is said to have become a high-constable.

At Isleham, east of Soham, a small early Norman chapel remains from the priory founded by Benedictines of St Jacut-sur-mer in Brittany. Its survival is something of a miracle, for the monks abandoned the place in 1254. A source of much beauty and interest, the church, St Andrew's, has been there since the fourteenth century. Remodelling was undertaken late in the following century when the lovely hammer-beam roof was given by Crystofer Peyton, member of an old Isleham family whose monuments are preserved in the church. There is a tomb-chest with brasses to Thomas Peyton (died 1484) and his two wives, one of whom, Margaret Bernard, brought Isleham to the Peytons. This association with the church and village is cherished by the Peyton family in America who gave St Andrew's a hand-carved oak screen. Of the Bernards, another old local family whose monuments may be seen in Isleham church, Sir Geoffrey went on crusade to the Holy Land with Prince Edward in the thirteenth century and Sir John, whose brass shows him in plate armour, fought at Agincourt.

At Fordham, a growing community off the A142, St Peter's Church has a few remains of the Norman period, but of its major features the Lady Chapel, with its beautiful windows, is surely the most memorable. Nothing survives of the Gilbertine priory founded here in the thirteenth century, Fordham Abbey, the red-brick house by the River Snail, dating from about 1790. Fordham rubs shoulders with Snailwell, whose church, also dedicated to St Peter, is distinguished by a Norman round tower of flint and pebble rubble. Evidence of even earlier human activity here, a cemetery of ten Bronze Age round barrows, was destroyed to make way for an airfield during the Second World War.

A pleasant model village, Chippenham has at its centre a partly Norman church of flint and pebble rubble. Near the porch lies Lord Farnborough, better known as Sir Thomas Erskine May, Clerk of the House of Commons for the fifteen years 1871-86, whose *Treatise on the Law, Privileges, Proceedings and Usage of Parliament* remains in constant use. Chippenham Park surrounds a red-brick mansion dating largely from 1886. We cannot leave this wooded corner of the county without mentioning Kennett, a small parish with an old church right away from the village and the roads.

Lying south of Kennett is Ashley, a small place with thatched and colour-washed cottages, whose nineteenth-century church was built with the help of the Marquis of Bute. His wife was a member of the North family. They had a large mansion in the adjoining village of Kirtling, where the partly Norman Church of All Saints includes a brick chapel built at the beginning of the sixteenth century by the first Baron North, who was also responsible for the great mansion whose gatehouse alone survives. Edward North, whose tomb-chest is in the family chapel, was a London merchant's son who gained riches and power and became Chancellor of the court of augmentations and Privy Councillor. His son Roger, second Baron North, M.P. for Cambridgeshire and Lord-lieutenant of the county, was visited by Queen Elizabeth at Kirtling in 1578.

Cheveley, Kirtling's northern neighbour, is close to Newmarket, in a pleasant wooded area where some of the country's finest stud farms and stables are situated. A growing village, it has an impressive church dedicated to St Mary and the Holy Host of Heaven. Woodditton, at the end of the great defensive bank of the Devil's Dyke, has two churches, the large flint Church of St Mary, with its brass to Henry English (died 1393) and his wife, and, in the hamlet of Saxon Street, the red and yellow brick Church of Holy Trinity, the Lord Manners Memorial Church, built by Diana Manners in 1876.

On the other side of the Devil's Dyke, to the west of the growing village of Stetchworth, is Dullingham, a farming village, whose half-timbered and thatched guildhall, with its oversailing upper floor, served as hall of the Guild of St John. St Mary's Church has monuments to members of the Jeaffreson family, including Lieutenant-General Christopher Jeaffreson (died 1824) and his wife, Henrietta Viscountess Gormanston. Burrough Green, a small village, has a flint church with monuments to members of the de Burgh and the Ingoldesthorpe families, a red-brick Elizabethan house (Burrough Green Hall), and a schoolhouse of 1714. At Westley Waterless the church, St Mary's, lost its round tower last century, when it collapsed, but still has its two fourteenth-century brasses, one to Sir John Creke, the other, one of the earliest brass portraits of a lady, to his tall and slender wife.

This area is, of course, within convenient reach of Cambridge, another place from which many journeys of exploration can be made. There are so many villages within a radius of ten to fifteen miles of its centre that only a small selection of them can be considered here. However, one hopes that readers will be tempted to venture forth and to allow themselves plenty of time to see not only these but other villages as well.

Impington, adjoining Cambridge at its northern edge, combines the old and the new. A fifteenth-century painting of St Christopher graces the north wall of St Andrew's Church and the Pepys and Turner arms decorate the chalice and paten of 1713. The Pepys had lived for many years at Impington Hall, and Samuel, he of the famous diary, came several times to see his elderly great-uncle Talbot at the big red house. One cannot help feeling that, had he been alive at the time, Samuel would have left us a moving account of the suffering at Impington in February 1799 of Elizabeth Woodcock, a farmer's wife, who, exhausted after pursuing her runaway horse, had fallen into a deep snowdrift and lay there helpless, only a mile from home, for eight days. Rescued by neighbours when her handkerchief was seen fluttering from a bush, she fought for life but died five months later. Since those early days Impington has, of course, undergone many changes, one of the most important being the erection, just before the Second World War, of its village college, a building described by Pevsner as one of the best of its date in England, if not the best.

Swavesey, to the north-west, has a large medieval church dedicated to St Andrew and an old manor house. The bench-ends in the church make a fascinating collection. Many of them were made in the nineteenth century but, like the medieval ones in the north aisle, they have carved and decorated edges and poppyheads showing saints, angels and animals. A pelican is swallowing a fish, an owl has a mouse in its beak, a dragon sports two heads, and there are many more. A big chest in the church was a thanks-offering from villagers threatened by serious floods in 1876. Some 200 years earlier men of Swavesey, this village on the very edge of the fenland, had talked of hanging some of the labourers engaged on the Bedford Level drainage scheme, who were, they claimed, usurping their ancient right to do such work. Today Swavesey is a peaceful place with only grassy banks and an overgrown moat as evidence of the castle that stood there in olden times, when it was considered necessary to have gallows in the village.

The name of Boxworth, Swavesey's neighbour, is associated throughout the farming world with its experimental husbandry farm whose work is described elsewhere in this book. What is not so well-known is the fact that nearly two and a half centuries ago St Peter's Church, at the north-east end of the village, became the last resting place of a remarkable man whose personal triumph over adversity could even now be a source of inspiration and encouragement to others. He was Nicholas Saunderson (or Sanderson) who, born in 1682, lost his eyes through smallpox in infancy. Despite this severe handicap, he was mathematical teacher at Cambridge by the age of twenty-five. Made a Master of Arts by special patent from Queen Anne in 1711, he was elected professor of mathematics and later to the fellowship of the Royal Society. Saunderson developed an acute sense of hearing and a delicate sense of touch (he was said to be able to detect false medals merely by touching them), but perhaps his greatest achievement was, as Lord Chesterfield put it, the outstanding way in which he taught other people to use their eyes.

Bourn, the historic place close to Boxworth, was dominated by a castle in Norman times. This has disappeared, but standing within its earthworks is Bourn Hall, an old red-brick house much altered last century, when a chimneypiece dated 1555, a staircase and other woodwork were introduced from Haslingfield Hall, the house built by Thomas Wendy, physician to Henry VIII. Standing on a slight rise above the brook that takes its name from this village, the Church of St Helen and St Mary, a cruciform building, embodies work of the twelfth and later centuries. Crowned by a quaint and crooked leaded spire, its tower of pebble rubble with stone dressings dates from the thirteenth century. Towards the end of that century Bourn Wood, on the A14, was the scene of a murder and afterwards, as a preventative measure, the roadside wood-banks were levelled, the ditches filled in, and bushes cleared away to a width of 60 feet. A reminder of a more pleasant activity, Bourn windmill, a post-mill known to have been bought and sold by deed in 1636, still stands, having been fully restored earlier this century.

About three miles south of the brook, as it flows eastward from Bourn, is Wimpole, another village of this area of scattered woods and ancient tracks. This is the site of Wimpole Hall, that great country mansion recently bequeathed to the National Trust, with an endowment, by Rudyard Kipling's daughter, Mrs Elsie Bambridge. Of red brick, the house was begun just before the middle of the seventeenth century for Sir Thomas Chicheley. Master-general of the ordnance, 1670–4, he served as high sheriff and also as Member of Parliament, twice for Cambridgeshire and three times for Cambridge town. But, living extravagantly, Sir Thomas was forced to sell Wimpole in 1686.

The Earl of Radnor bought the house and spent so much on the property, altering and extending it, that some people regarded him as the original builder. In 1710 the earl sold the house to the Duke of Newcastle, who died the following year, leaving it to his daughter Henrietta. She married Edward Harley, later second Earl of Oxford, who carried out further work at Wimpole, adding a projecting wing to house the great collection of manuscripts and books started by his father, Robert Harley, first Earl of Oxford. Edward Harley, who earned the reputation of being cultured but indolent, sold Wimpole to the Lord Chancellor, Philip Yorke, first Earl of Hardwicke, in 1740 to pay off a debt of £100,000.

The new owner, who made his own alterations to the house and the gardens and grounds, had risen from obscurity to his high office. He had worked hard to transform the part of the law known as equity, but his legislative measures against Scotland, including proscription of the tartan, had best not be mentioned to nationalists north of the border. The first Earl's successors held important offices of various kinds. The fourth Earl, Charles Philip Yorke, became an admiral and served in government. Queen Victoria liked him very much. He seemed to be so straightforward and took the greatest care of her on board ship. He entertained Queen Victoria and Prince Albert at Wimpole in 1843, a visit which prompted Lord Melbourne to tell the Queen that Lord Hardwicke, to whom he was "very partial", "always is and has been very civil and good natured to Lord Melbourne". St Andrew's Church, standing to the east of the house, has a rich collection of monuments to certain of the people just mentioned and to many others too. At Arrington, to the west, the Hardwicke Arms Hotel dates from the eighteenth century and one hopes that, with the opening of Wimpole to the public, many more people will learn about the great family whose name it bears.

One cannot avoid history or figures of the past in Cambridgeshire and, as it happens, three Sir George Downings, father, son and grandson, are buried in the church at Croydon, Arrington's neighbour. The first, who was Samuel Pepys's employer for a time, received a grant of land near Whitehall in London and thus left his name to one of the world's most famous streets. His grandson founded Downing College, Cambridge.

But we must move on to Bassingbourn, the border village adjoining Royston, where housing development has occurred since the Second World War and where one of the county's village colleges opened in 1954. The Church of St Peter and St Paul, a building of flint and stone rubble, has a number of features of interest, particularly its fourteenth-century chancel. Before he died in 1931, Sir Sydney George Holland, third baronet and second Viscount Knutsford, whose joy was "to help all in distress and to bring happiness into the lives of others", chose a corner of the churchyard as his last resting place. Today he is remembered as a dedicated hospital administrator and reformer. He worked hard, as its chairman, for Poplar Hospital from 1891 until 1896 and served, again as chairman, London Hospital from 1896 until his death, raising £5 million and helping considerably to raise the standard of nursing and administration. One wonders what he would have said of one title bestowed upon him: 'Prince of Beggars'.

Duxford, the next village selected for this survey, lies east of Bassingbourn, not far from the county border. Again, as happens in so many parts of England, the ancient and the modern rub shoulders. Olden times are represented by St Peter's Church, with its Norman tower, St John's, a deserted church with Norman features, and the thirteenth-century chapel of St John's Hospital. Modern architects have used contemporary materials to create laboratories and other buildings for industrial purposes. And in recent years the Imperial War Museum has made use of Duxford airfield, housing there a large aircraft collection, including a Spitfire, a Flying Fortress, a Vampire fighter, and many others.

At Whittlesford, Duxford's neighbour in the north, the Belgae, who were active in these parts in the Iron Age, buried their rulers in some state at Chronicle Hill. Very little evidence of their presence remains, but the Church of St Mary and St Andrew still displays much Norman work and the half-timbered guildhall at the main crossroads, an attractive building in itself, is a link with more recent times.

The straggling riverside village of Linton, along the county border to the east of Whittlesford, was the site of an Iron Age settlement and an important Anglo-Saxon cemetery has been excavated there. Nowadays, a mixture of old and new, it is the kind of place where one must walk and use one's eyes, in order not to miss anything. Chaundlers in the High Street, with its pargetted front, is often thought to be the best house in the place, but its neighbour, the half-timbered Bell Inn, is well worth seeing, as is so much else here. Linton also has its church, St Mary's, a fine building of flint and stone, a village college opened in 1937, modern housing, some light industry, and pleasant walks around Rivey Hill, one with a delightful view over the Cam valley.

Balsham, immediately north of Linton, is a grand place for outdoor people whose maps will show them just how close it is to the Roman Road and the Fleam Dyke, both splendid places for walking and rambling. The village, quietly set in farming country, has in Holy Trinity, its church with the thirteenth-century tower, reminders of Hugh de Balsham, founder of Peterhouse, Cambridge, Thomas Sutton, founder of Charterhouse, and other benefactors.

In their different ways, these generous individuals were men of action, and it seems fitting that one should end this book by urging readers to get out and about in Cambridgeshire. They will surely find in its villages abundant evidence of the county's quiet beauty and character and may well be moved to help in the protection and conservation of some small part of our priceless heritage.

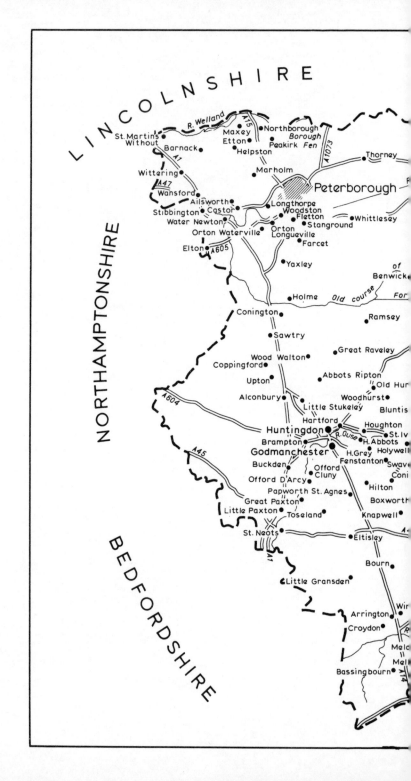

INDEX

Abbots Ripton, 89, 186
Acco Co. Ltd, 85
Addenbrooke, John, 25
Adrian, Lord, 173
Aero Research, 28
Ailsworth, 41
Alcock, John, 145, 167
——, Thomas, 39
Alconbury, 186
Aldreth, 38
Andrewes, Lancelot, 169
Anglesey Abbey, 33-4, 99, 110-11
Anjou, Margaret of, 19
Aragon, Catherine of, 151, 168
Arrington, 196
Arthur Rickwood Exp. Husbandry Farm, 48, 56, 57
Arundel, Thomas, 19, 32, 166
Ascham, Roger, 113
Ashley, 192
Ashton, A. E. & N., & Co. Ltd, 70-1

Babington, Charles Cardale, 100
Babraham, 21, 61-2, 139
Baker Perkins Ltd, 73, 74-5, 152-4, 155
Balsham, Hugh de, 18, 165, 198
Balsham, 70, 198
Bambridge, Mrs Elsie, 195
Barlow, Thomas, 185
Barnack, 14, 180
Barnes, Joshua, 37
Barnet, John, 166
Barnwell, 16, 138
Barrington, 30, 68, 81
Barrow, Henry, 21
Bassingbourn, 24, 197
Bateman, William, 18

Beaufort, Lady Margaret, 20, 181
Bedford, first Duke of, 177
——, fourth Earl of, 22, 177-8
Bedfordshire & Huntingdonshire Naturalists' Trust, 89, 90, 92, 98
Bennett, William Sterndale, 142-3
Benson, Arthur Christopher, 118, 135
——, Robert Hugh, 135
Bentley, Richard, 170
Benwick, 16, 45, 184
Bernard family, 191
Biffen, Rowland Harry, 59
Biggs, Dr P. M., 63
Blomfield, Sir Arthur, 186-7
Bluntisham, 37-8
Bottisham, 27, 34
Bourchier, Thomas, 166-7
Bourn, 31, 195
Boxworth, 62, 101, 194
Boxworth Exp. Husbandry Farm, 56-7
Bragg, Sir Lawrence, 172
Brampton, 184, 185
Braunston, Thomas de, 44
Brihtnoth, 147
British Sugar Corporation, 49-50
British Welding Research Association, 28
Brooke, Rupert, 31-2, 81
Brotherhood, Peter, Ltd, 73-4, 154, 155
Broughton, Huttleston, 33-4, 110
Brown, Lancelot ('Capability'), 180, 187-8
——, Potto, 36-7
Browne, Edward Harold, 171
Bruyne, Dr N. A. de, 28, 80
Buck, Thomas, 176
Buckden, 185-6

Burghley, Lord, 22, 176, 180
Burrough Green, 193
Burwell, 17, 34-5, 85
Butler, Lord, 107

Caius, John, 21
Cam, River, 30-5, 39, 105, 115
Cambridge, 12, 14-23, 25-7, 32, 57-8, 67, 69, 71-2, 75-80, 82-5, 89, 99, 100-2, 106-9, 111-18, 125-43
Cambridge Evening News, 110, 115
Cambridge Instrument Co., 27, 79-80
Cambridge University Press, 71-2
Cambridgeshire & Isle of Ely Naturalists' Trust, 38, 87-8, 90-2, 97-8, 100
Cantabrian, 82-3
Car Dyke, 12, 33
Carey, Rev. William, 136
Cartwright, Thomas, 21
Castor, 16, 41
Caux, John de, 161
Cavendish Laboratory, 26-7, 171-2
Cecil family, 180
Cement companies, 68
Cenwulf, Bishop, 150
Chain, Sir Ernst Boris, 174
Chambers, John, 161
Charles I, King, 22-3, 143, 169, 178, 186, 187
—— II, King, 23, 24
Chatteris, 45, 46, 51, 55
Cherry Hinton, 11, 68
Chesterton, 32
Chettisham, 40
Cheveley, 192-3
Chicheley, Sir Thomas, 195
Chippenham, 11, 192
Chippenham Fen, 94, 96
Chivers, 55
Christ's College, 20, 168, 174
Ciba-Geigy (UK) Ltd, 70
Clare, Elizabeth de, 18, 19
——, Gilbert de, 190
——, John, 181-2
Clare College, 18
Clarkson, Thomas, 43-4

Clavering, Robert, 162
Claypole, John, 181
Clerk-Maxwell, James, 171
Clough, Anne, 26
Cnut, King, 14, 15
Coke, Sir William, 32
Coldham, 91
Cole, Rev. William, 33
Colledge, John, 39
Conington, 187
Cook, Captain James, 133
Coolidge, John Calvin, 39
Coote, George, 30
Coppingford, 186
Corpus Christi College, 18-19, 170
Cottenham, 39
Cotton family, 187
Coveney, 189
Cowper, William, 36
Cox, Richard, 169
Cozy-Shel (Insulation) Co., 70
Cranmer, Thomas, 21, 168, 169
Crauden, John de, 146
Crick, Dr Francis, 174
Cromwell, Elizabeth, 181, 191
——, Henry, 35
——, Sir Oliver, 22
——, Oliver, 22, 23, 36, 37, 39, 43, 147, 177, 181, 191
Crosfield Electronics, 73
Cross, Dr B. A., 62
Croydon, 196
Cumberland, Richard, 162

Daly, Prof. Ivan de Burgh, 62
Darwin, Sir Horace, 27, 79
Davys, George, 163
D'Aye, Elizabeth, 191
Daye, Stephen, 176
Dee, Francis, 162
Defoe, Daniel, 182
Devil's Dyke, 34, 87, 88, 193
Devonshire, Duke of, 26, 171
Dirac, Prof. Paul, 174
Doddington, 45, 183-4
Doket, Andrew, 19
Dorman Sprayer Co., 69-70

Dove, Thomas, 162
Downing, Sir George, 196-7
Downing College, 25, 197
Dullingham, 193
Dunster, Henry, 176
Duport, James, 152
Durobrivae, 12, 40
Duxford, 28, 70, 80, 197

Eadgar, King, 150
Earith, 38
East Anglian Waterways Association, 46
East Midland Allied Press Group, 72-3
East of England Show, 64-5, 109
Eastern Counties Leather Co. Ltd, 86
Eccles, Sir John, 173
Edleston family, 185
Edward (The Confessor), King, 15
—— (The Elder), King, 13
—— I, King, 17-18, 31
—— II, King, 18, 165
—— III, King, 18, 146, 165, 166
—— IV, King, 19, 20, 166, 167
—— V, King, 20, 167, 168
—— VI, King, 20, 168, 169
Elgood & Sons Ltd, 69
Elizabeth I, Queen, 21-2, 113, 161, 169, 183, 192
Elm, 43
Elton, 15
Ely, 11, 13-17, 20, 25-6, 39-40, 49, 69-71, 85-6, 90-1, 108, 109, 111, 114, 116, 144-9
Emmanuel College, 21, 131, 173, 174, 176
Ermenhilda, St, 164
Ermine Street, 12, 40
Essex, James (Junior), 131
Etheldreda, St, 13, 14, 147, 163-4
Ethelred, King, 14
Ethelwold, St, 150
Etton, 182
Eustace, Bishop, 147, 165

Fairbairn, Steve, 115
Fairhaven, First Lord, 33-4, 110

Fawcett, Henry, 31
Felix, St, 13, 191
Felton, Nicholas, 169
Fen Ditton, 32
Fenstanton, 187-8
Fisons, 30, 70
Fitzwilliam, Sir William, 182, 183
Fleam Dyke, 32, 87-8, 198
Fleetwood, William, 170
Fletton, 15, 67
Fordham John, 166
Fordham, 191-2
Forster, E. M., 175
Fortrey, James, 189-90
Fox, George, 135-6
Friday Bridge, 43
Fulbourn Fen, 96-7

Gaddum, Sir John, 62
Gardiner, Stephen, 168
Garrett, Millicent, 31
George I, King, 170
—— III, King, 162-3
Gibbons, Orlando, 142
Gibbs, James, 128
Girton, 62, 111
Girton College, 26
Godmanchester, 12, 36
Gonville, Edmund, 18
Gonville and Caius College, 18, 21, 131, 173
Goodrich, Thomas, 168
Gordon family, 41
Grafham Water, 36, 67-8, 98, 116, 117
Grant Instruments (Cambridge) Ltd, 81-2
Granta, River, 32
Grantchester, 31-2, 81
Grays Group, 83-4
Great Ouse, River, 35-40, 46, 104, 105
Great Paxton, 14-15, 35
Great Raveley, 52, 89
Green, John, 185
Greene, Thomas, 170
Greenwood, John, 21
Grey, Lady Jane, 20
——, Dr William, 167

Gunning, Dr Peter, 143
Gurteens, 86
Guthlac, St, 42
Gyrth, Earl, 15

Hainault, Philippa of, 146
Hardwicke, Earls of, 196
Harley family, 196
Harlock, Ebenezer William, 148
Harston, 30
Hartford, 36
Harvard, John, 176
Haslingfield, 30, 195
Hauxton, 70
Hayley Wood, 88-9
Heffers Group, 72
Helpston, 182
Hemingfords, The, 37
Henry I, King, 16, 164
—— II, King, 17, 165
—— III, King, 17, 145, 161, 165
—— IV, King, 19, 166
—— VI, King, 19, 166, 167
—— VII, King, 16, 20, 39, 166, 167, 181
—— VIII, King, 20, 30, 71, 161, 168, 195
Henshaw, Joseph, 152
Hereward the Wake, 15, 37, 38, 39, 150
Hervey, Bishop, 146, 164
Heton, Martin, 169
Hewish, Prof. Antony, 173
Hill, Prof. Archibald, 173
——, Octavia, 43
Hilton, 188
Hinchcliffe, John, 163
Hinchingbrooke House, 22, 184-5
Hinxton, 29
Histon, 55
Hobbs, Sir John ('Jack'), 137
Hobson, Thomas, 130-1
Hodgkin, Sir Alan, 173
Holcroft, Francis, 24
Holland, Sir Sydney George, 197
Holywell, 37
Hooper, John, 168
Horningsea, 32
Hose, Charles, 115

Hotham, John, 165-6
Hotpoint, 75
Houghton, 36-7
Houghton Poultry Research Station, 62-3
Howland, Richard, 161-2
Huddleston family, 21
Hullier, John, 21
Huntingdon, 13, 15-16, 17, 23, 36
Huxley, Sir Andrew, 173

Ickleton, 16, 91-2
Ihlee, Frederick Charles, 153-4
Impington, 27-8, 193-4
Institute of Animal Physiology, 29, 61-2
Isleham, 11, 191

James I, King, 22, 151, 162, 187
—— II, King, 24, 162, 169, 170, 190
Jeaffreson family, 193
Jenyns family, 34
Jesus College, 16, 20, 114, 115, 136, 168, 171
John, King, 17, 34, 139, 165
Josephson, Prof. Brian, 173

Kelsall, Roger, 136
Kendrew, Sir John, 174
Kennett, 192
Kennett, White, 162
Kenulf, Bishop, 150
Keynes, Lord, 141
——, Dr Richard, 62
Kilkenny, William of, 165
King's College, 19, 142-3, 175
Kirtling, 192
Knutsford, Viscount, 197
Krebs, Sir Hans, 174
Kyneburga, St. 41

Landbeach, 33
Laney, Benjamin, 145, 169
Langham, Simon, 166
Lark, River, 40
Latimer, Hugh, 21, 134
Legate, John, 176

Lesney Products, 71
Linton, 27, 79, 120-1, 197-8
Little Downham, 189
Little Gransden, 88
Little Paxton, 35
Littleport, 25, 38, 40, 52, 55, 177
Little Stukeley, 184
Lloyd, William, 162
Lode, 33
London Brick Co. Ltd, 67-8
Longchamp, William, 165
Longthorne, William de, 187
Longthorpe, 12, 41, 52
Lurmark, 70
Lyne-Stephens, Mrs 135

Macmillan, Daniel, 72
Madan, Spencer, 163
Madingley, 28
Magdalene College, 20, 32, 118, 176
Magee, William Connor, 163
Mallory family, 188
Mandeville, Geoffrey de, 16-17, 34-5, 164
March, 21, 26, 42, 55, 183, 184
Marholm, 182
Marsh, Herbert, 163
Marshall, Sir Arthur, 185
Marshall of Cambridge, 75-6
Martin, Prof. Archer, 173-4
Mary, Queen, 20-1, 168, 169
—— Queen of Scots, 151, 182
Mawson, Matthias, 170
Maxey, 181
May, Sir Thomas Erskine, 192
Melbourn, 23, 24
Meldreth, 30
Mepal, 48, 189-90
Milton, 32-3
Monks Wood, 88, 89, 186
Montagu, Sir Edward, 185
Moore, John, 170
Morris, Henry, 27
Morton, John, 167, 168
Morton's Leam, 41, 44, 167
Mott, Sir Nevill, 172
Moyne, Sir William de, 187

National Institute of Agricultural Botany, 27, 57-8, 59, 60
National Seed Development Organization, 60
Nene, River, 12, 40-5, 46
New Bedford River, 38, 189
Newnham College, 26
Newton, 60
Nigel, Bishop, 164
Norrish, Ronald, 174
North family, 192
Northborough, 181
Northwold, Hugh of, 17, 145

Oakington, 24
Oddy, Joseph, 24
Offords, The, 35-6
Old Bedford River, 22, 38, 177, 178
Old Hurst, 188
Old West River, 35, 38-9, 46
Orme, Sir Humphrey, 152
Ortons, The, 41
Osland, Henry, 24
Ouse Washes, 38, 92-4, 98
Over, 37
Oxford, Earls of, 196

Paines of St Neots, 68-9
Palmer, Edward Henry, 143
Papworth, John Buonarotti, 35
Papworth St Agnes, 188
Parker, Edward, 137
Parry, Thomas Gambier, 144
Parsons, John, 163
Patrick, Simon, 170
Peada, Under-king, 13, 41, 161
Peakirk, 70, 102-4
Peckover House, 24-5, 43
Pelham, George, 185
Pembroke College, 18
Penry, John, 21, 162
Pepys, Samuel, 184-5, 193, 196
Perkins Engines, 70, 74, 154, 155
Perse, Dr Stephen, 143
Perutz, Dr Max, 174
Peterborough, 13-15, 17, 26, 41, 49, 50, 52, 64, 67, 69-75, 85-6, 111-12, 114, 118, 123, 149-60

Peterborough Die Casting Co., 75
Peterhouse, 18, 165, 173, 198
Peyton, Sir John, 177
—— family, 191
Piers, William, 162
Pippard, Sir Brian, 171
Plant Breeding Institute, 50, 58-60
Pole, David, 161
Popham, Sir John, 177
Porter, Sir George, 174
Potto, Samuel, 130
Prickwillow, 40
Pye Group, 27, 76-9

Queens' College, 19, 177

Radnor, Earl of, 196
Ramsey, 14, 16, 45
Rawley, William, 33
Ray, John, 23, 100
Rayleigh, third Baron, 171-2
Reach, 34
Redman, Richard, 168
Reinald, Abbot, 132-3
Rhee, River, 30-1
Richard I, King, 165
—— II, King, 19, 166
—— III, King, 20, 166, 167, 168
Ridel, Geoffrey, 165
Ridley, Bishop, 21
Root Harvesters, 70
Rottenburg, Henry, 82-3
Royal Society for the Protection of
    Birds, 38, 92-3
Russell, Bertrand, 175
——, Francis, 177, 178
——, William, 177, 178
Rutherford, Lord, 27, 172
Ryle, Sir Martin, 174

St Catherine's College, 19
St Ives, 22, 37
St John's College, 20, 143, 168, 173, 174,
    176
St Martin's Without, 180
St Neots, 14, 35, 68-9, 85
Sandwich, First Earl of, 185

Sanger, Dr Frederick, 174
Saunderson, Nicholas, 194-5
Sawston, 21, 27, 70, 84-5, 86
Sawtry, 186
Scambler, Edmund, 161
Scott Christopher, 135
——, Sir Giles Gilbert, 128
See, William, 117
Séez, John de, 150
Selwyn College, 26
Sexburga, St, 164
Shelford, 31
Shepherd, Lambert Charles, 115-16
Shepreth, 81
Siberch, John, 176
Sidgwick, Henry, 26
Sidney Sussex College, 21
Simeon, Abbot, 16
——, Rev. Charles, 133
Simplex of Cambridge Ltd, 70
Smart, William ('Turkey'), 117
Smedleys, 54-5
Smith, Sir Harry George Wakelyn, 42
Snailwell, 192
Soham, 13, 190-1
Sparke, Rev. Edward Bowyer, 147
Spicers Ltd, 84-5
Spillers-French Milling Ltd, 69
Stamford Baron, 180
Stanground, 15
Stanley, James, 168
Stapleford, 91
Stephen, King, 16, 17, 164
Stetchworth, 193
Steward, Robert, 147
Stibbington, 40
Stittle, John, 133, 136
Stow-cum-Quy Fen, 96
Stretham, 39
Strutt, John William, 171-2
Stuntney, 39
Sutton, Thomas, 198
Sutton, 190
Swaffhams, The, 34
Swavesey, 194
Sweyn Forkbeard, King, 14
Synge, Prof. Richard, 173-4

Taylor, Jeremy, 143
Techne (Cambridge) Ltd, 80-1
Tenison, Thomas, 39
Terrick, Richard, 162-3
Thetford, 39
Thirlby, Thomas, 168-9
Thomas, John, 162
——, Thomas, 176
Thomson, Sir Joseph John, 26-7, 172
Thoresby, Ralph, 45
Thorney, 13, 14, 41-2, 46
Thornton, Nigel de, 127
Thorpe, Sir William de, 181
Todd, Lord, 174
Towers, John, 162
Townshend, Sir Charles, 183-4
Trevelyan, G. M., 175-6
Trinity College, 18, 20-3, 170-5
Trinity Hall, 18, 31, 168
Trumpington, 31, 58-60
Turner, Francis, 169-70
Turton, Thomas, 170-1
Tye, Christopher, 183

Udall, John, 21
Upton, 186
Upwell, 46, 177

Valence, Mary de, 18
Vermuyden, Sir Cornelius, 22-3, 38, 44, 46, 177, 178
Victoria, Queen, 163, 196

Walsingham, Alan de, 144, 146
Walters, Dr Max, 99-100
Waltheof, Earl, 15
Wandlebury, 11, 88, 111
Wansford, 40
Ward, Peter, 81, 82
Waterbeach, 12, 33
Water Newton, 12, 40

Watson, John, 174
Webb, Jonas, 139
Webber, E. Berry, 155
Welch, Edmund, 178
Well Stream, 44
Wendy, Thomas, 30, 195
Wentworth, 190
Werburga, St. 164
West, Nicholas, 168
Westley Waterless, 193
White, Thomas, 162
Whittlesey, 41, 42, 67, 70
Whittlesford, 70, 197
Wicken, 13, 35
—— Fen, 94, 95-6
Wilburton, 39
Wildfowl Trust, 38, 93, 102-4
Wilkins, Prof. Maurice, 173
William I, King, 15-16, 150, 190
—— II (Rufus), King 16
—— III, King, 24, 162, 170
Willingham, 38-9
Wimblington, 55-6, 184
Wimpole, 195-6
Wisbech, 17, 24-6, 43-5, 54-5, 69, 85
—— St Mary, 43
Witcham, 190
Witchford, 190
Withburga, St, 164
Wittering, 14
Wodelarke, Robert, 19
Woodcock, Elizabeth, 193-4
Woodditton, 193
Woodford, James Russell, 171
Woodhurst, 188-9
Wood Walton, 16, 94-5
Wren, Matthew, 146, 169
Wynn, Edward, 146
Wyton, 36

Yaxley, 52
Yorke family, 196